the AMAZING SPIDER-MAN

BLACK CAT

AMAZING SPIDER-MAN PRESENTS: BLACK CAT
Writer: **JEN VAN METER**
Artists: **JAVIER PULIDO** & **JAVIER RODRIGUEZ**
Colorist: **MATT HOLLINGSWORTH** WITH **JAVIER RODRIGUEZ**
Letterer: **VC'S JOE CARAMAGNA**
Cover Art: **AMANDA CONNER** & **CHRISTINA STRAIN**

"THE ROOT OF ALL ANNOYANCE"
Writer: **CHRIS YOST**
Penciler: **MICHAEL RYAN**
Inker: **DANNY MIKI**
Colorist: **JOHN RAUCH**
Letterer: **JARED K. FLETCHER**
Cover Art: **JASON LEVESQUE**
Editor: **JODY LEHEUP**
Special thanks to Chris Allo

"THE OTHER WOMAN"
Writer: **JOE KELLY**
Artist/Letterer: **JM KEN NIIMURA**
Cover Art: **ED MCGUINNESS, DEXTER VINES** & **MORRY HOLLOWELL**

Assistant Editor: **THOMAS BRENNAN** Editor: **STEPHEN WACKER**
Executive Editor: **TOM BREVOORT**

Collection Editor: **JENNIFER GRÜNWALD** • Editorial Assistants: **JAMES EMMETT** & **JOE HOCHSTEIN**
Assistant Editors: **ALEX STARBUCK** & **NELSON RIBEIRO**
Editors, Special Projects: **MARK D. BEAZLEY** Senior Editor, Special Projects: **JEFF YOUNGQUIST**
Senior Vice President of Sales: **DAVID GABRIEL**

Editor In Chief: **JOE QUESADA** • Publisher: **DAN BUCKLEY** • Executive Producer: **ALAN FINE**

Black Cat, aka Felicia Hardy, is a sexy super-human with the ability to bring bad fortune to anyone in her vicinity. Like her father Walter Hardy (A.k.a. The Cat), she is a master burglar and extremely agile, but Felicia's misdeeds never extend past thievery. In fact, she often employs her feline skills to help Spider-Man, a friend with whom she shares a romantic and crime-fighting past.

Now their paths have crossed again, and a strictly masks-on physical relationship has developed. Felicia is also working for the Mayor's office as Mayor Jameson's head of investigations.

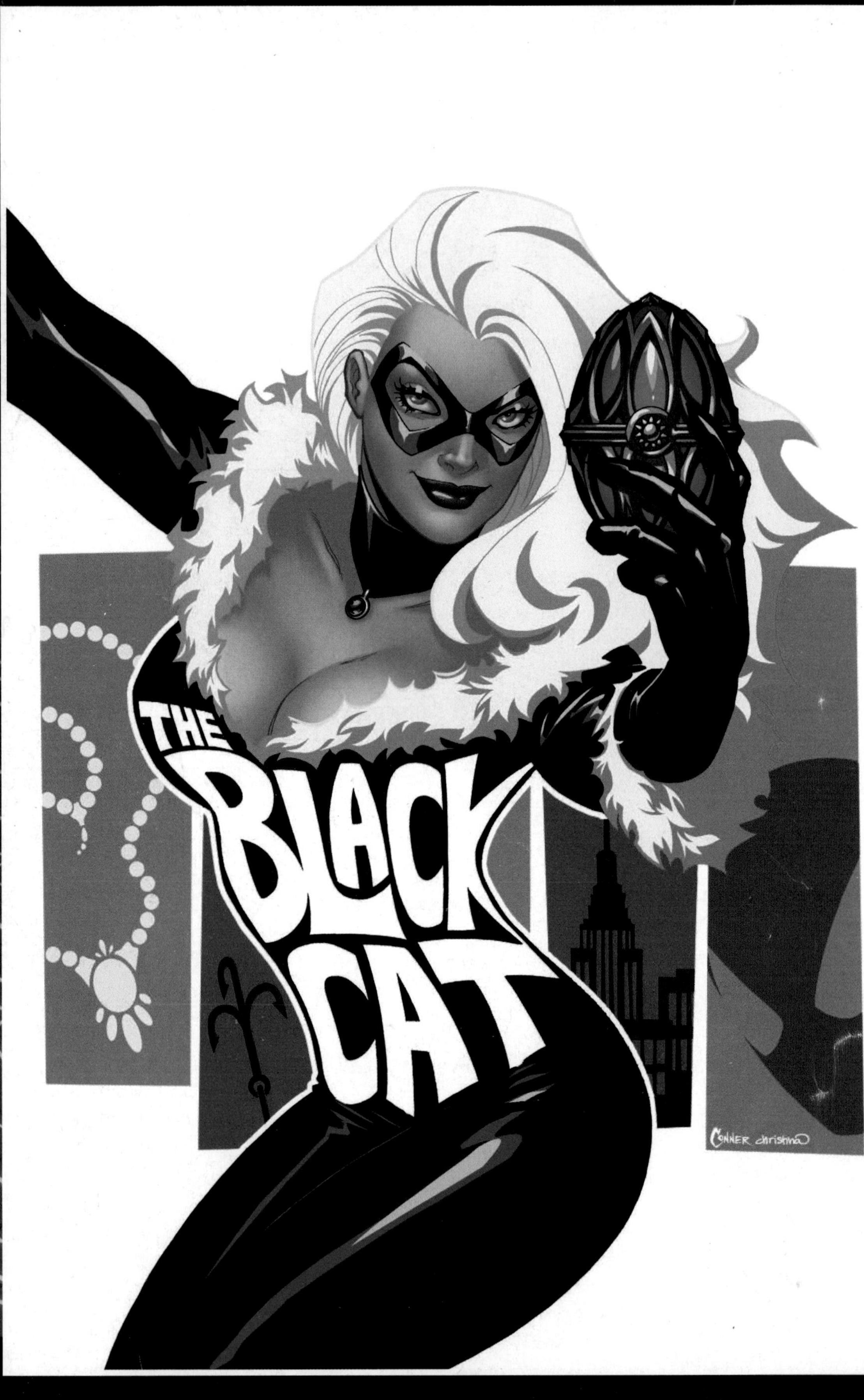
THE
BLACK
CAT
CONNER christina

AMAZING SPIDER-MAN PRESENTS: BLACK CAT #1

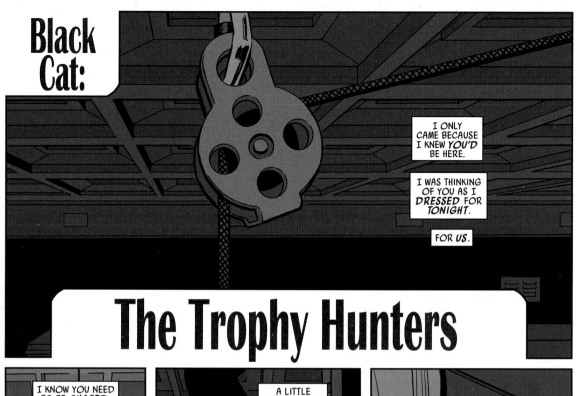

Black Cat:

I ONLY CAME BECAUSE I KNEW *YOU'D* BE HERE.

I WAS THINKING OF YOU AS I *DRESSED* FOR *TONIGHT*.

FOR *US*.

The Trophy Hunters

I KNOW YOU NEED TO BE *CHASED*. THAT'S OKAY.

I *LIKE* THE FLIRTATION.

A LITTLE MANEUVERING... JUST TO GET YOU *ALONE*.

Part One

IT'S EXQUISITE. SO *CLOSE* I CAN ALMOST *TASTE* YOU, AND--

KRSH

Jen Van Meter
writer
Javier Pulido
artist
Matt Hollingsworth
colors
Vc's Joe Caramagna
letters

--AND THEN SOME DAMN *DRUNK* BARGES IN LOOKING FOR THE *JOHN*.

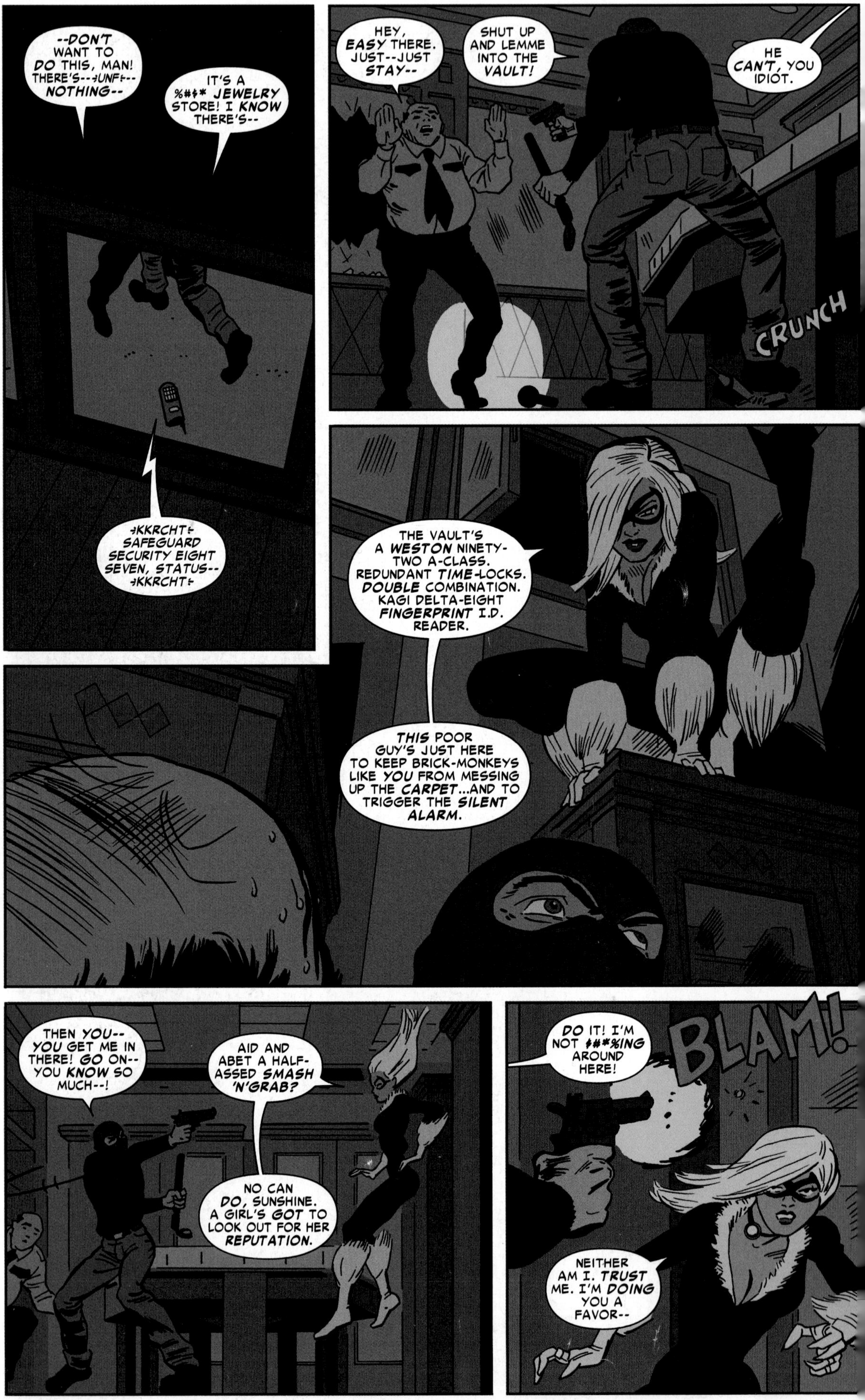
--DON'T WANT TO DO THIS, MAN! THERE'S--+UNF+-- NOTHING--
IT'S A %#$* JEWELRY STORE! I KNOW THERE'S--
+KKRCHT+ SAFEGUARD SECURITY EIGHT SEVEN, STATUS-- +KKRCHT+
HEY, EASY THERE. JUST--JUST STAY--
SHUT UP AND LEMME INTO THE VAULT!
HE CAN'T, YOU IDIOT.
CRUNCH
THE VAULT'S A WESTON NINETY-TWO A-CLASS. REDUNDANT TIME-LOCKS. DOUBLE COMBINATION. KAGI DELTA-EIGHT FINGERPRINT I.D. READER.
THIS POOR GUY'S JUST HERE TO KEEP BRICK-MONKEYS LIKE YOU FROM MESSING UP THE CARPET...AND TO TRIGGER THE SILENT ALARM.
THEN YOU--YOU GET ME IN THERE! GO ON--YOU KNOW SO MUCH--!
AID AND ABET A HALF-ASSED SMASH 'N'GRAB?
NO CAN DO, SUNSHINE. A GIRL'S GOT TO LOOK OUT FOR HER REPUTATION.
DO IT! I'M NOT $#*%ING AROUND HERE!
BLAM!
NEITHER AM I. TRUST ME. I'M DOING YOU A FAVOR--

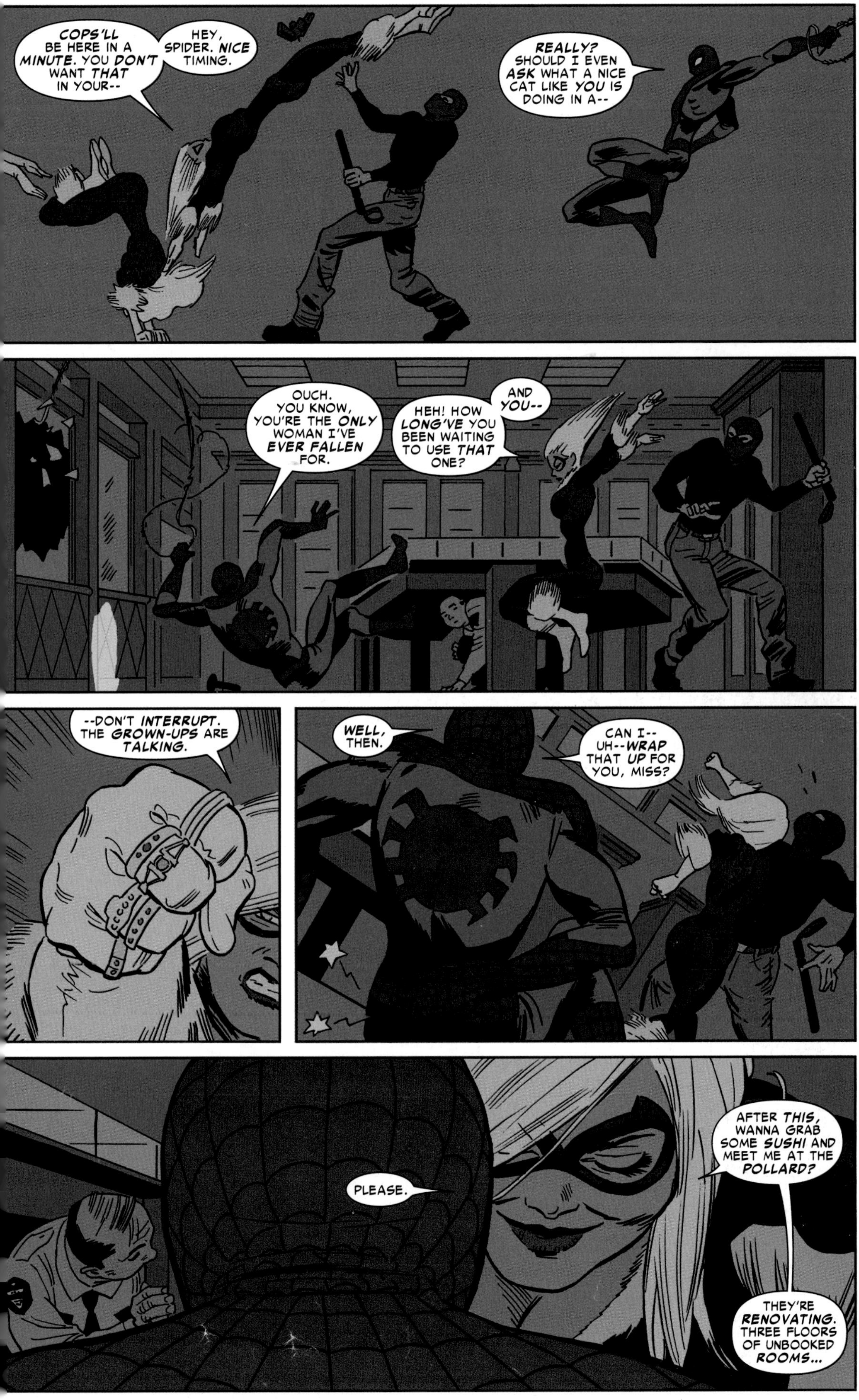

HEY, SPIDER. NICE TIMING.
COPS'LL BE HERE IN A MINUTE. YOU DON'T WANT THAT IN YOUR--
REALLY? SHOULD I EVEN ASK WHAT A NICE CAT LIKE YOU IS DOING IN A--
OUCH. YOU KNOW, YOU'RE THE ONLY WOMAN I'VE EVER FALLEN FOR.
HEH! HOW LONG'VE YOU BEEN WAITING TO USE THAT ONE?
AND YOU--
--DON'T INTERRUPT. THE GROWN-UPS ARE TALKING.
WELL, THEN.
CAN I-- UH--WRAP THAT UP FOR YOU, MISS?
AFTER THIS, WANNA GRAB SOME SUSHI AND MEET ME AT THE POLLARD?
PLEASE.
THEY'RE RENOVATING. THREE FLOORS OF UNBOOKED ROOMS...

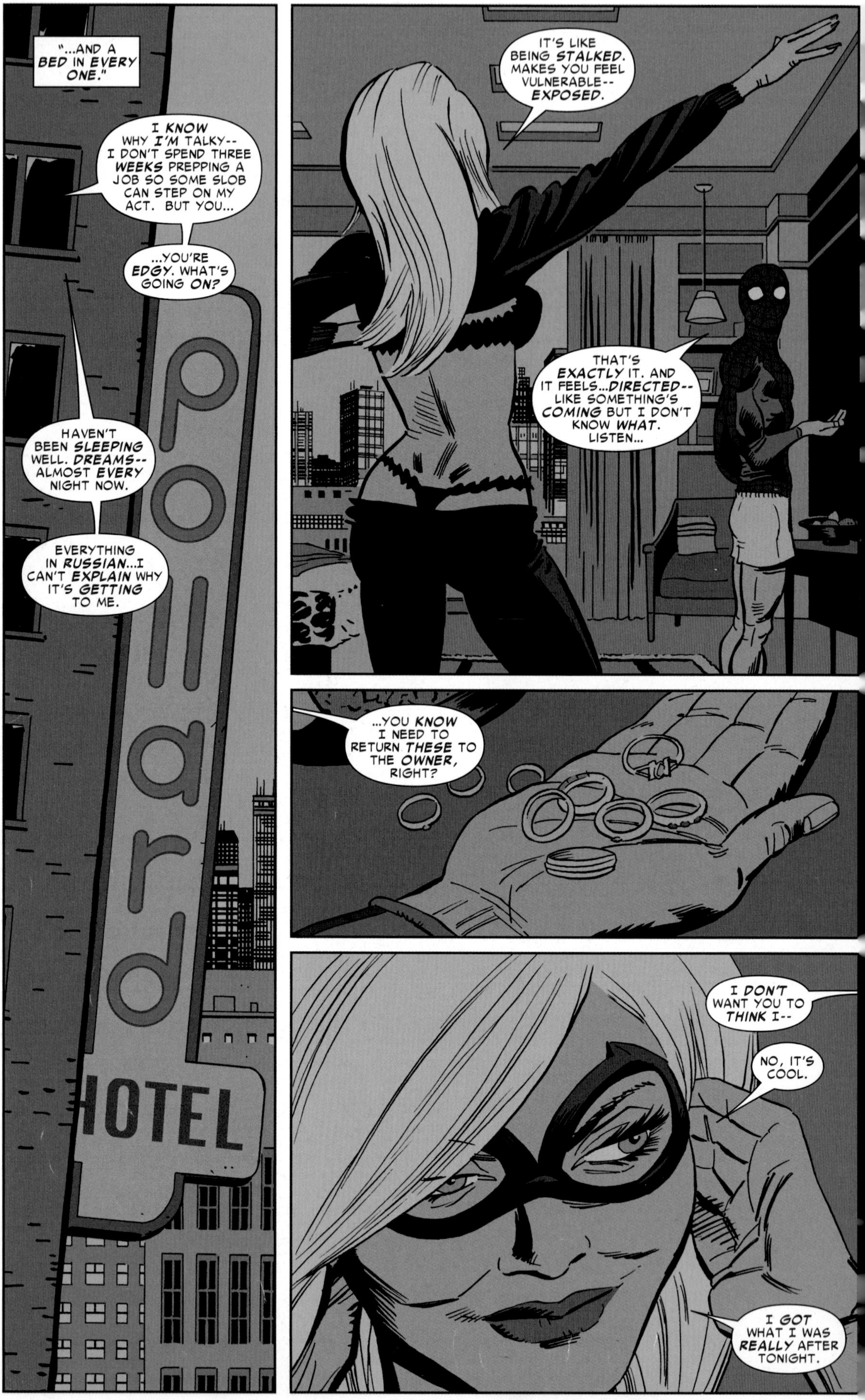
"...AND A BED IN EVERY ONE."
I KNOW WHY I'M TALKY-- I DON'T SPEND THREE WEEKS PREPPING A JOB SO SOME SLOB CAN STEP ON MY ACT. BUT YOU...
...YOU'RE EDGY. WHAT'S GOING ON?
HAVEN'T BEEN SLEEPING WELL. DREAMS-- ALMOST EVERY NIGHT NOW.
EVERYTHING IN RUSSIAN...I CAN'T EXPLAIN WHY IT'S GETTING TO ME.
HOTEL
IT'S LIKE BEING STALKED. MAKES YOU FEEL VULNERABLE-- EXPOSED.
THAT'S EXACTLY IT. AND IT FEELS...DIRECTED-- LIKE SOMETHING'S COMING BUT I DON'T KNOW WHAT. LISTEN...
...YOU KNOW I NEED TO RETURN THESE TO THE OWNER, RIGHT?
I DON'T WANT YOU TO THINK I--
NO, IT'S COOL.
I GOT WHAT I WAS REALLY AFTER TONIGHT.

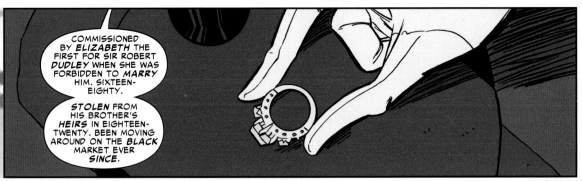

COMMISSIONED BY *ELIZABETH* THE FIRST FOR SIR ROBERT *DUDLEY* WHEN SHE WAS FORBIDDEN TO *MARRY* HIM. SIXTEEN-EIGHTY.

STOLEN FROM HIS BROTHER'S *HEIRS* IN EIGHTEEN-TWENTY. BEEN MOVING AROUND ON THE *BLACK* MARKET EVER *SINCE.*

IT *COULD* BE THE *BEST* OFFER WILL COME FROM ONE OF THE BRITISH *MUSEUMS...IF* WE CAN DEMONSTRATE ITS LEGITIMACY.

AND THE *REVERE* WEDDING BANDS?

HAD TO SACRIFICE *PAWNS* TO KEEP THE *QUEEN.* ANOTHER TIME, MAYBE.

THE GOLDSMITH'S *MARK* IS STILL CLEAR... *ENGRAVING'S* WORN...

HAVE YOU GIVEN ANY *THOUGHT* TO THE *RUSSIANS?*

THE-- WHAT DO YOU *MEAN?*

THE IMPERIAL *FABERGÉ* COLLECTION IS COMING TO THE *FRITTZ* MUSEUM. I HAVE A *CLIENT* WHO ASKED...

OH, *THAT.* I DON'T KNOW... THE FRITT'S NEVER BEEN MUCH *FUN.*

YOU MIND IF I HANG ONTO *THIS* WHILE YOU LOOK FOR A BUYER? I KIND OF *HATE* TO SAY GOODBYE SO *SOON.*

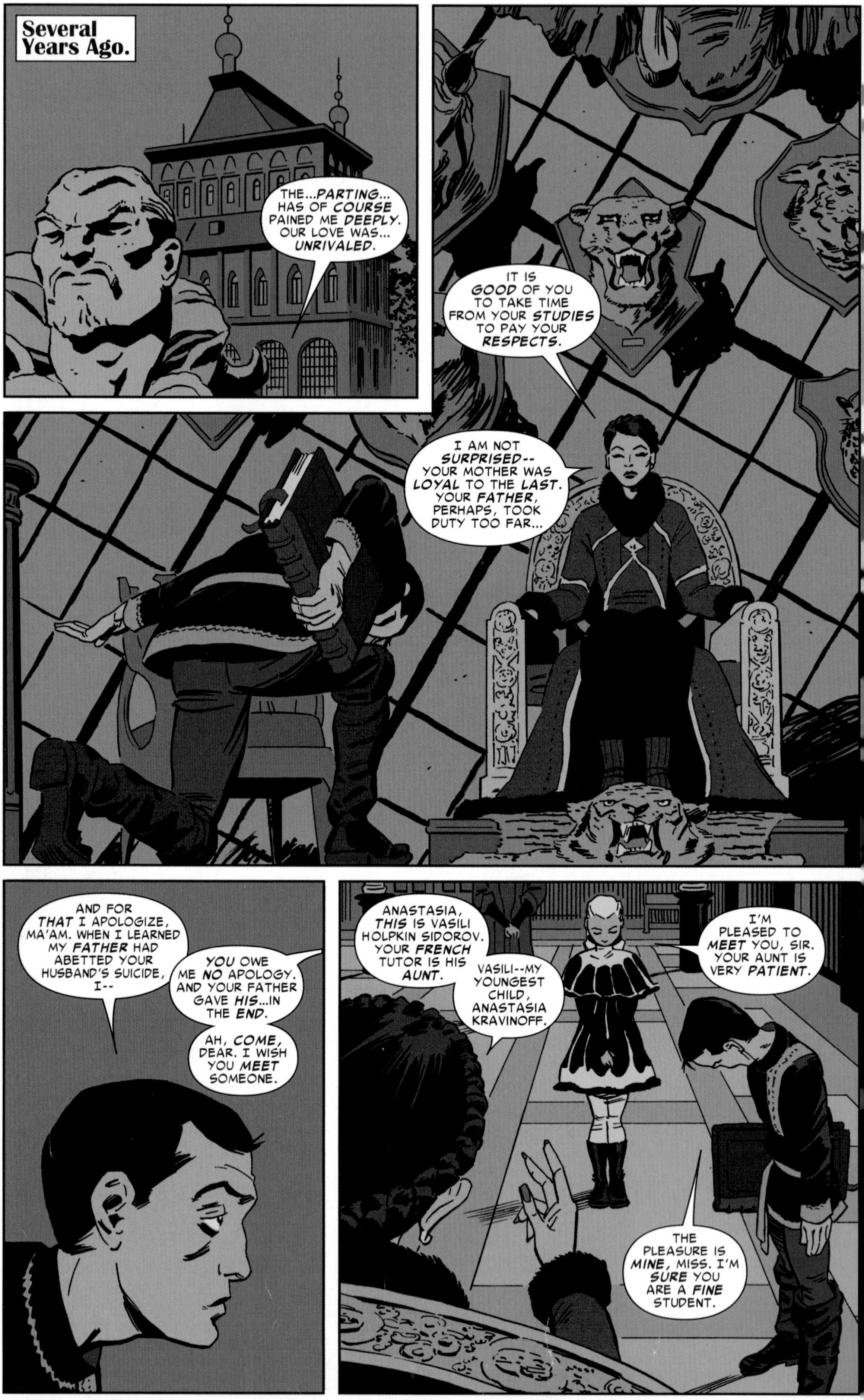
Several Years Ago.
THE...PARTING... HAS OF COURSE PAINED ME DEEPLY. OUR LOVE WAS... UNRIVALED.
IT IS GOOD OF YOU TO TAKE TIME FROM YOUR STUDIES TO PAY YOUR RESPECTS.
I AM NOT SURPRISED-- YOUR MOTHER WAS LOYAL TO THE LAST. YOUR FATHER, PERHAPS, TOOK DUTY TOO FAR...
AND FOR THAT I APOLOGIZE, MA'AM. WHEN I LEARNED MY FATHER HAD ABETTED YOUR HUSBAND'S SUICIDE, I--
YOU OWE ME NO APOLOGY. AND YOUR FATHER GAVE HIS...IN THE END.
AH, COME, DEAR. I WISH YOU MEET SOMEONE.
ANASTASIA, THIS IS VASILI HOLPKIN SIDOROV. YOUR FRENCH TUTOR IS HIS AUNT.
VASILI--MY YOUNGEST CHILD, ANASTASIA KRAVINOFF.
I'M PLEASED TO MEET YOU, SIR. YOUR AUNT IS VERY PATIENT.
THE PLEASURE IS MINE, MISS. I'M SURE YOU ARE A FINE STUDENT.

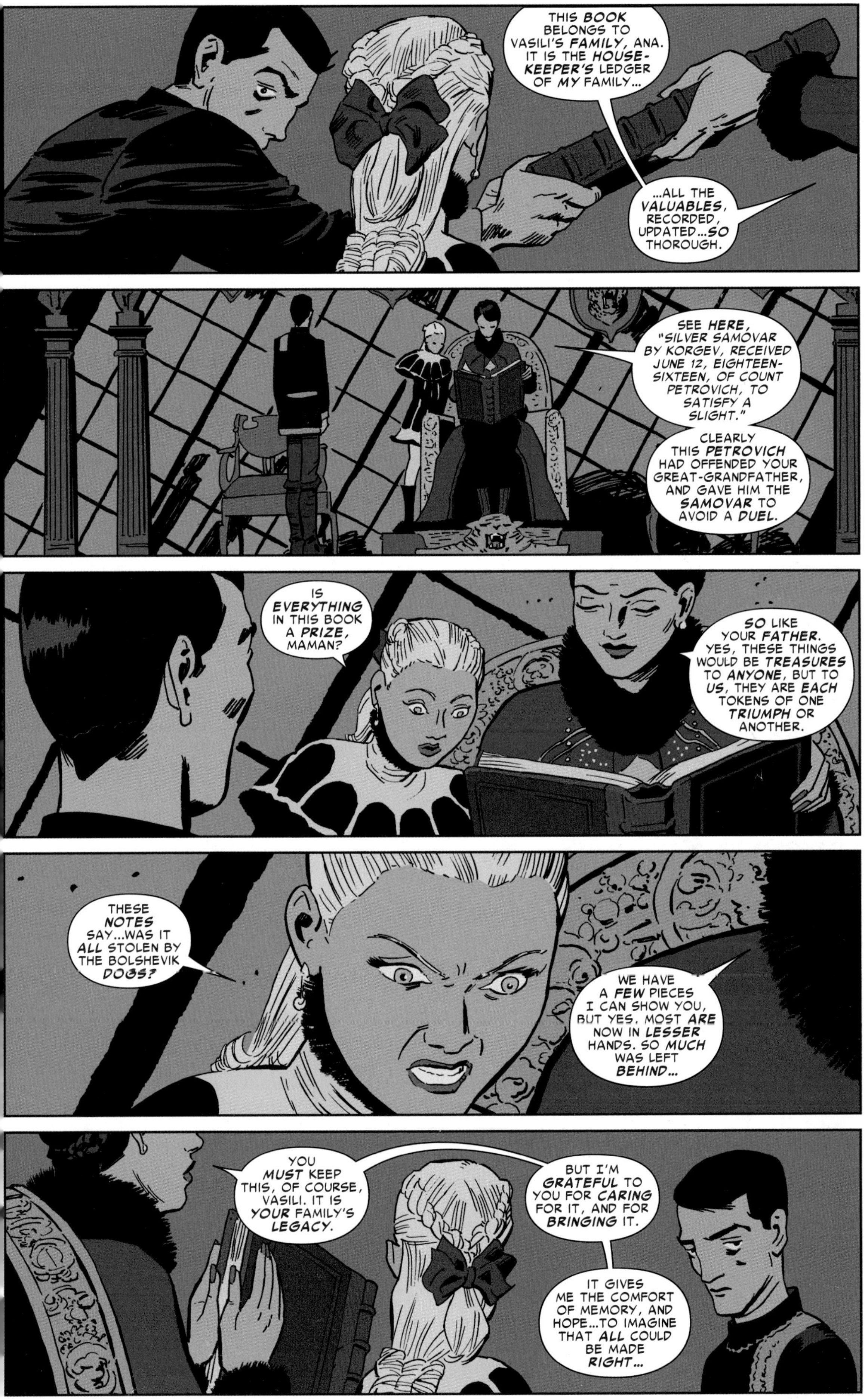
THIS BOOK BELONGS TO VASILI'S FAMILY, ANA. IT IS THE HOUSE-KEEPER'S LEDGER OF MY FAMILY...
...ALL THE VALUABLES, RECORDED, UPDATED...SO THOROUGH.
SEE HERE, "SILVER SAMOVAR BY KORGEV, RECEIVED JUNE 12, EIGHTEEN-SIXTEEN, OF COUNT PETROVICH, TO SATISFY A SLIGHT."
CLEARLY THIS PETROVICH HAD OFFENDED YOUR GREAT-GRANDFATHER, AND GAVE HIM THE SAMOVAR TO AVOID A DUEL.
IS EVERYTHING IN THIS BOOK A PRIZE, MAMAN?
SO LIKE YOUR FATHER. YES, THESE THINGS WOULD BE TREASURES TO ANYONE, BUT TO US, THEY ARE EACH TOKENS OF ONE TRIUMPH OR ANOTHER.
THESE NOTES SAY...WAS IT ALL STOLEN BY THE BOLSHEVIK DOGS?
WE HAVE A FEW PIECES I CAN SHOW YOU, BUT YES. MOST ARE NOW IN LESSER HANDS. SO MUCH WAS LEFT BEHIND...
YOU MUST KEEP THIS, OF COURSE, VASILI. IT IS YOUR FAMILY'S LEGACY.
BUT I'M GRATEFUL TO YOU FOR CARING FOR IT, AND FOR BRINGING IT.
IT GIVES ME THE COMFORT OF MEMORY, AND HOPE...TO IMAGINE THAT ALL COULD BE MADE RIGHT...

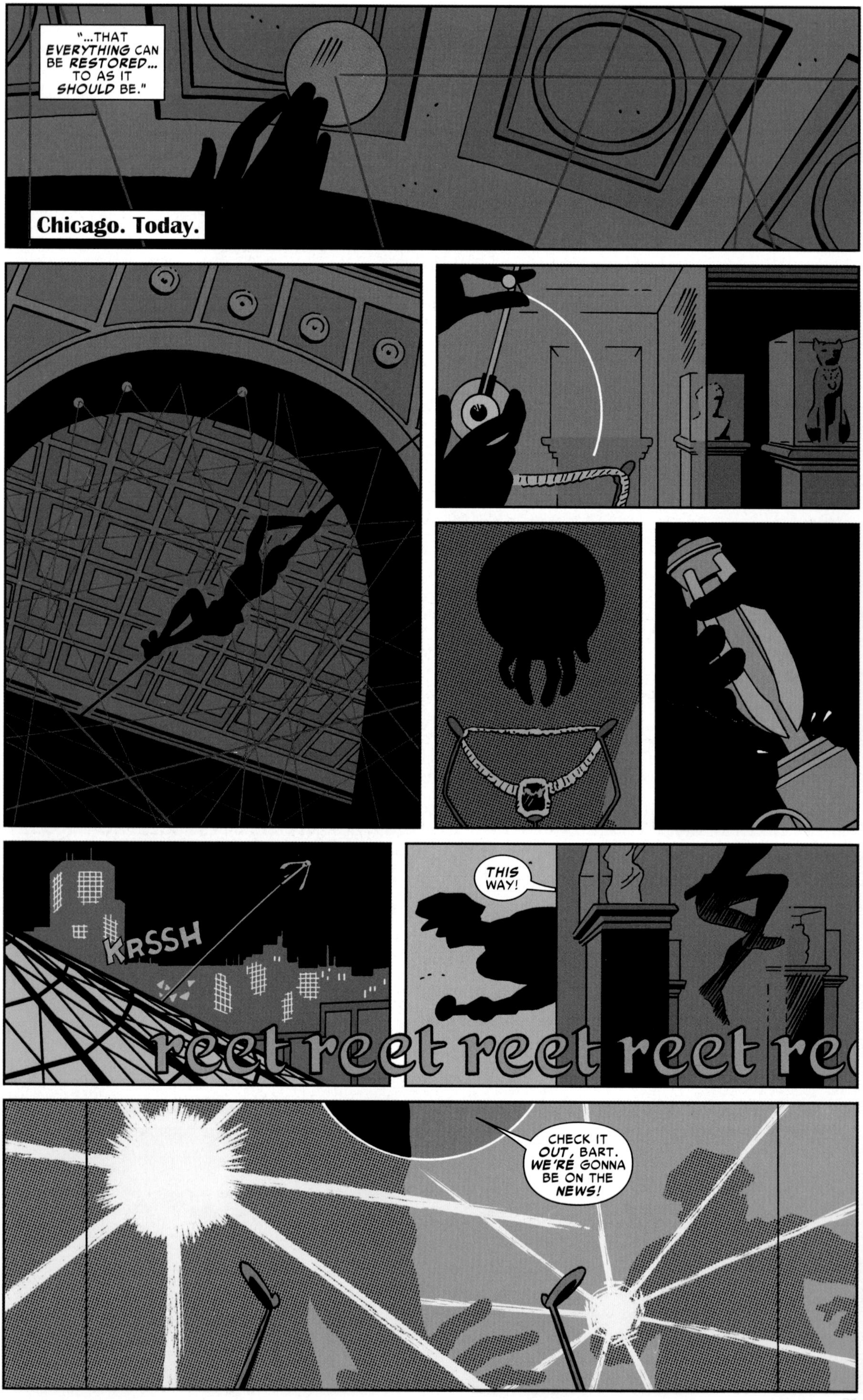
"...THAT EVERYTHING CAN BE RESTORED... TO AS IT SHOULD BE."
Chicago. Today.
KRSSH
THIS WAY!
reet reet reet reet re
CHECK IT OUT, BART. WE'RE GONNA BE ON THE NEWS!

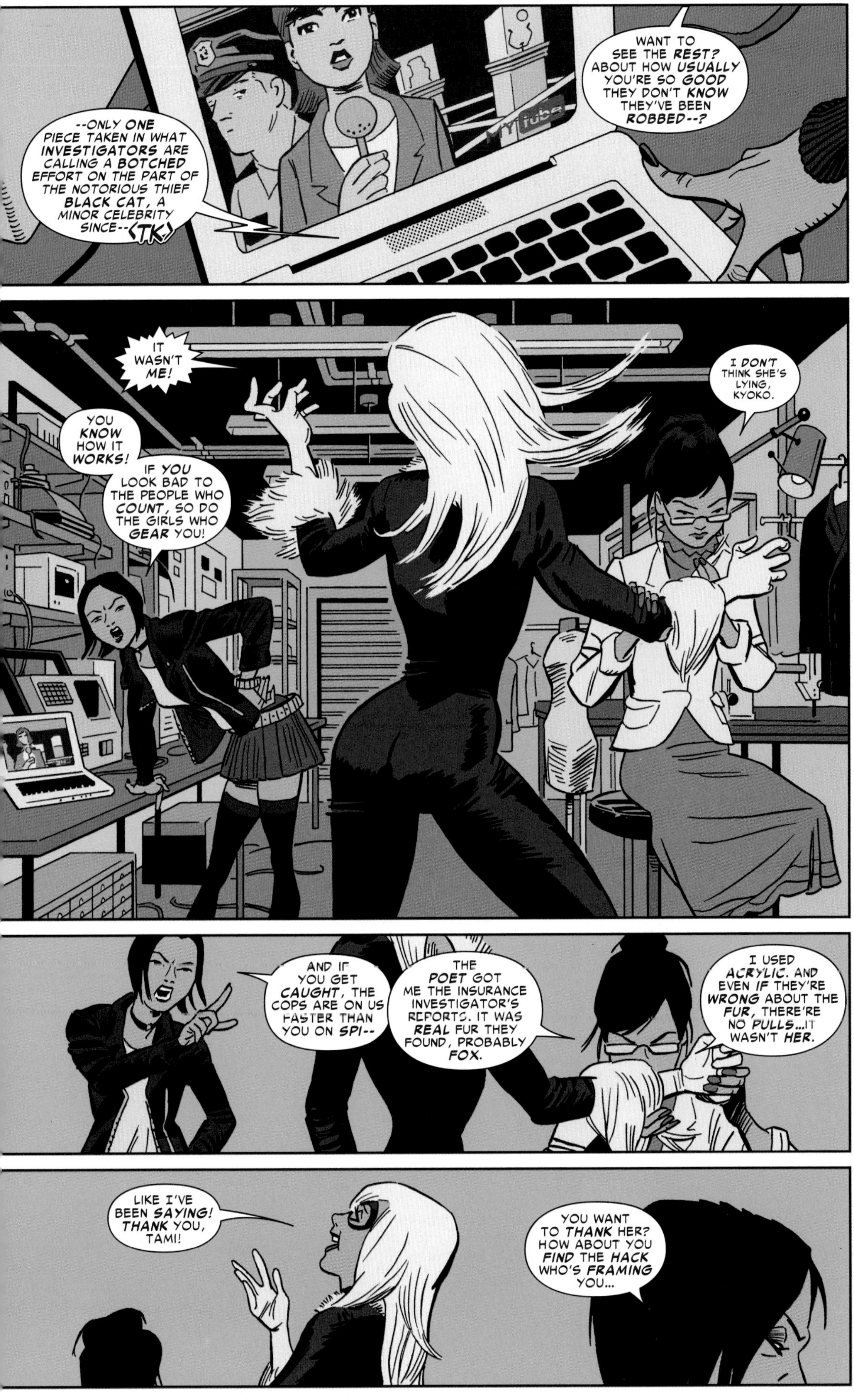
--ONLY ONE PIECE TAKEN IN WHAT INVESTIGATORS ARE CALLING A BOTCHED EFFORT ON THE PART OF THE NOTORIOUS THIEF BLACK CAT, A MINOR CELEBRITY SINCE--<TK>
MYtube
WANT TO SEE THE REST? ABOUT HOW USUALLY YOU'RE SO GOOD THEY DON'T KNOW THEY'VE BEEN ROBBED--?
IT WASN'T ME!
YOU KNOW HOW IT WORKS!
IF YOU LOOK BAD TO THE PEOPLE WHO COUNT, SO DO THE GIRLS WHO GEAR YOU!
I DON'T THINK SHE'S LYING, KYOKO.
AND IF YOU GET CAUGHT, THE COPS ARE ON US FASTER THAN YOU ON SPI--
THE POET GOT ME THE INSURANCE INVESTIGATOR'S REPORTS. IT WAS REAL FUR THEY FOUND, PROBABLY FOX.
I USED ACRYLIC. AND EVEN IF THEY'RE WRONG ABOUT THE FUR, THERE'RE NO PULLS...IT WASN'T HER.
LIKE I'VE BEEN SAYING! THANK YOU, TAMI!
YOU WANT TO THANK HER? HOW ABOUT YOU FIND THE HACK WHO'S FRAMING YOU...

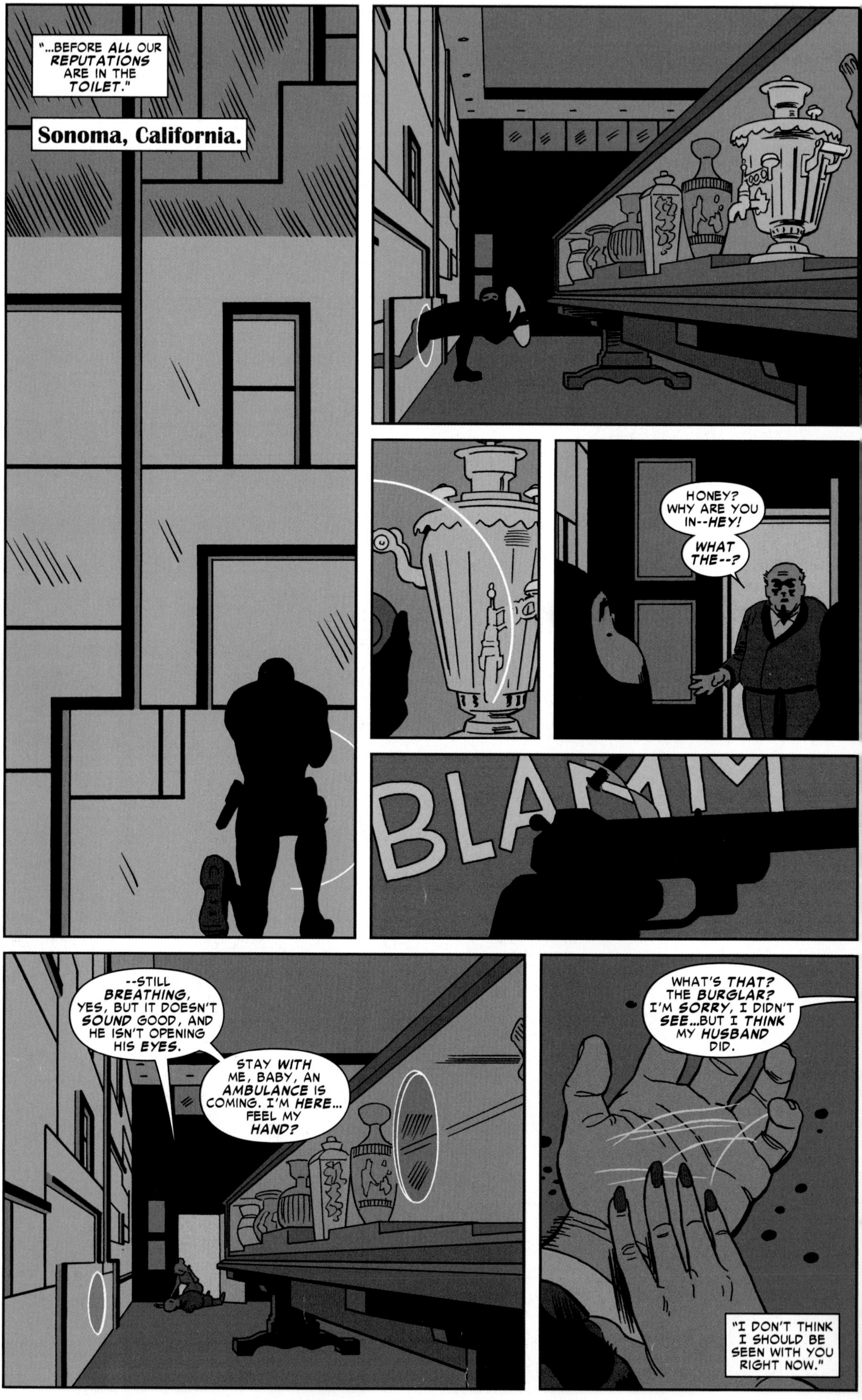
"...BEFORE ALL OUR REPUTATIONS ARE IN THE TOILET."
Sonoma, California.
HONEY? WHY ARE YOU IN--HEY!
WHAT THE--?
BLAMM
--STILL BREATHING, YES, BUT IT DOESN'T SOUND GOOD, AND HE ISN'T OPENING HIS EYES.
STAY WITH ME, BABY, AN AMBULANCE IS COMING. I'M HERE... FEEL MY HAND?
WHAT'S THAT? THE BURGLAR? I'M SORRY, I DIDN'T SEE...BUT I THINK MY HUSBAND DID.
"I DON'T THINK I SHOULD BE SEEN WITH YOU RIGHT NOW."

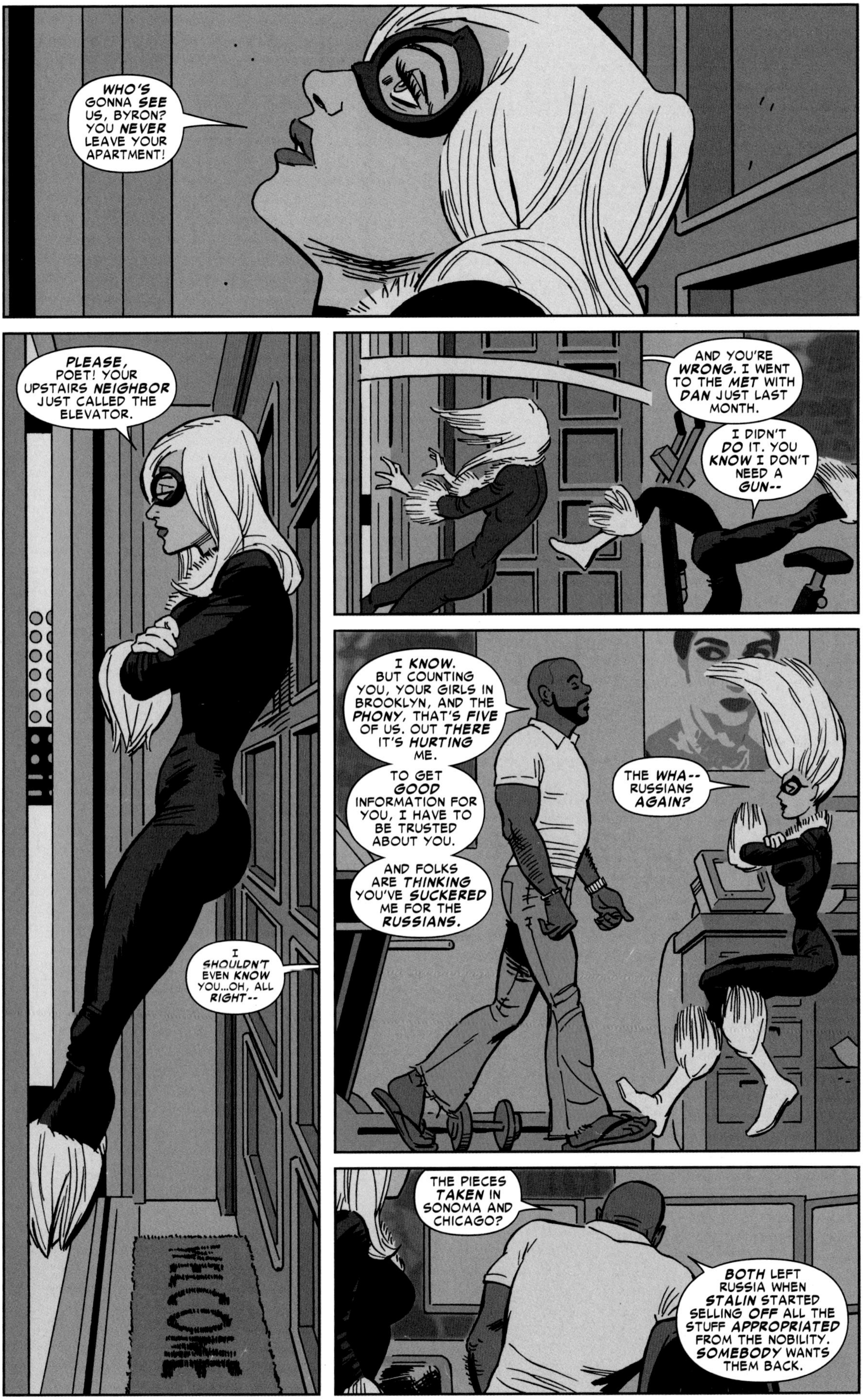
WHO'S GONNA SEE US, BYRON? YOU NEVER LEAVE YOUR APARTMENT!
PLEASE, POET! YOUR UPSTAIRS NEIGHBOR JUST CALLED THE ELEVATOR.
I SHOULDN'T EVEN KNOW YOU...OH, ALL RIGHT--
AND YOU'RE WRONG. I WENT TO THE MET WITH DAN JUST LAST MONTH.
I DIDN'T DO IT. YOU KNOW I DON'T NEED A GUN--
I KNOW. BUT COUNTING YOU, YOUR GIRLS IN BROOKLYN, AND THE PHONY, THAT'S FIVE OF US. OUT THERE IT'S HURTING ME.
TO GET GOOD INFORMATION FOR YOU, I HAVE TO BE TRUSTED ABOUT YOU.
AND FOLKS ARE THINKING YOU'VE SUCKERED ME FOR THE RUSSIANS.
THE WHA-- RUSSIANS AGAIN?
THE PIECES TAKEN IN SONOMA AND CHICAGO?
BOTH LEFT RUSSIA WHEN STALIN STARTED SELLING OFF ALL THE STUFF APPROPRIATED FROM THE NOBILITY. SOMEBODY WANTS THEM BACK.

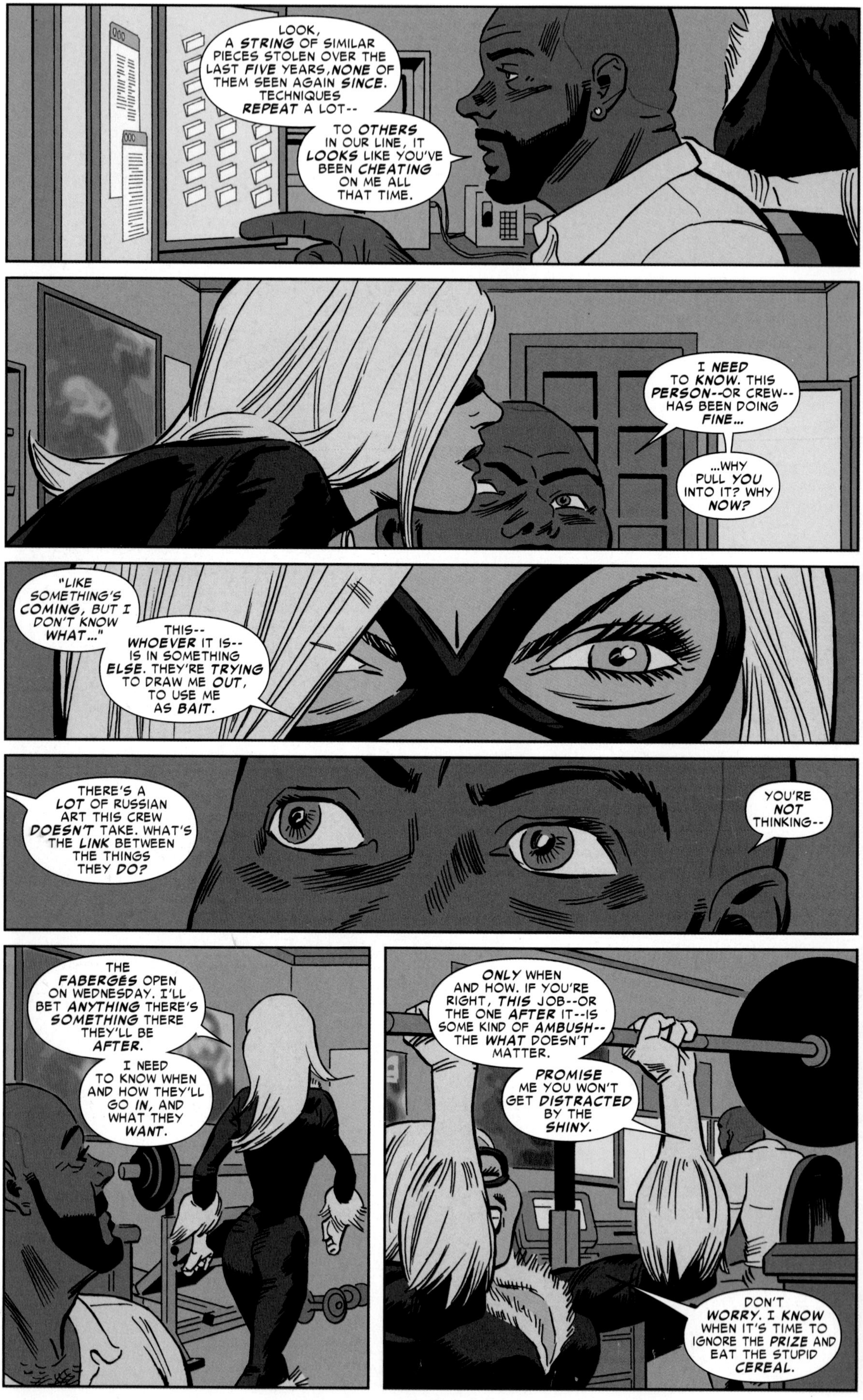
LOOK, A STRING OF SIMILAR PIECES STOLEN OVER THE LAST FIVE YEARS, NONE OF THEM SEEN AGAIN SINCE. TECHNIQUES REPEAT A LOT--
TO OTHERS IN OUR LINE, IT LOOKS LIKE YOU'VE BEEN CHEATING ON ME ALL THAT TIME.
I NEED TO KNOW. THIS PERSON--OR CREW--HAS BEEN DOING FINE...
...WHY PULL YOU INTO IT? WHY NOW?
"LIKE SOMETHING'S COMING, BUT I DON'T KNOW WHAT..."
THIS--WHOEVER IT IS--IS IN SOMETHING ELSE. THEY'RE TRYING TO DRAW ME OUT, TO USE ME AS BAIT.
THERE'S A LOT OF RUSSIAN ART THIS CREW DOESN'T TAKE. WHAT'S THE LINK BETWEEN THE THINGS THEY DO?
YOU'RE NOT THINKING--
THE FABERGES OPEN ON WEDNESDAY. I'LL BET ANYTHING THERE'S SOMETHING THERE THEY'LL BE AFTER.
I NEED TO KNOW WHEN AND HOW THEY'LL GO IN, AND WHAT THEY WANT.
ONLY WHEN AND HOW. IF YOU'RE RIGHT, THIS JOB--OR THE ONE AFTER IT--IS SOME KIND OF AMBUSH--THE WHAT DOESN'T MATTER.
PROMISE ME YOU WON'T GET DISTRACTED BY THE SHINY.
DON'T WORRY. I KNOW WHEN IT'S TIME TO IGNORE THE PRIZE AND EAT THE STUPID CEREAL.

"THEY'LL EXPECT *YOU* TO USE THE *SKYLIGHTS*--IT'S YOUR *STYLE*..."

"... BUT YOUR *IMPOSTER*-- FOUR TO ONE ODDS THEY'LL USE THE *DUCTS.*"

"SECURITY IS *MOSTLY* HUMAN BECAUSE OF THE *AGE* OF THE *BUILDING*..."

"ONCE THE *TARGET'S* DISABLED THE *MOTION* SENSORS, YOU'RE *GOLDEN*."

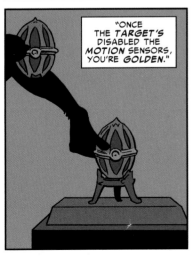

"*WEIGHT* ALARMS IN THE *CASES* MEANS PROBABLY AN *AERIAL RIG.* THEY'LL BE *VULNERABLE*."

"HIT THEM *EARLY,* AND REMEMBER WHAT YOU *SAID*..."

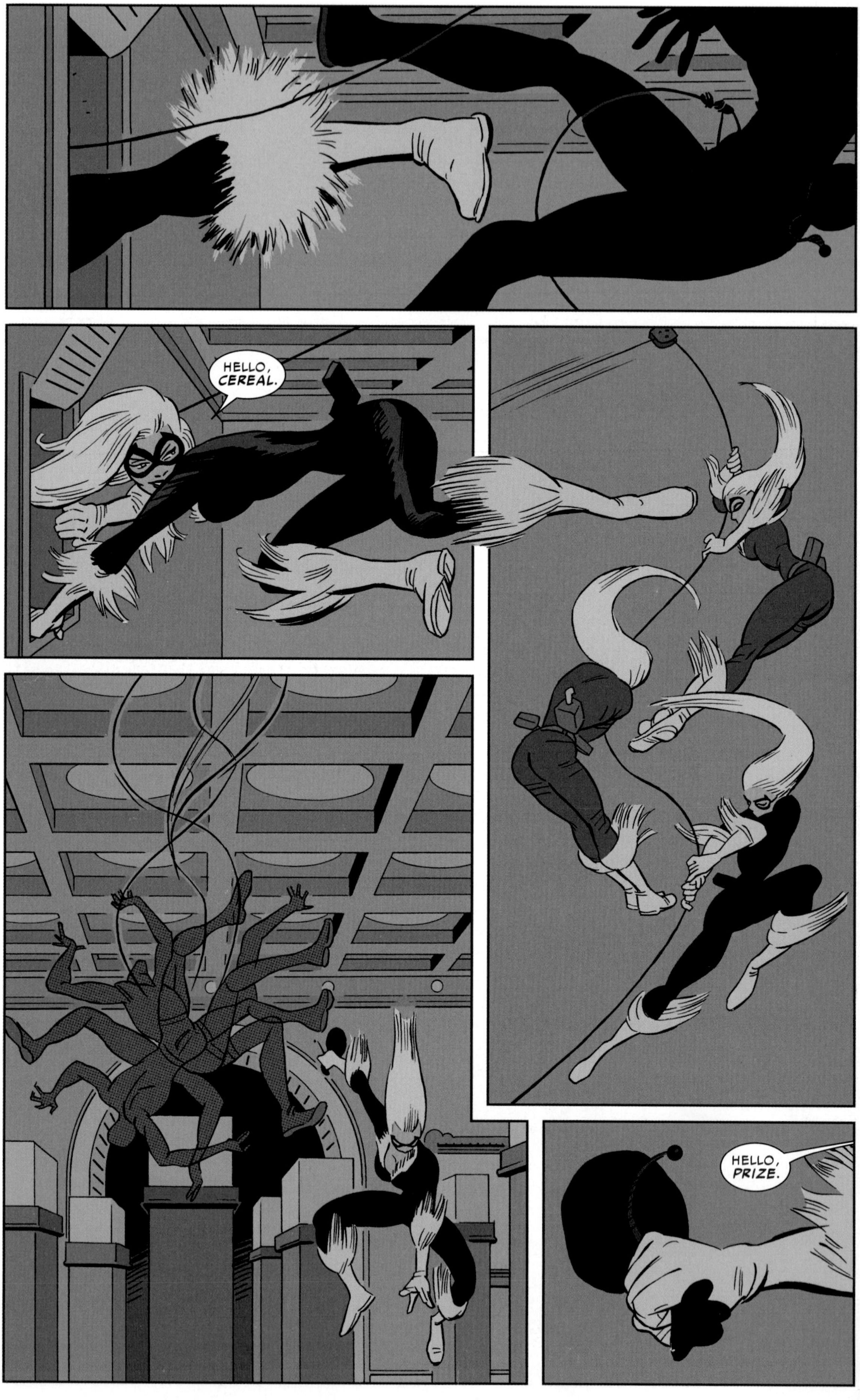
HELLO, CEREAL.
HELLO, PRIZE.

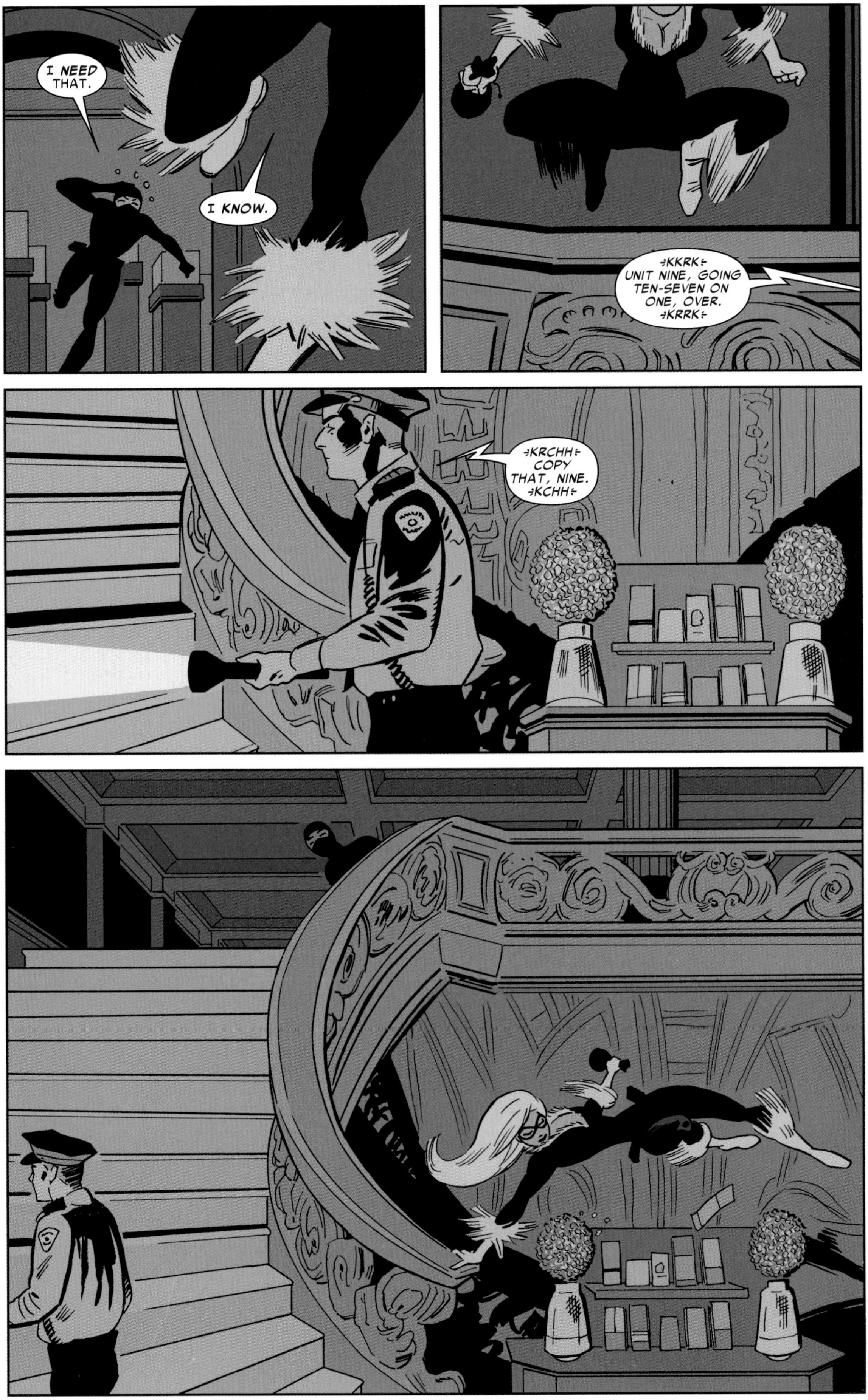
I NEED THAT.
I KNOW.
⊰KKRK⊱ UNIT NINE, GOING TEN-SEVEN ON ONE, OVER. ⊰KRRK⊱
⊰KRCHH⊱ COPY THAT, NINE. ⊰KCHH⊱

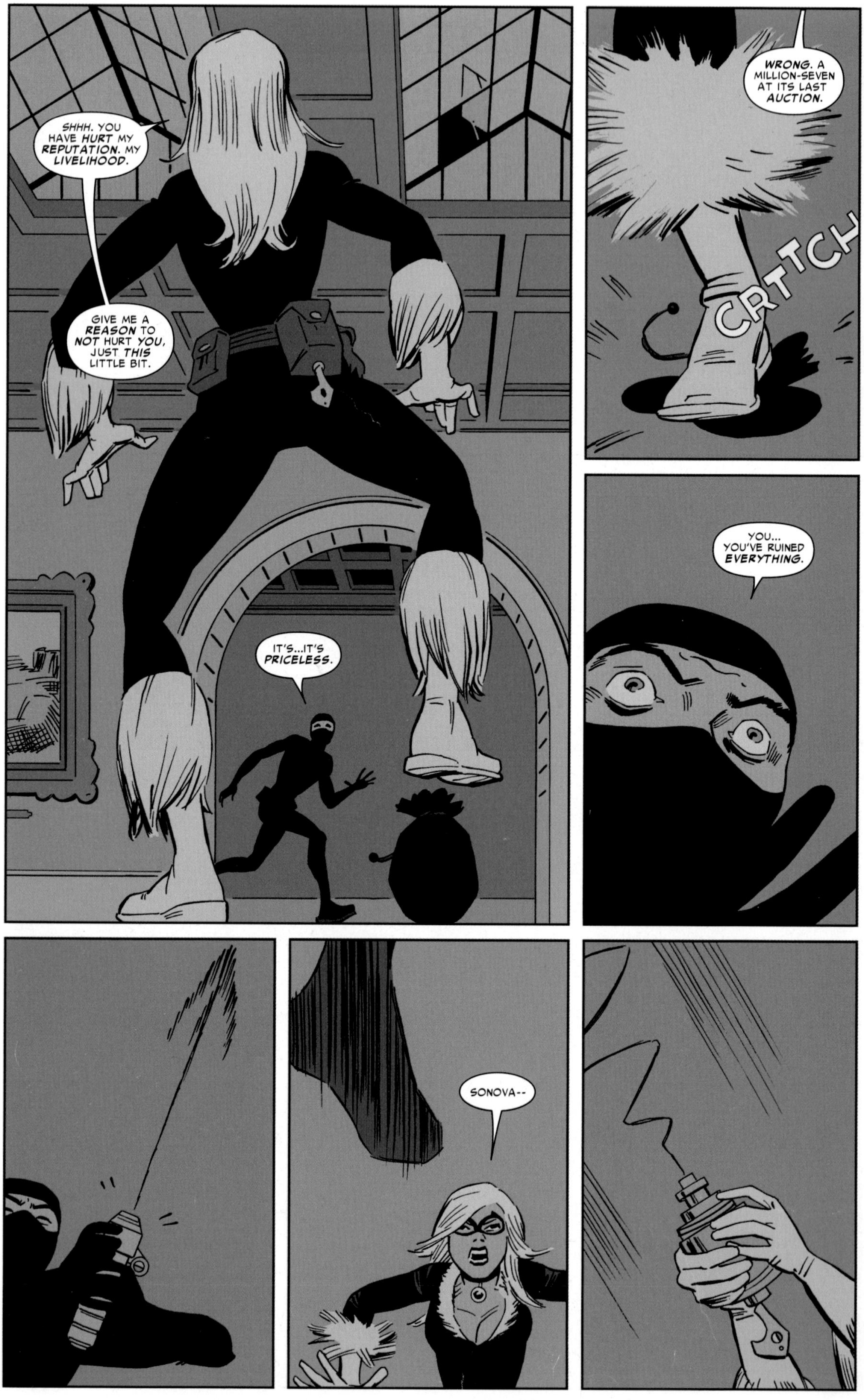
SHHH. YOU HAVE HURT MY REPUTATION. MY LIVELIHOOD.
GIVE ME A REASON TO NOT HURT YOU, JUST THIS LITTLE BIT.
IT'S...IT'S PRICELESS.
WRONG. A MILLION-SEVEN AT ITS LAST AUCTION.
CRTTCH
YOU... YOU'VE RUINED EVERYTHING.
SONOVA--

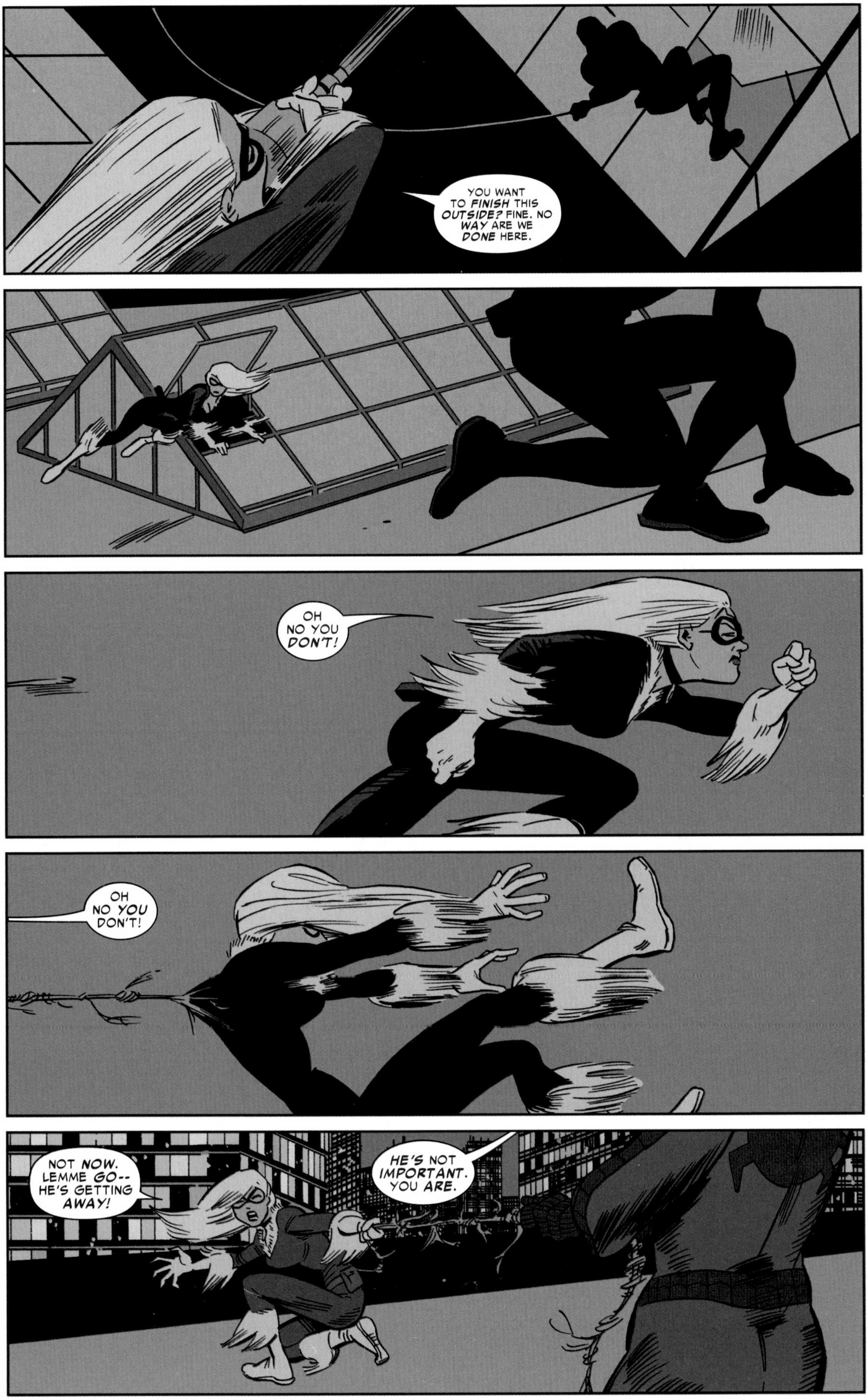

YOU WANT TO FINISH THIS OUTSIDE? FINE. NO WAY ARE WE DONE HERE.
OH NO YOU DON'T!
OH NO YOU DON'T!
NOT NOW. LEMME GO-- HE'S GETTING AWAY!
HE'S NOT IMPORTANT. YOU ARE.

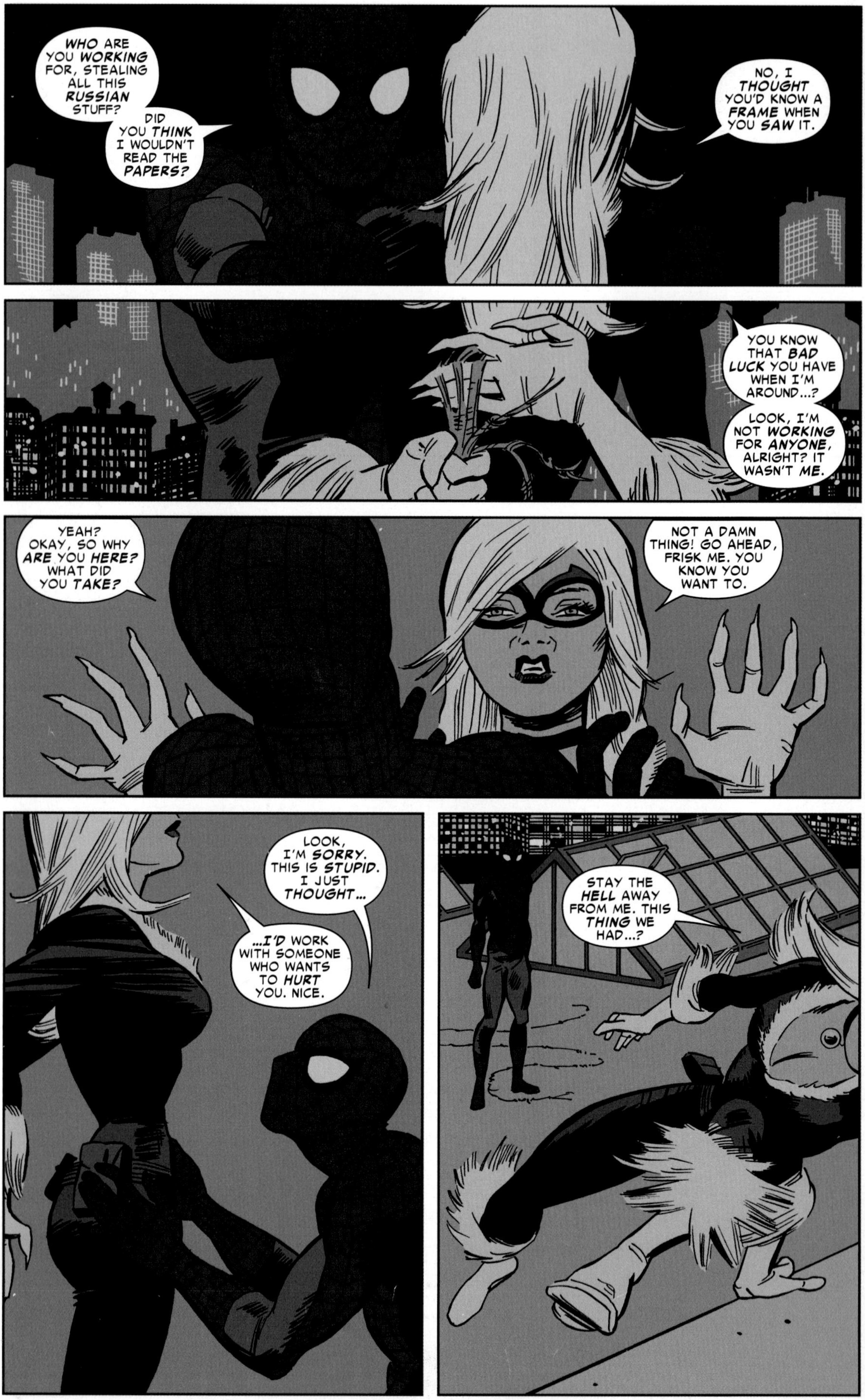
WHO ARE YOU WORKING FOR, STEALING ALL THIS RUSSIAN STUFF?
DID YOU THINK I WOULDN'T READ THE PAPERS?
NO, I THOUGHT YOU'D KNOW A FRAME WHEN YOU SAW IT.
YOU KNOW THAT BAD LUCK YOU HAVE WHEN I'M AROUND...?
LOOK, I'M NOT WORKING FOR ANYONE, ALRIGHT? IT WASN'T ME.
YEAH? OKAY, SO WHY ARE YOU HERE? WHAT DID YOU TAKE?
NOT A DAMN THING! GO AHEAD, FRISK ME. YOU KNOW YOU WANT TO.
LOOK, I'M SORRY. THIS IS STUPID. I JUST THOUGHT...
...I'D WORK WITH SOMEONE WHO WANTS TO HURT YOU. NICE.
STAY THE HELL AWAY FROM ME. THIS THING WE HAD...?

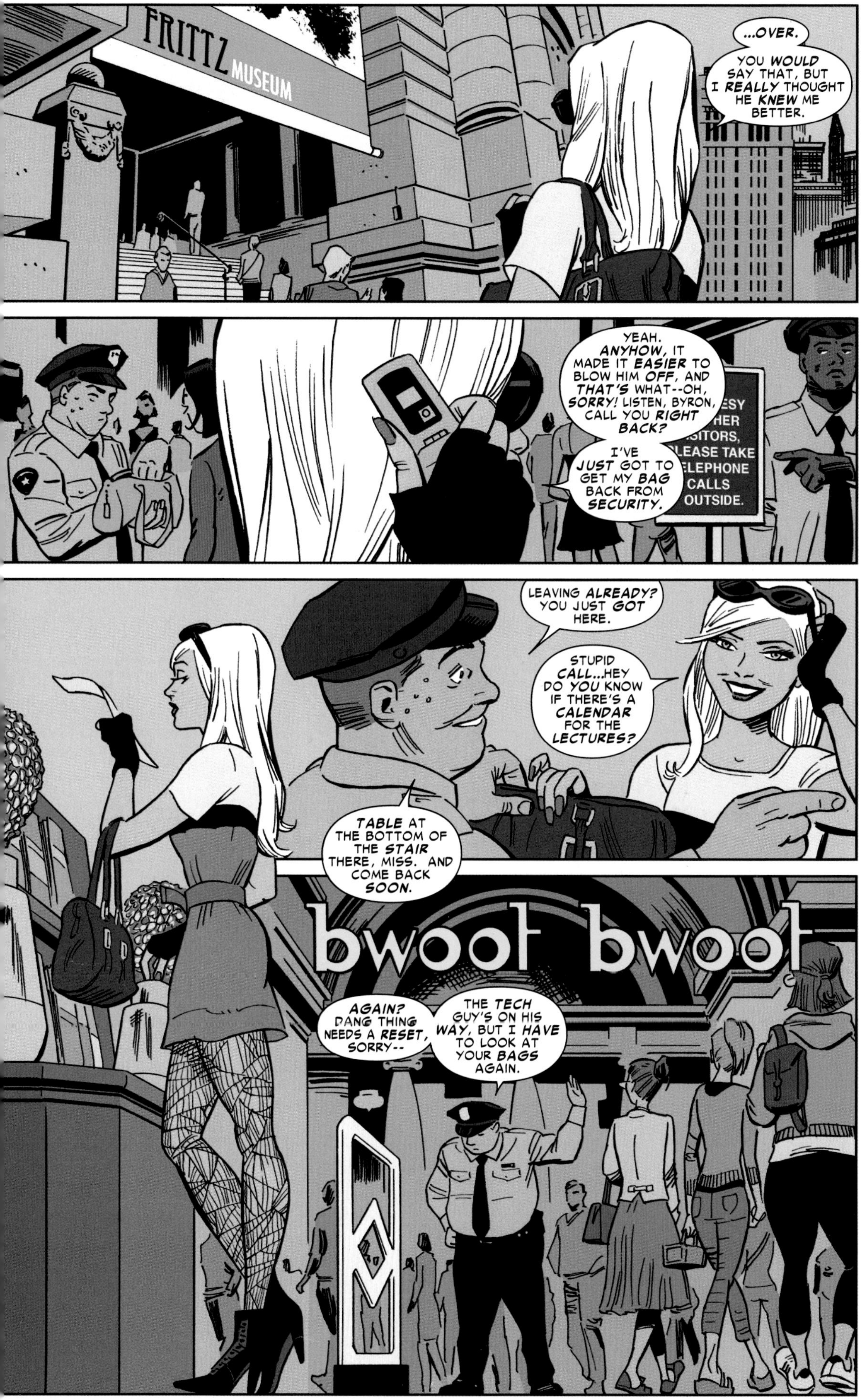
FRITTZ MUSEUM
...OVER.
YOU WOULD SAY THAT, BUT I REALLY THOUGHT HE KNEW ME BETTER.
YEAH. ANYHOW, IT MADE IT EASIER TO BLOW HIM OFF, AND THAT'S WHAT--OH, SORRY! LISTEN, BYRON, CALL YOU RIGHT BACK?
I'VE JUST GOT TO GET MY BAG BACK FROM SECURITY.
LEAVING ALREADY? YOU JUST GOT HERE.
STUPID CALL...HEY DO YOU KNOW IF THERE'S A CALENDAR FOR THE LECTURES?
TABLE AT THE BOTTOM OF THE STAIR THERE, MISS. AND COME BACK SOON.
bwoot bwoot
AGAIN? DANG THING NEEDS A RESET, SORRY--
THE TECH GUY'S ON HIS WAY, BUT I HAVE TO LOOK AT YOUR BAGS AGAIN.

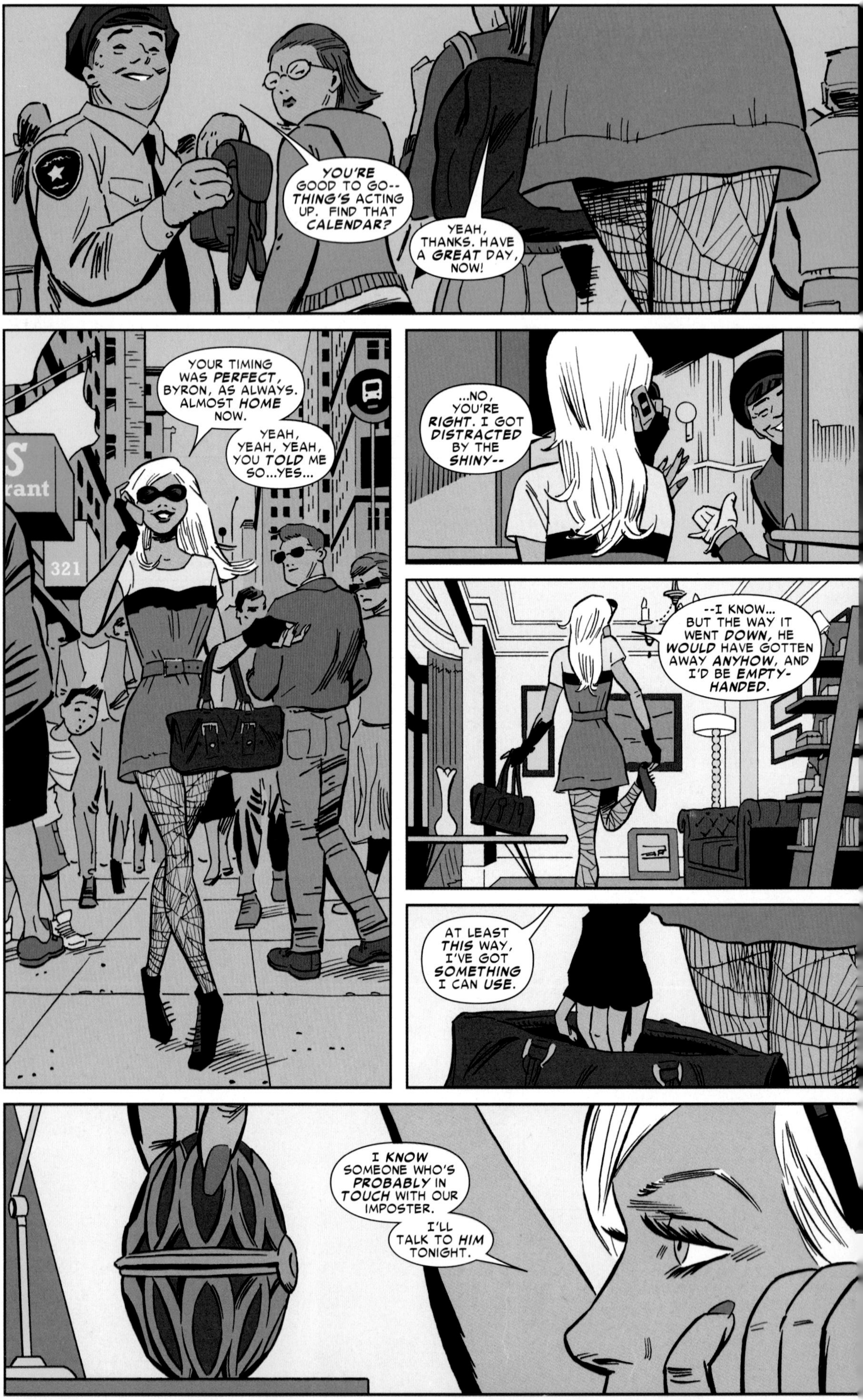
YOU'RE GOOD TO GO-- THING'S ACTING UP. FIND THAT CALENDAR?
YEAH, THANKS. HAVE A GREAT DAY, NOW!
YOUR TIMING WAS PERFECT, BYRON, AS ALWAYS. ALMOST HOME NOW.
YEAH, YEAH, YEAH, YOU TOLD ME SO...YES...
...NO, YOU'RE RIGHT. I GOT DISTRACTED BY THE SHINY--
--I KNOW... BUT THE WAY IT WENT DOWN, HE WOULD HAVE GOTTEN AWAY ANYHOW, AND I'D BE EMPTY-HANDED.
AT LEAST THIS WAY, I'VE GOT SOMETHING I CAN USE.
I KNOW SOMEONE WHO'S PROBABLY IN TOUCH WITH OUR IMPOSTER.
I'LL TALK TO HIM TONIGHT.

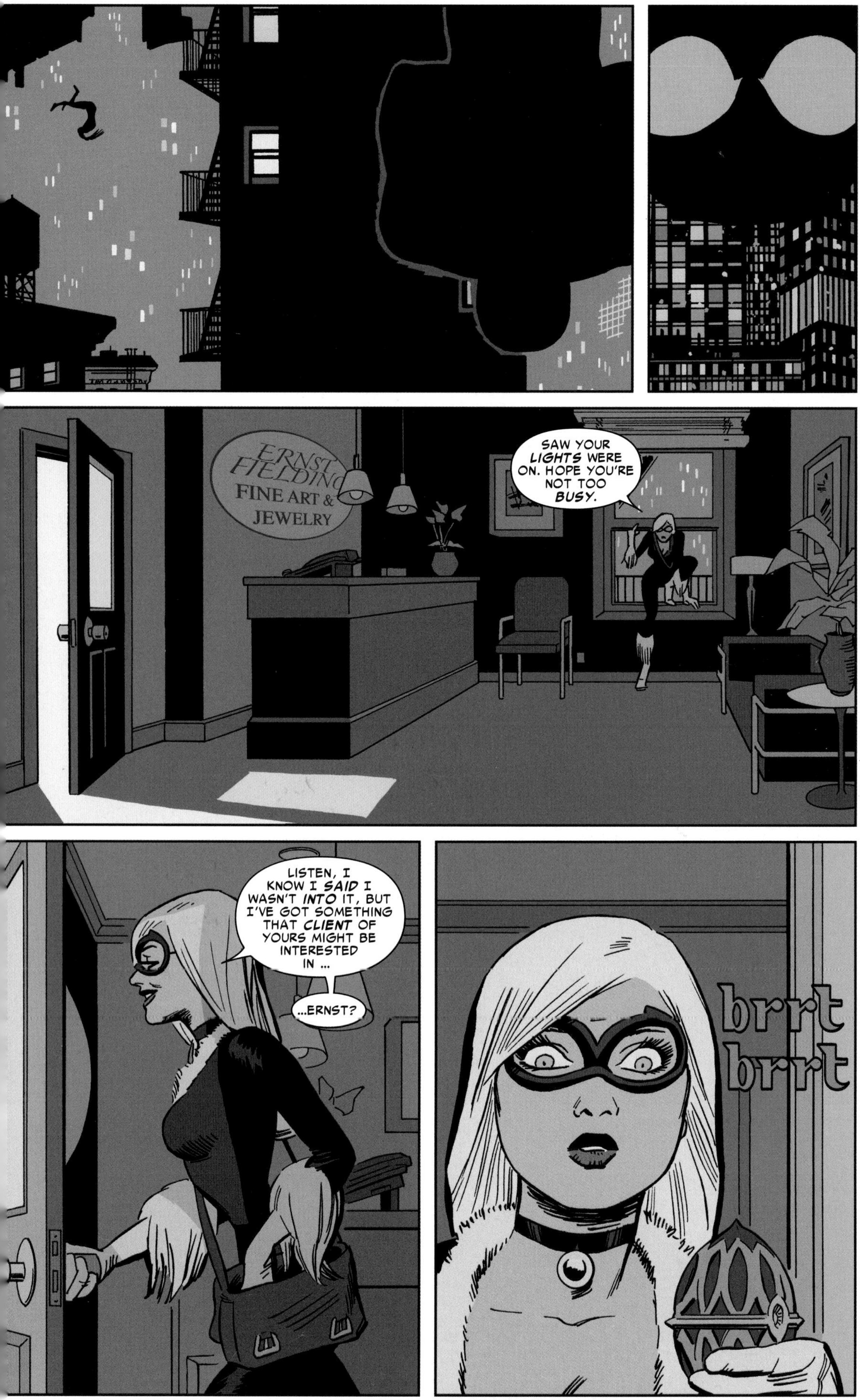
ERNST FIELDING FINE ART & JEWELRY
SAW YOUR LIGHTS WERE ON. HOPE YOU'RE NOT TOO BUSY.
LISTEN, I KNOW I SAID I WASN'T INTO IT, BUT I'VE GOT SOMETHING THAT CLIENT OF YOURS MIGHT BE INTERESTED IN ...
...ERNST?
brrt brrt

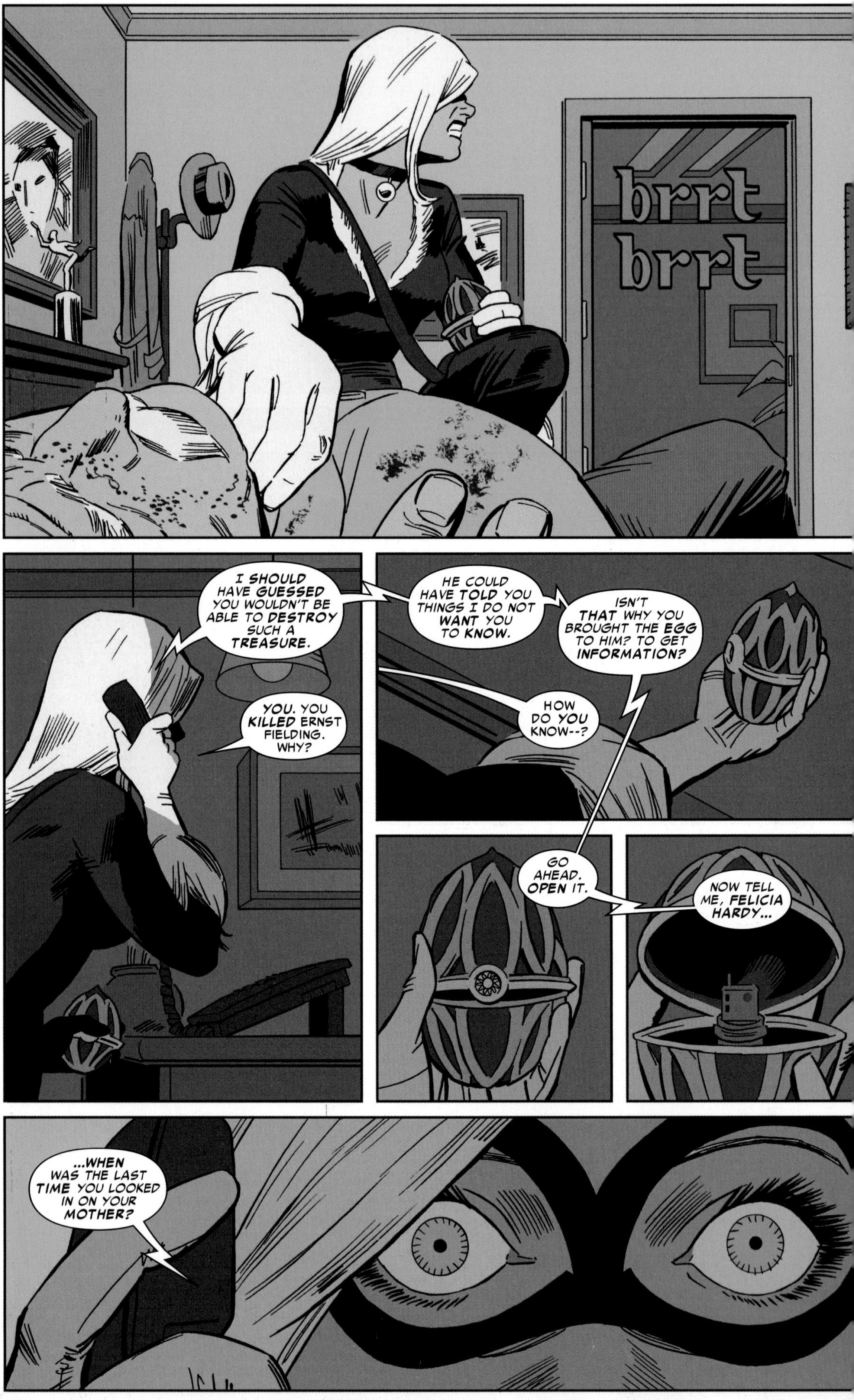

brrt brrt
I SHOULD HAVE GUESSED YOU WOULDN'T BE ABLE TO DESTROY SUCH A TREASURE.
YOU. YOU KILLED ERNST FIELDING. WHY?
HE COULD HAVE TOLD YOU THINGS I DO NOT WANT YOU TO KNOW.
ISN'T THAT WHY YOU BROUGHT THE EGG TO HIM? TO GET INFORMATION?
HOW DO YOU KNOW--?
GO AHEAD. OPEN IT.
NOW TELL ME, FELICIA HARDY...
...WHEN WAS THE LAST TIME YOU LOOKED IN ON YOUR MOTHER?

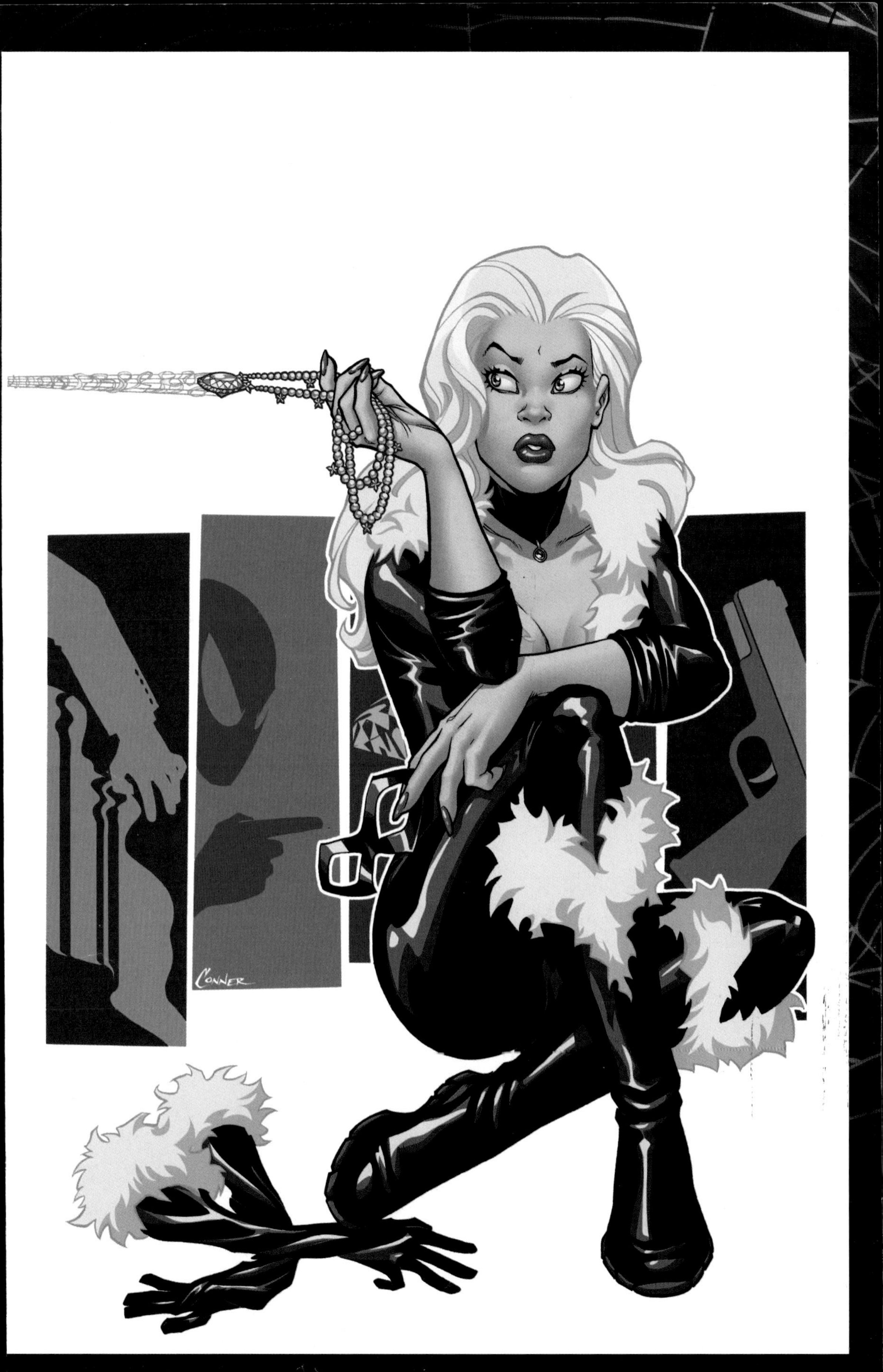
CONNER

AMAZING SPIDER-MAN PRESENTS: BLACK CAT #2

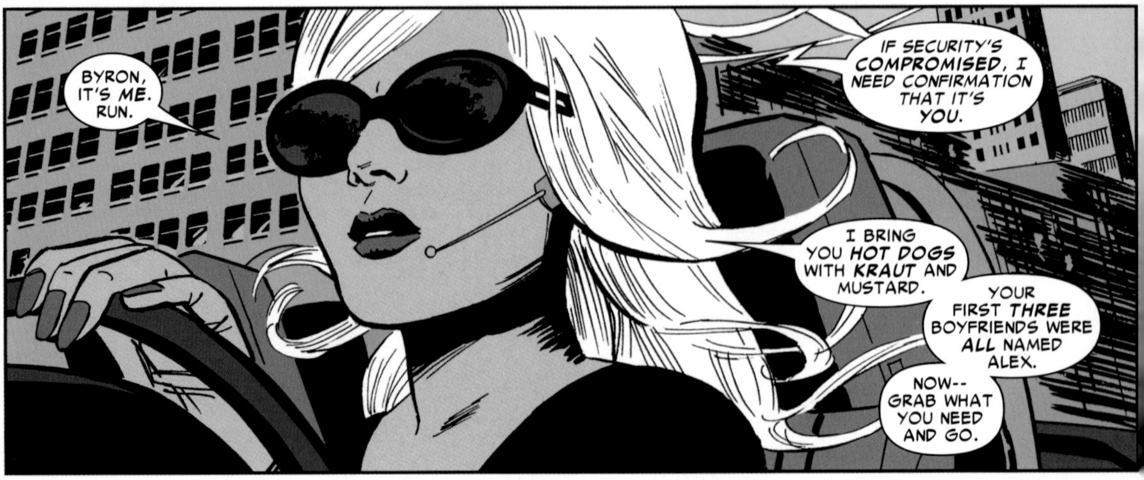
BYRON, IT'S ME. RUN.
IF SECURITY'S COMPROMISED, I NEED CONFIRMATION THAT IT'S YOU.
I BRING YOU HOT DOGS WITH KRAUT AND MUSTARD.
YOUR FIRST THREE BOYFRIENDS WERE ALL NAMED ALEX.
NOW-- GRAB WHAT YOU NEED AND GO.

TOM BRENNAN
ASST. EDITOR

STEPHEN WACKER
EDITOR

TOM BREVOORT
EXEC. EDITOR

JOE QUESADA
EDITOR IN CHIEF

DAN BUCKLEY
PUBLISHER

ALAN FINE
EXEC. PRODUCER

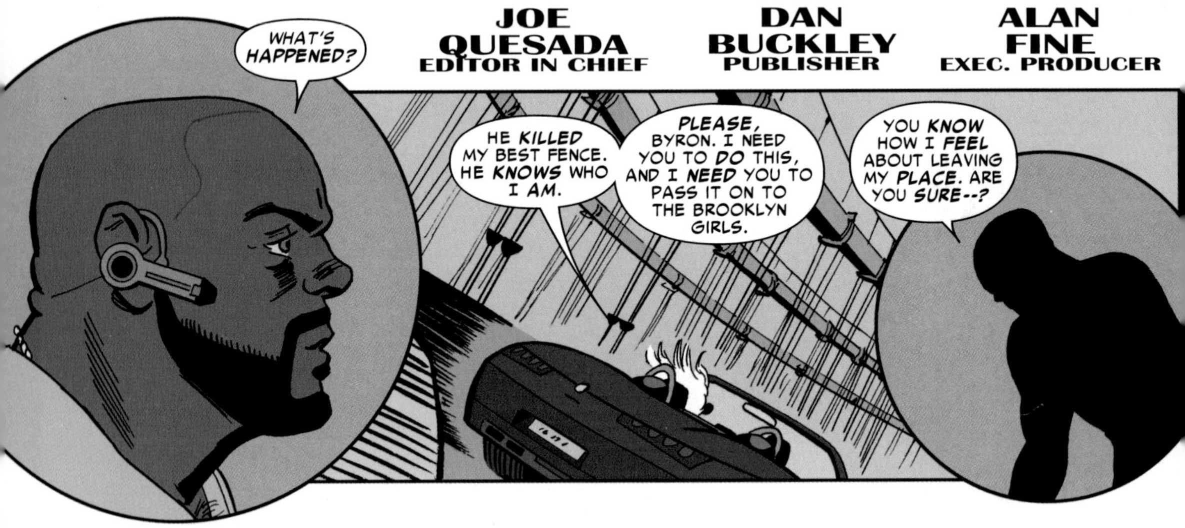
WHAT'S HAPPENED?
HE KILLED MY BEST FENCE. HE KNOWS WHO I AM.
PLEASE, BYRON. I NEED YOU TO DO THIS, AND I NEED YOU TO PASS IT ON TO THE BROOKLYN GIRLS.
YOU KNOW HOW I FEEL ABOUT LEAVING MY PLACE. ARE YOU SURE--?

MATT HOLLINGSWORTH
COLOR ART

VC'S JOE CARAMAGNA
LETTERS

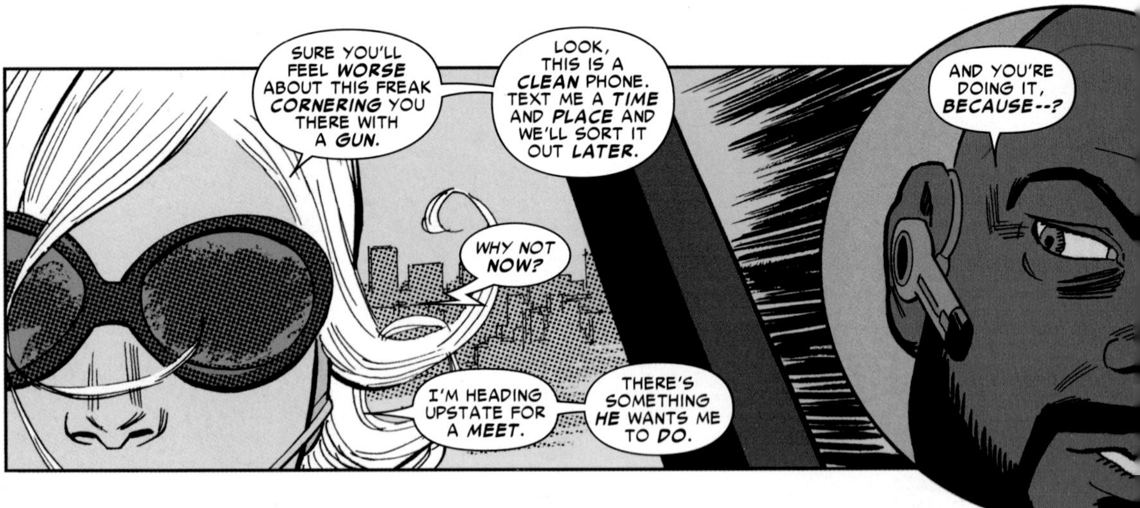
SURE YOU'LL FEEL WORSE ABOUT THIS FREAK CORNERING YOU THERE WITH A GUN.
LOOK, THIS IS A CLEAN PHONE. TEXT ME A TIME AND PLACE AND WE'LL SORT IT OUT LATER.
AND YOU'RE DOING IT, BECAUSE--?
WHY NOT NOW?
I'M HEADING UPSTATE FOR A MEET.
THERE'S SOMETHING HE WANTS ME TO DO.

JEN VAN METER
WRITER

JAVIER PULIDO
ARTIST, pg. 1-17

JAVIER RODRIGUEZ
ARTIST, pg. 18-23

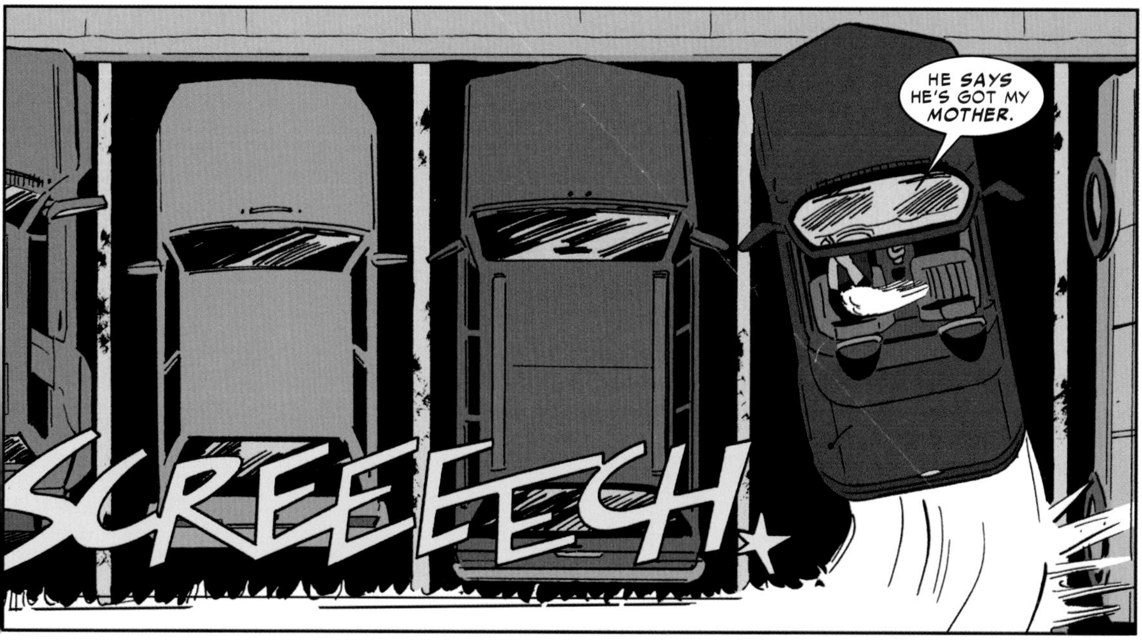

HE SAYS HE'S GOT MY MOTHER.
SCREEEECH

Black Cat: The Trophy Hunters Part Two

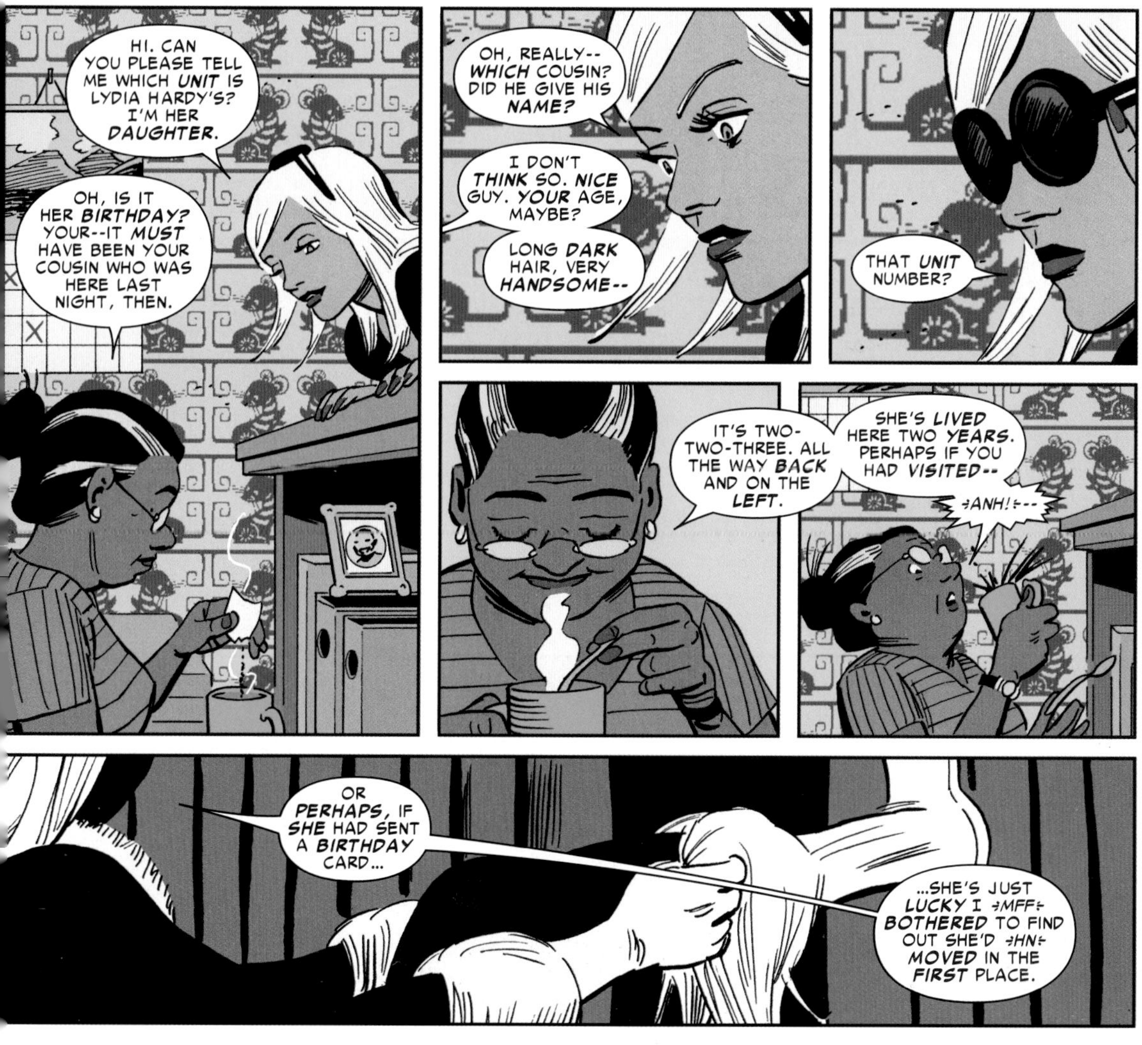

HI. CAN YOU PLEASE TELL ME WHICH UNIT IS LYDIA HARDY'S? I'M HER DAUGHTER.
OH, IS IT HER BIRTHDAY? YOUR--IT MUST HAVE BEEN YOUR COUSIN WHO WAS HERE LAST NIGHT, THEN.
OH, REALLY--WHICH COUSIN? DID HE GIVE HIS NAME?
I DON'T THINK SO. NICE GUY. YOUR AGE, MAYBE?
LONG DARK HAIR, VERY HANDSOME--
THAT UNIT NUMBER?
IT'S TWO-TWO-THREE. ALL THE WAY BACK AND ON THE LEFT.
SHE'S LIVED HERE TWO YEARS. PERHAPS IF YOU HAD VISITED--
ANH!
OR PERHAPS, IF SHE HAD SENT A BIRTHDAY CARD...
...SHE'S JUST LUCKY I MFF BOTHERED TO FIND OUT SHE'D HN MOVED IN THE FIRST PLACE.

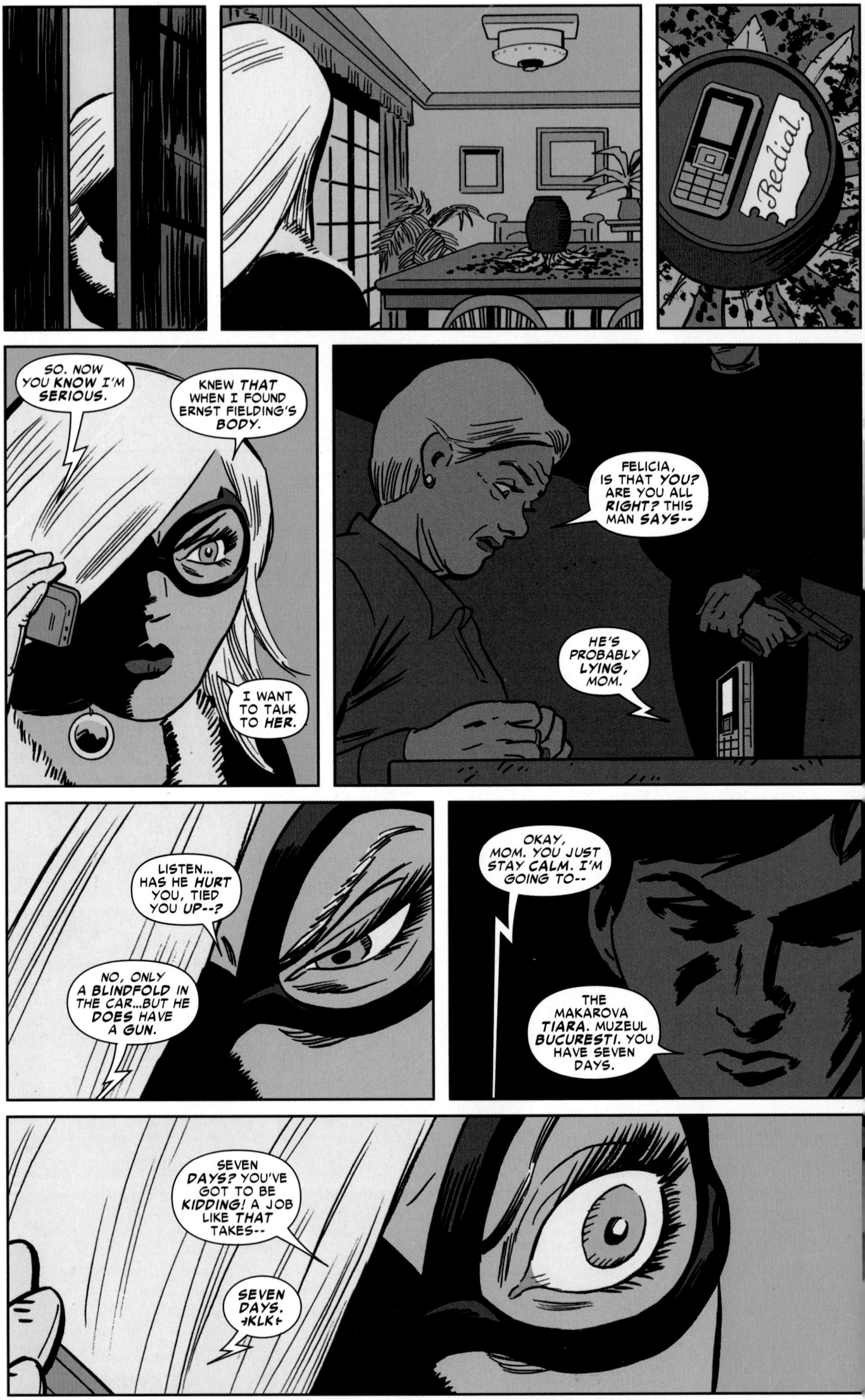
Redial.
SO. NOW YOU KNOW I'M SERIOUS.
KNEW THAT WHEN I FOUND ERNST FIELDING'S BODY.
I WANT TO TALK TO HER.
FELICIA, IS THAT YOU? ARE YOU ALL RIGHT? THIS MAN SAYS--
HE'S PROBABLY LYING, MOM.
LISTEN... HAS HE HURT YOU, TIED YOU UP--?
NO, ONLY A BLINDFOLD IN THE CAR...BUT HE DOES HAVE A GUN.
OKAY, MOM. YOU JUST STAY CALM. I'M GOING TO--
THE MAKAROVA TIARA. MUZEUL BUCURESTI. YOU HAVE SEVEN DAYS.
SEVEN DAYS? YOU'VE GOT TO BE KIDDING! A JOB LIKE THAT TAKES--
SEVEN DAYS.
KLK

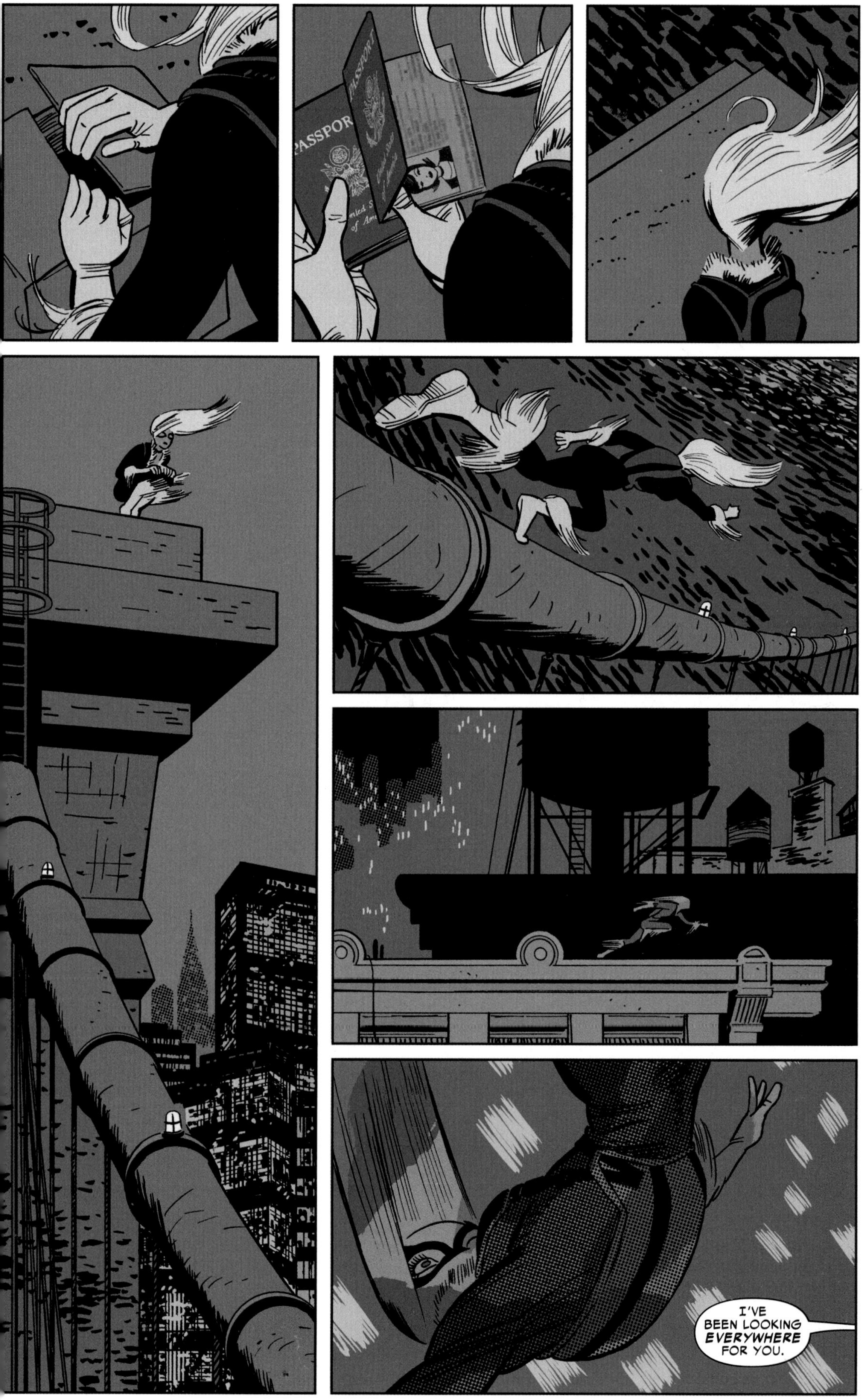
PASSPORT
PASSPORT
I'VE BEEN LOOKING *EVERYWHERE* FOR YOU.

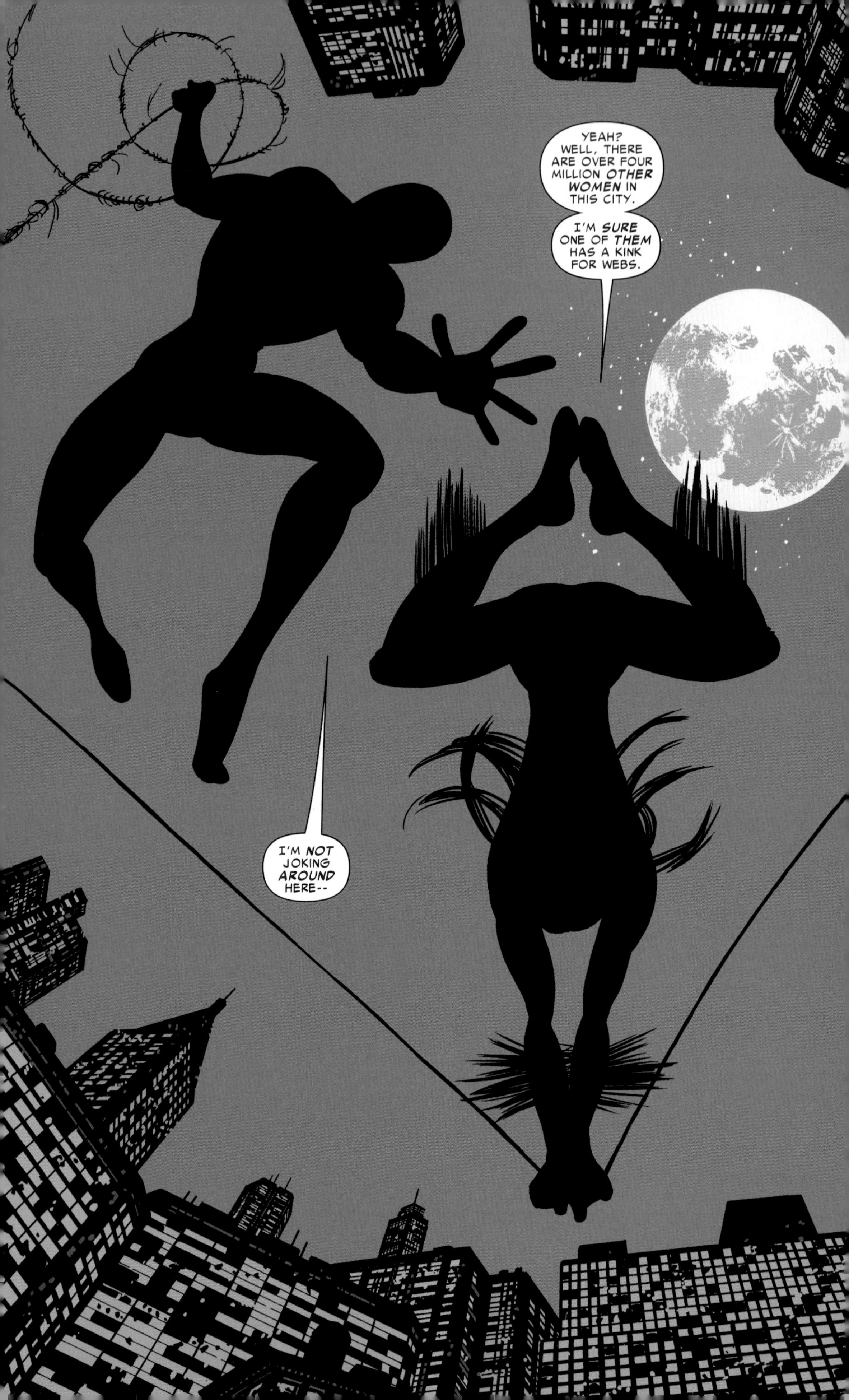
YEAH? WELL, THERE ARE OVER FOUR MILLION OTHER WOMEN IN THIS CITY.
I'M SURE ONE OF THEM HAS A KINK FOR WEBS.
I'M NOT JOKING AROUND HERE--

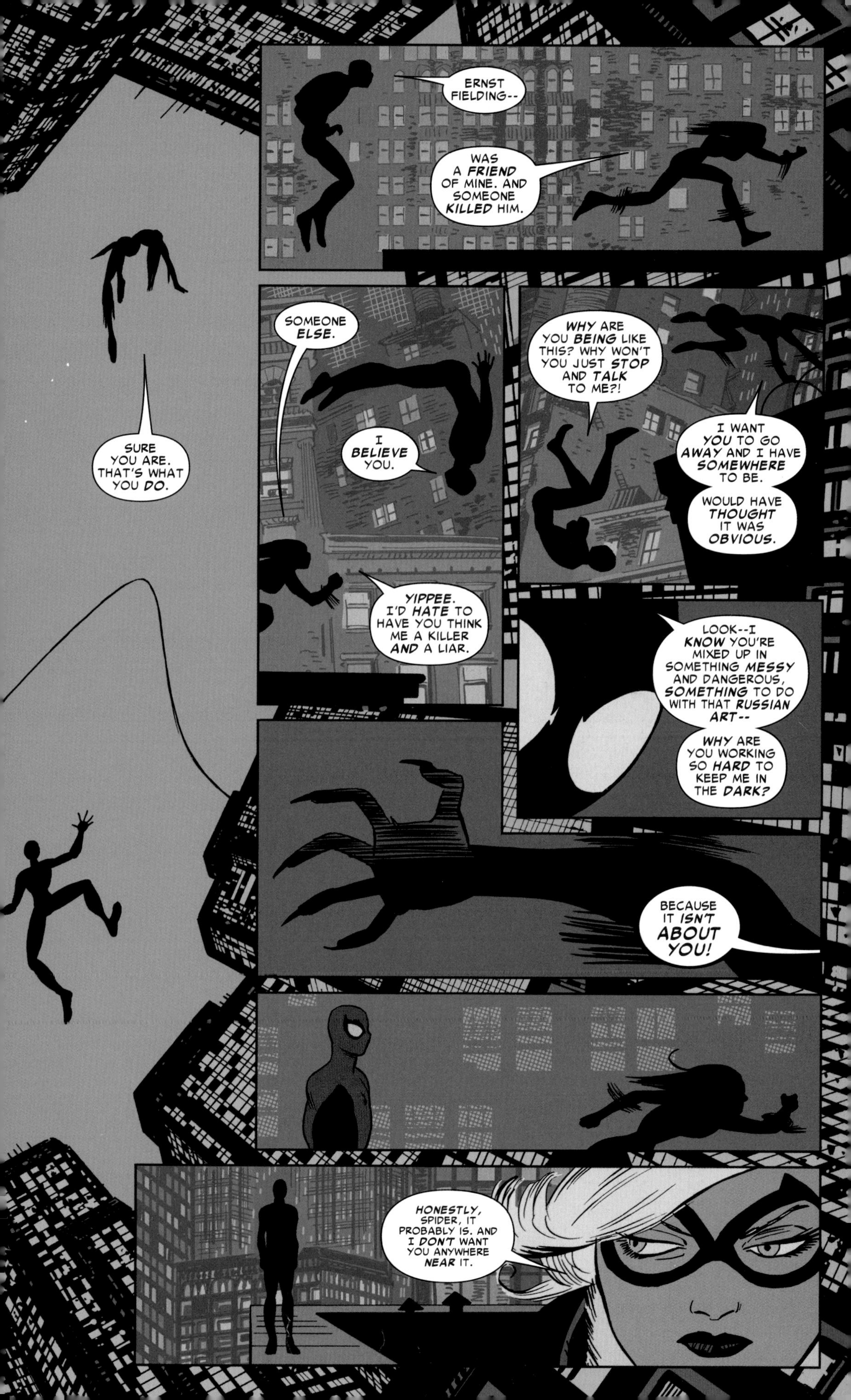
ERNST FIELDING--
WAS A FRIEND OF MINE. AND SOMEONE KILLED HIM.
SURE YOU ARE. THAT'S WHAT YOU DO.
SOMEONE ELSE.
I BELIEVE YOU.
YIPPEE. I'D HATE TO HAVE YOU THINK ME A KILLER AND A LIAR.
WHY ARE YOU BEING LIKE THIS? WHY WON'T YOU JUST STOP AND TALK TO ME?!
I WANT YOU TO GO AWAY AND I HAVE SOMEWHERE TO BE.
WOULD HAVE THOUGHT IT WAS OBVIOUS.
LOOK--I KNOW YOU'RE MIXED UP IN SOMETHING MESSY AND DANGEROUS, SOMETHING TO DO WITH THAT RUSSIAN ART--
WHY ARE YOU WORKING SO HARD TO KEEP ME IN THE DARK?
BECAUSE IT ISN'T ABOUT YOU!
HONESTLY, SPIDER, IT PROBABLY IS. AND I DON'T WANT YOU ANYWHERE NEAR IT.

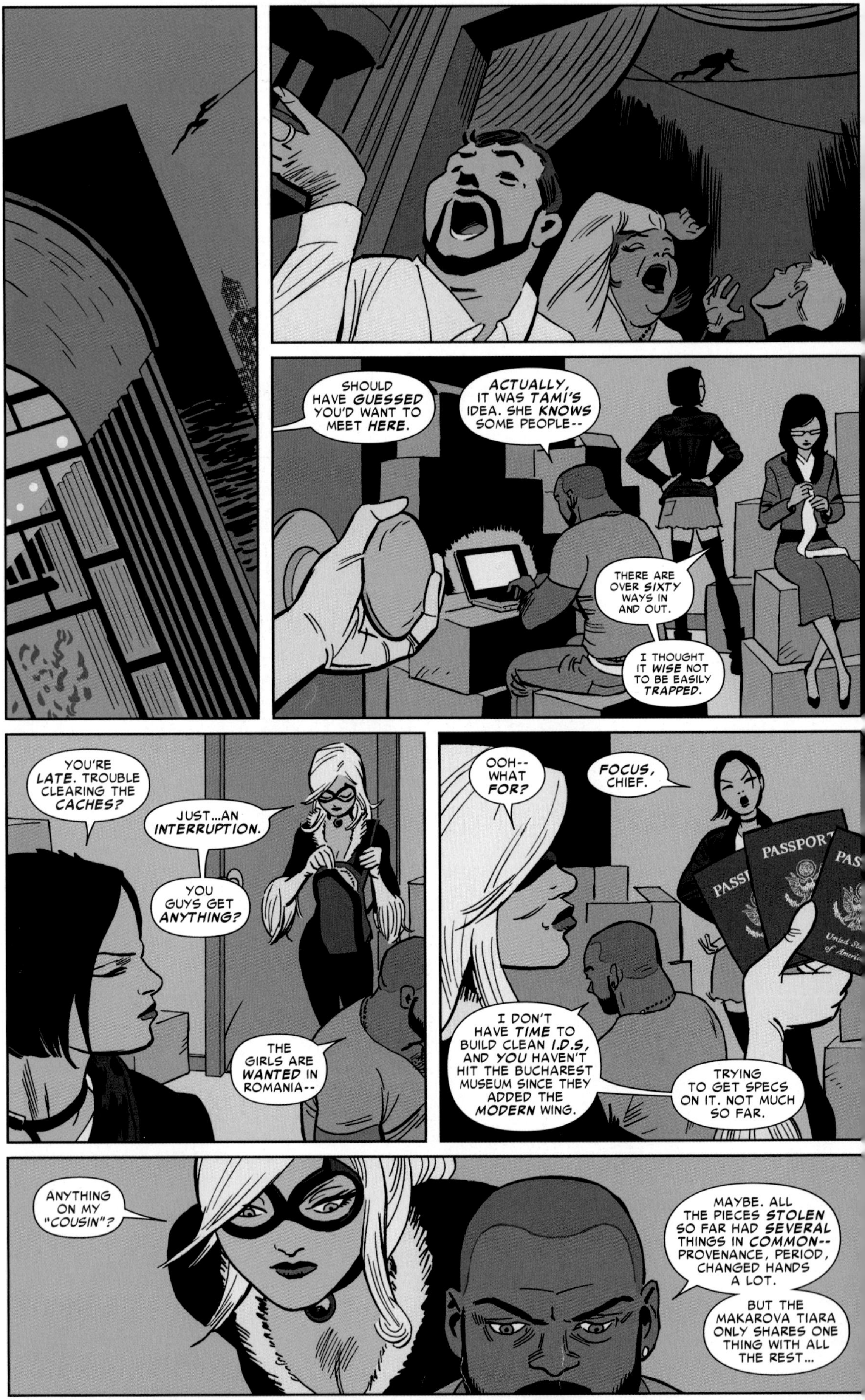

SHOULD HAVE GUESSED YOU'D WANT TO MEET HERE.
ACTUALLY, IT WAS TAMI'S IDEA. SHE KNOWS SOME PEOPLE--
THERE ARE OVER SIXTY WAYS IN AND OUT.
I THOUGHT IT WISE NOT TO BE EASILY TRAPPED.
YOU'RE LATE. TROUBLE CLEARING THE CACHES?
JUST...AN INTERRUPTION.
YOU GUYS GET ANYTHING?
THE GIRLS ARE WANTED IN ROMANIA--
OOH-- WHAT FOR?
FOCUS, CHIEF.
PASSPORT
I DON'T HAVE TIME TO BUILD CLEAN I.D.S, AND YOU HAVEN'T HIT THE BUCHAREST MUSEUM SINCE THEY ADDED THE MODERN WING.
TRYING TO GET SPECS ON IT. NOT MUCH SO FAR.
ANYTHING ON MY "COUSIN"?
MAYBE. ALL THE PIECES STOLEN SO FAR HAD SEVERAL THINGS IN COMMON-- PROVENANCE, PERIOD, CHANGED HANDS A LOT.
BUT THE MAKAROVA TIARA ONLY SHARES ONE THING WITH ALL THE REST...

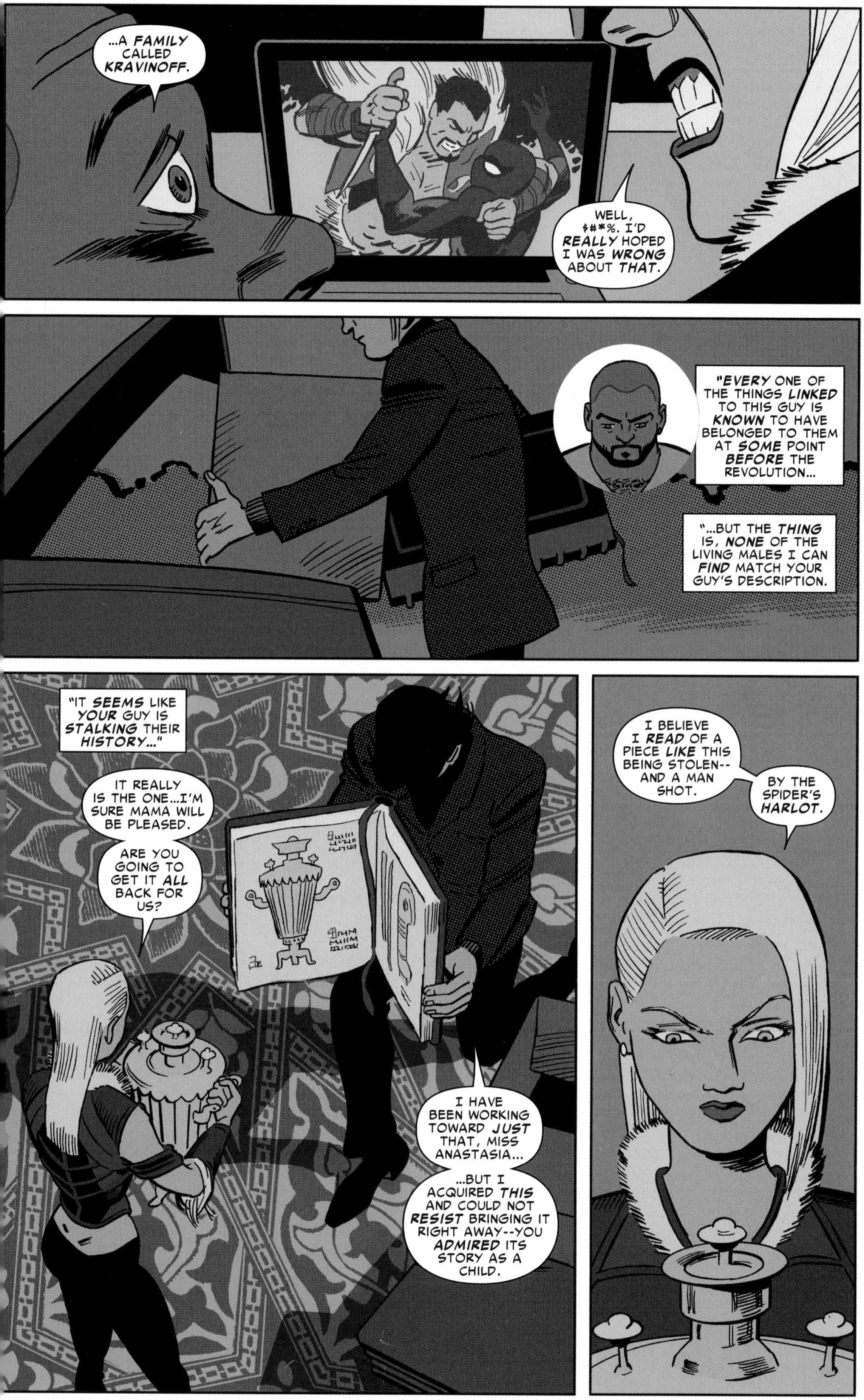
...A FAMILY CALLED KRAVINOFF.
WELL, $#*%. I'D REALLY HOPED I WAS WRONG ABOUT THAT.
"EVERY ONE OF THE THINGS LINKED TO THIS GUY IS KNOWN TO HAVE BELONGED TO THEM AT SOME POINT BEFORE THE REVOLUTION...
"...BUT THE THING IS, NONE OF THE LIVING MALES I CAN FIND MATCH YOUR GUY'S DESCRIPTION.
"IT SEEMS LIKE YOUR GUY IS STALKING THEIR HISTORY..."
IT REALLY IS THE ONE...I'M SURE MAMA WILL BE PLEASED.
ARE YOU GOING TO GET IT ALL BACK FOR US?
I HAVE BEEN WORKING TOWARD JUST THAT, MISS ANASTASIA...
...BUT I ACQUIRED THIS AND COULD NOT RESIST BRINGING IT RIGHT AWAY--YOU ADMIRED ITS STORY AS A CHILD.
I BELIEVE I READ OF A PIECE LIKE THIS BEING STOLEN--AND A MAN SHOT.
BY THE SPIDER'S HARLOT.

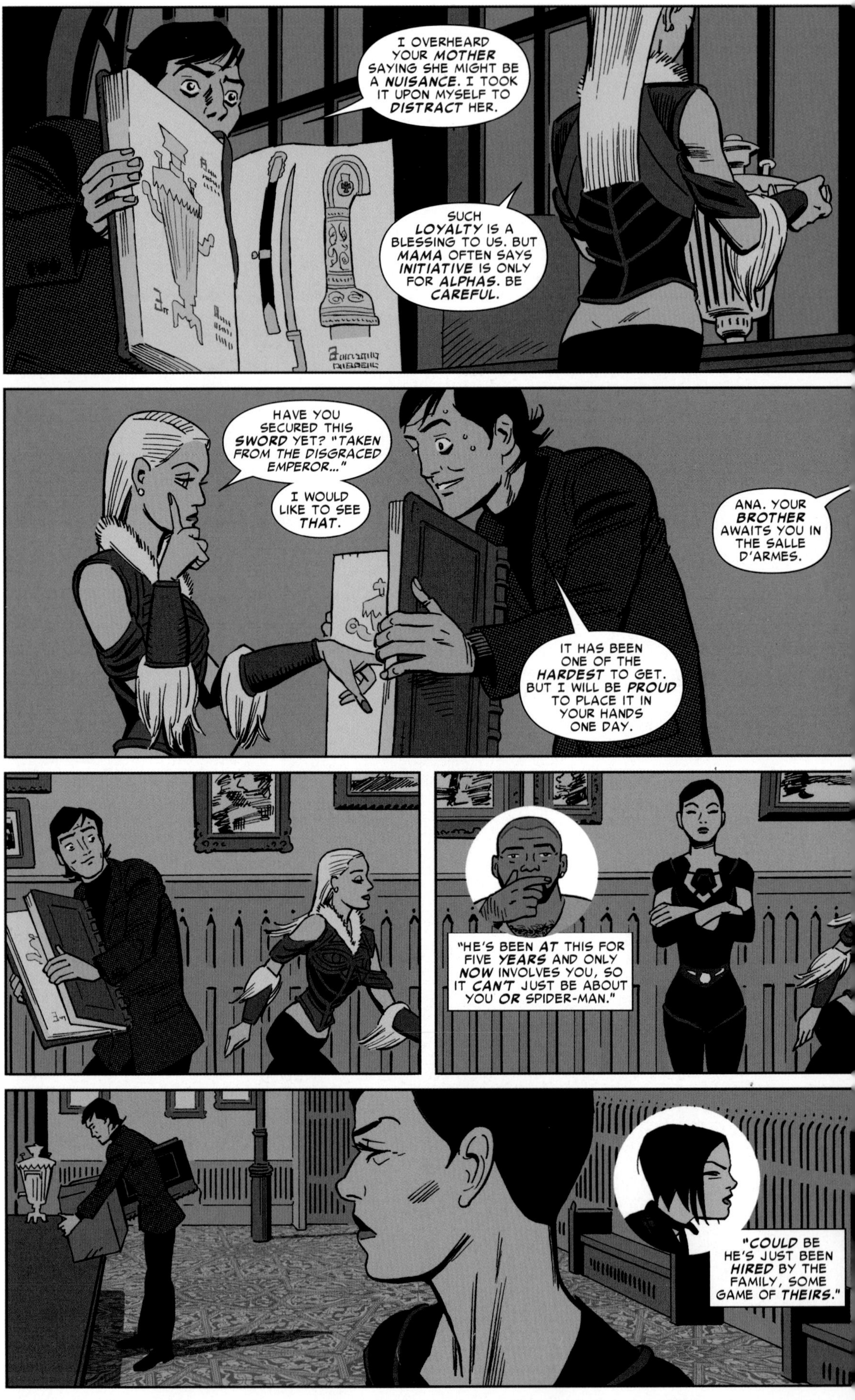
I OVERHEARD YOUR MOTHER SAYING SHE MIGHT BE A NUISANCE. I TOOK IT UPON MYSELF TO DISTRACT HER.
SUCH LOYALTY IS A BLESSING TO US. BUT MAMA OFTEN SAYS INITIATIVE IS ONLY FOR ALPHAS. BE CAREFUL.
HAVE YOU SECURED THIS SWORD YET? "TAKEN FROM THE DISGRACED EMPEROR..."
I WOULD LIKE TO SEE THAT.
IT HAS BEEN ONE OF THE HARDEST TO GET. BUT I WILL BE PROUD TO PLACE IT IN YOUR HANDS ONE DAY.
ANA. YOUR BROTHER AWAITS YOU IN THE SALLE D'ARMES.
"HE'S BEEN AT THIS FOR FIVE YEARS AND ONLY NOW INVOLVES YOU, SO IT CAN'T JUST BE ABOUT YOU OR SPIDER-MAN."
"COULD BE HE'S JUST BEEN HIRED BY THE FAMILY, SOME GAME OF THEIRS."

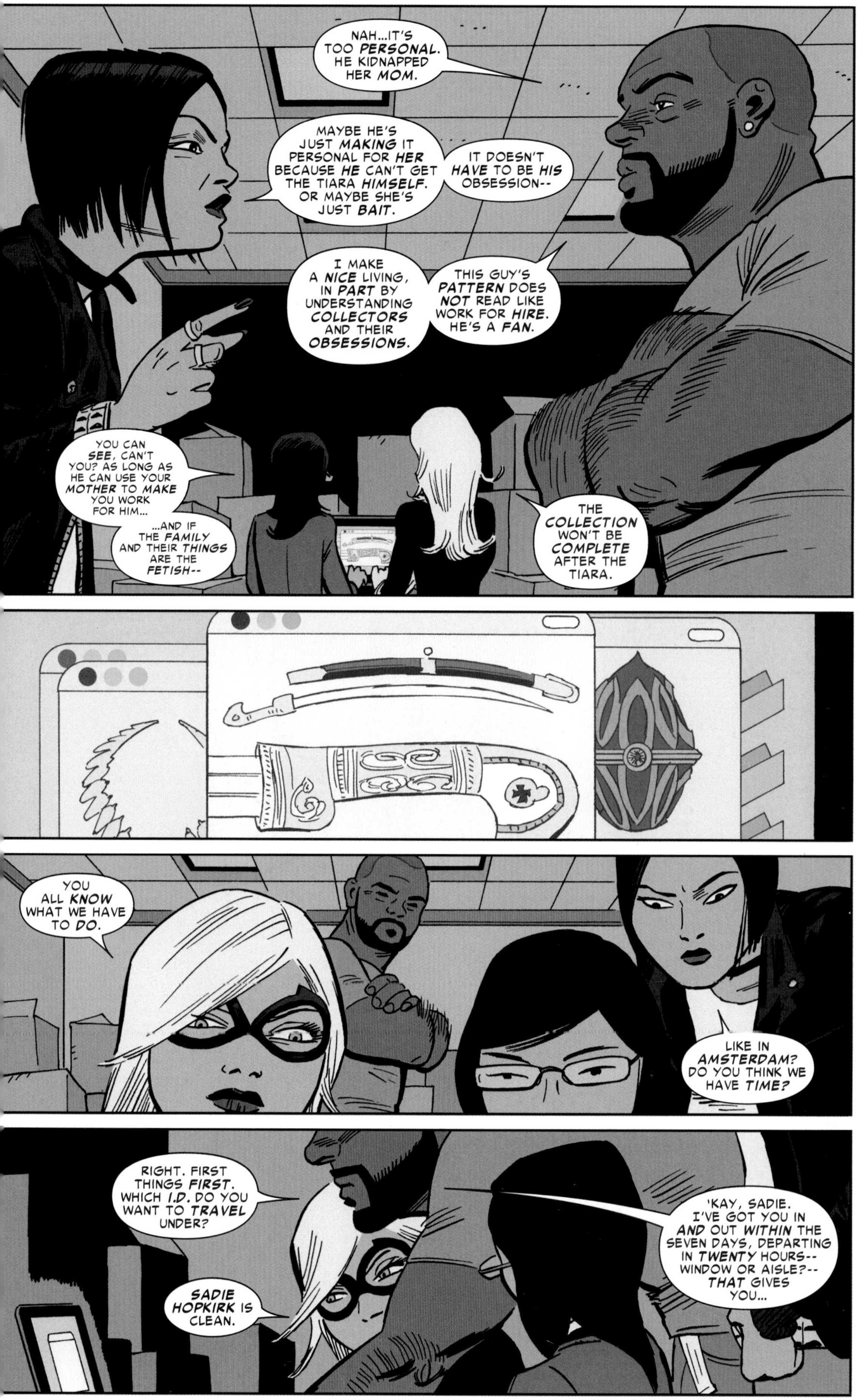
NAH...IT'S TOO PERSONAL. HE KIDNAPPED HER MOM.
MAYBE HE'S JUST MAKING IT PERSONAL FOR HER BECAUSE HE CAN'T GET THE TIARA HIMSELF. OR MAYBE SHE'S JUST BAIT.
IT DOESN'T HAVE TO BE HIS OBSESSION--
I MAKE A NICE LIVING, IN PART BY UNDERSTANDING COLLECTORS AND THEIR OBSESSIONS.
THIS GUY'S PATTERN DOES NOT READ LIKE WORK FOR HIRE. HE'S A FAN.
YOU CAN SEE, CAN'T YOU? AS LONG AS HE CAN USE YOUR MOTHER TO MAKE YOU WORK FOR HIM...
...AND IF THE FAMILY AND THEIR THINGS ARE THE FETISH--
THE COLLECTION WON'T BE COMPLETE AFTER THE TIARA.
YOU ALL KNOW WHAT WE HAVE TO DO.
LIKE IN AMSTERDAM? DO YOU THINK WE HAVE TIME?
RIGHT. FIRST THINGS FIRST. WHICH I.D. DO YOU WANT TO TRAVEL UNDER?
SADIE HOPKIRK IS CLEAN.
'KAY, SADIE. I'VE GOT YOU IN AND OUT WITHIN THE SEVEN DAYS, DEPARTING IN TWENTY HOURS-- WINDOW OR AISLE?-- THAT GIVES YOU...

"...A LITTLE UNDER *THREE DAYS* IN *ROMANIA*."

BUCURESTI

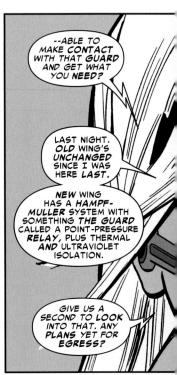

--ABLE TO MAKE *CONTACT* WITH THAT *GUARD* AND GET WHAT YOU *NEED*?

LAST NIGHT. *OLD WING'S UNCHANGED* SINCE I WAS HERE *LAST*.

NEW WING HAS A *HAMPF-MULLER* SYSTEM WITH SOMETHING *THE GUARD* CALLED A POINT-PRESSURE *RELAY*, PLUS THERMAL *AND* ULTRAVIOLET ISOLATION.

GIVE US A SECOND TO *LOOK* INTO THAT. ANY *PLANS* YET FOR *EGRESS*?

EU TE VA PLATI *OPTZEKI* EURO PENTRU ASTA.

SALBATIC. NOUAZEKI.

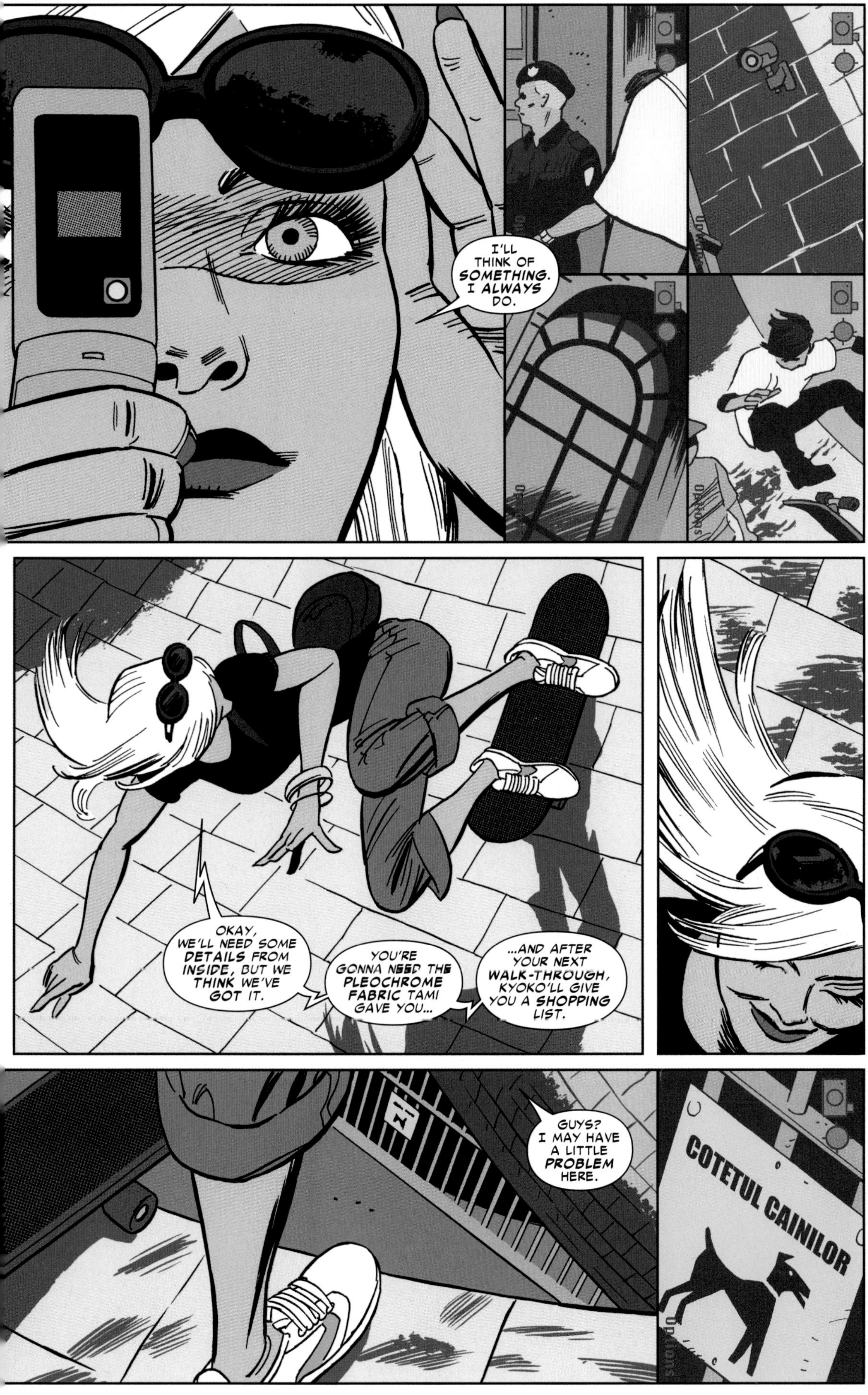
I'LL THINK OF SOMETHING. I ALWAYS DO.
OKAY, WE'LL NEED SOME DETAILS FROM INSIDE, BUT WE THINK WE'VE GOT IT.
YOU'RE GONNA NEED THE PLEOCHROME FABRIC TAMI GAVE YOU...
...AND AFTER YOUR NEXT WALK-THROUGH, KYOKO'LL GIVE YOU A SHOPPING LIST.
GUYS? I MAY HAVE A LITTLE PROBLEM HERE.
COTETUL CAINILOR

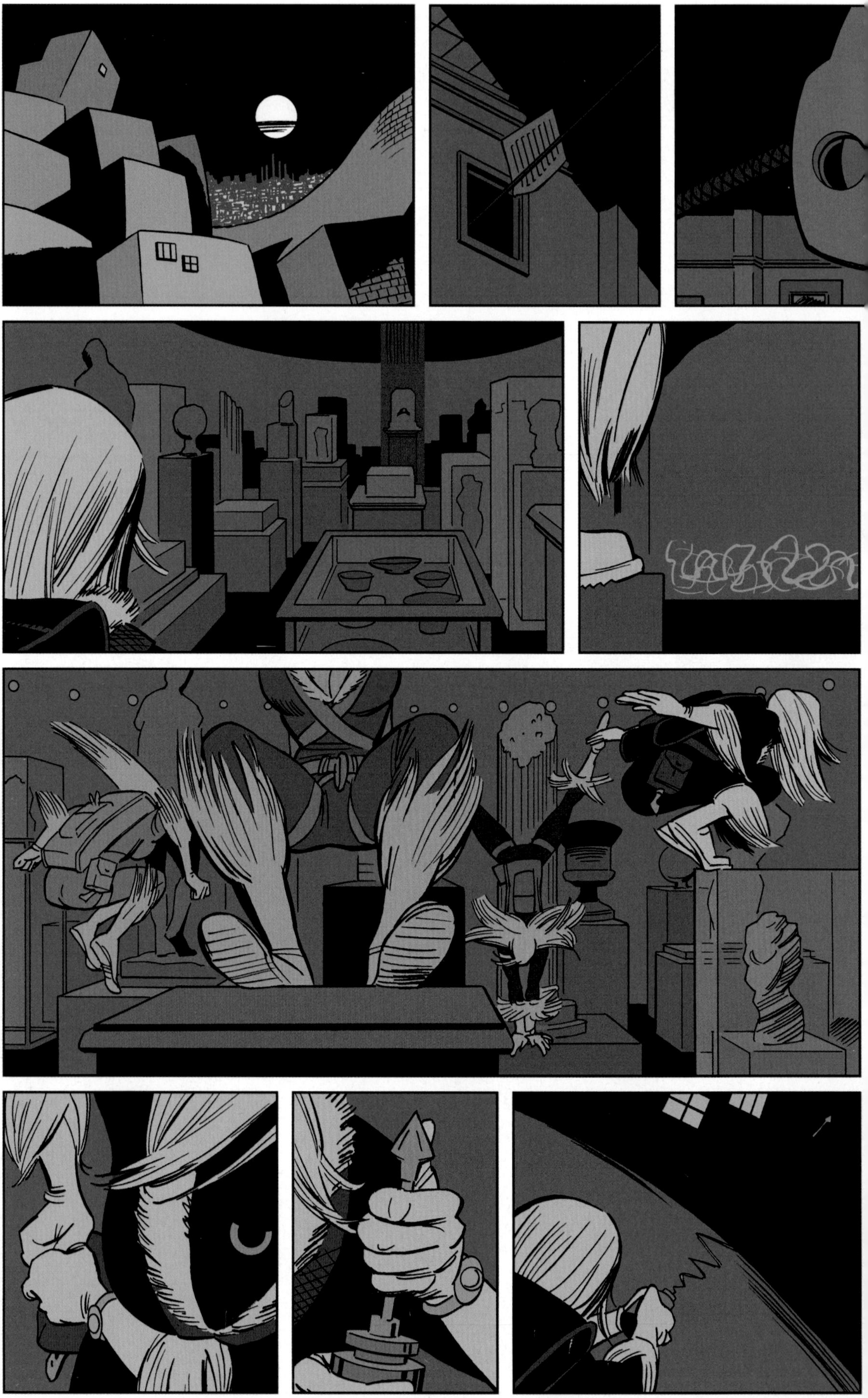

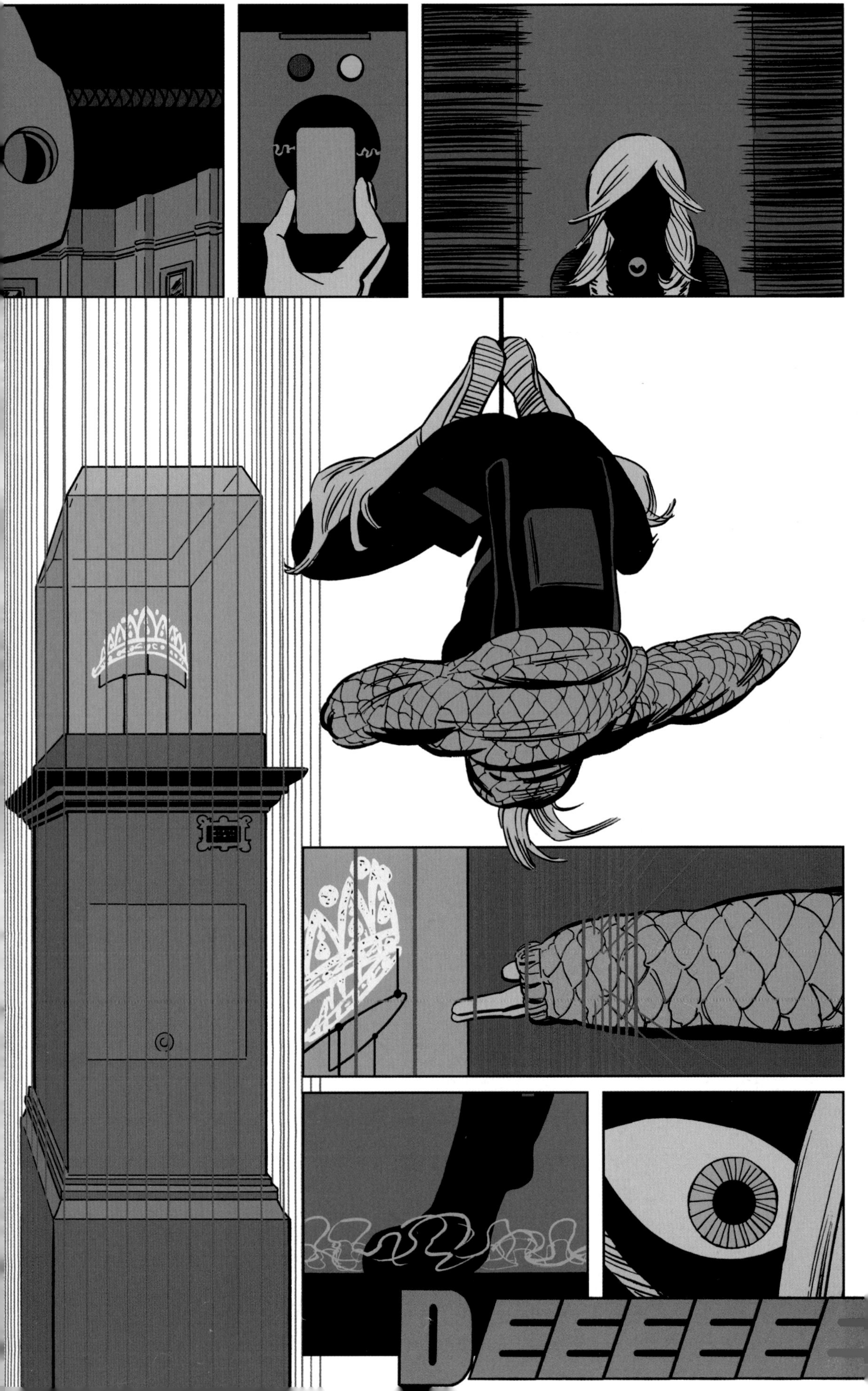
DEEEEEE

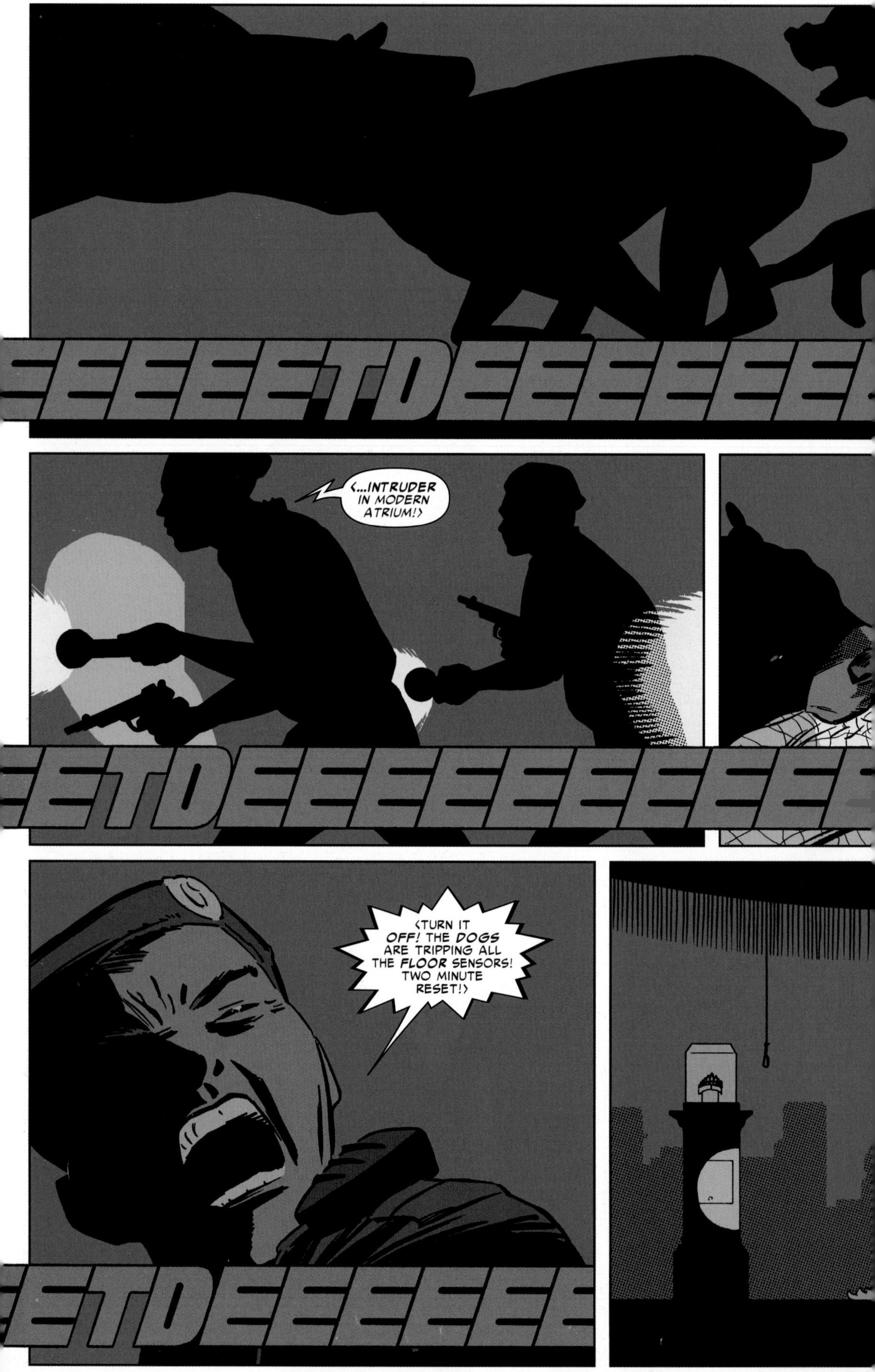

EEEEETDEEEEEEEE
‹...INTRUDER IN MODERN ATRIUM!›
ETDEEEEEEEEEEEE
‹TURN IT OFF! THE DOGS ARE TRIPPING ALL THE FLOOR SENSORS! TWO MINUTE RESET!›
ETDEEEEEEE

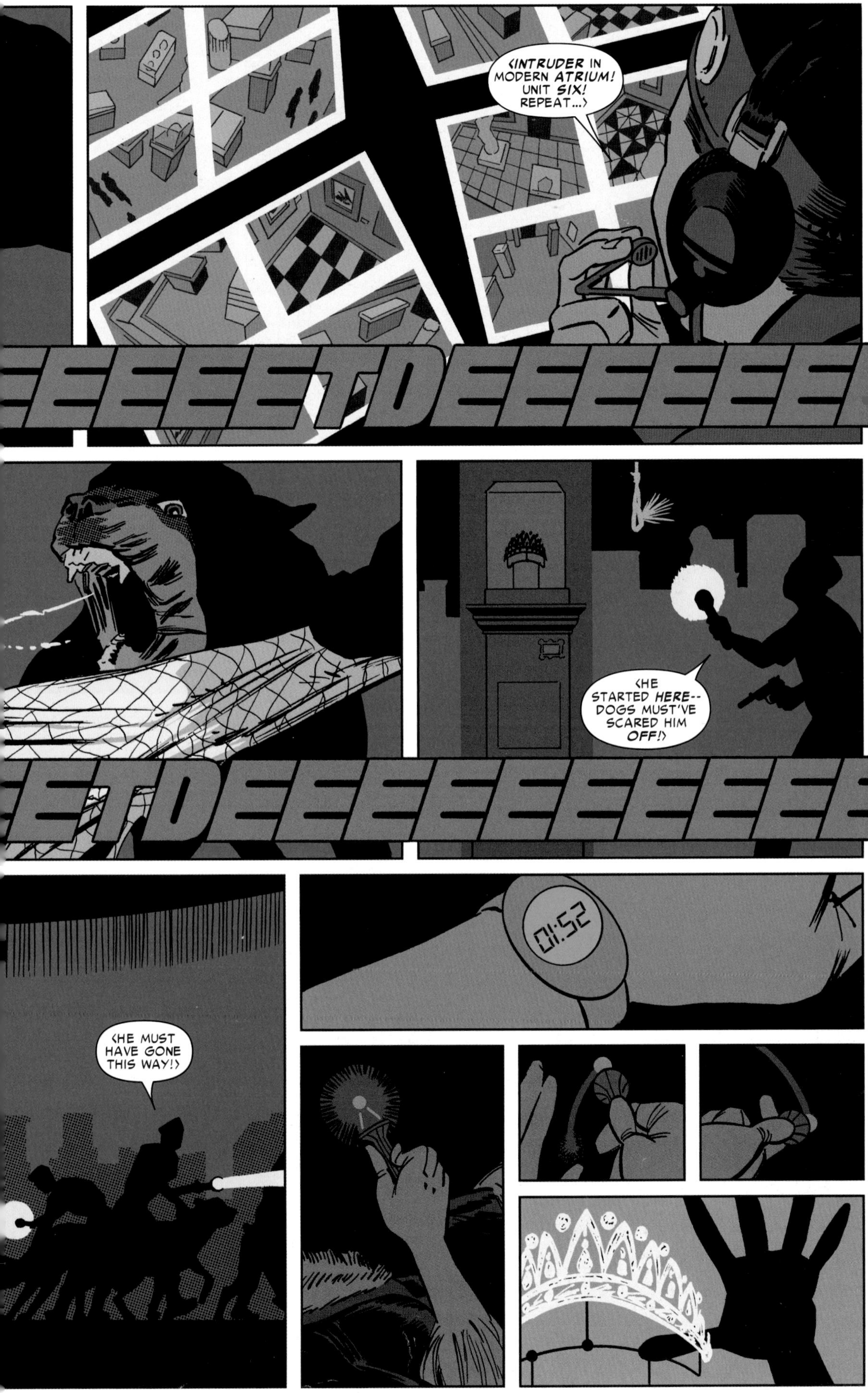
‹INTRUDER IN MODERN ATRIUM! UNIT SIX! REPEAT...›
EEEEETDEEEEEEEEE
‹HE STARTED HERE-- DOGS MUST'VE SCARED HIM OFF!›
EETDEEEEEEEEEEE
01:52
‹HE MUST HAVE GONE THIS WAY!›

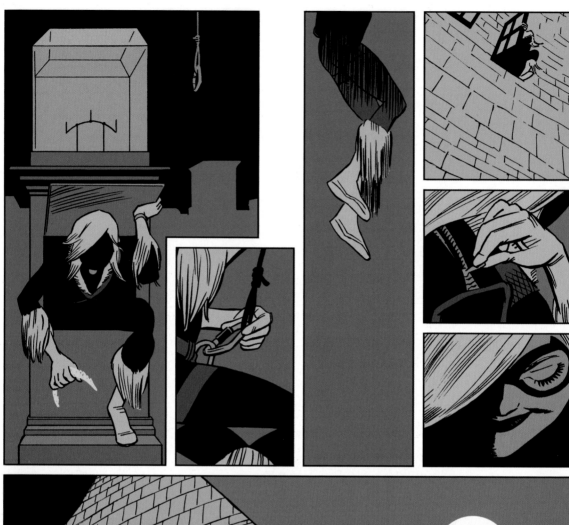

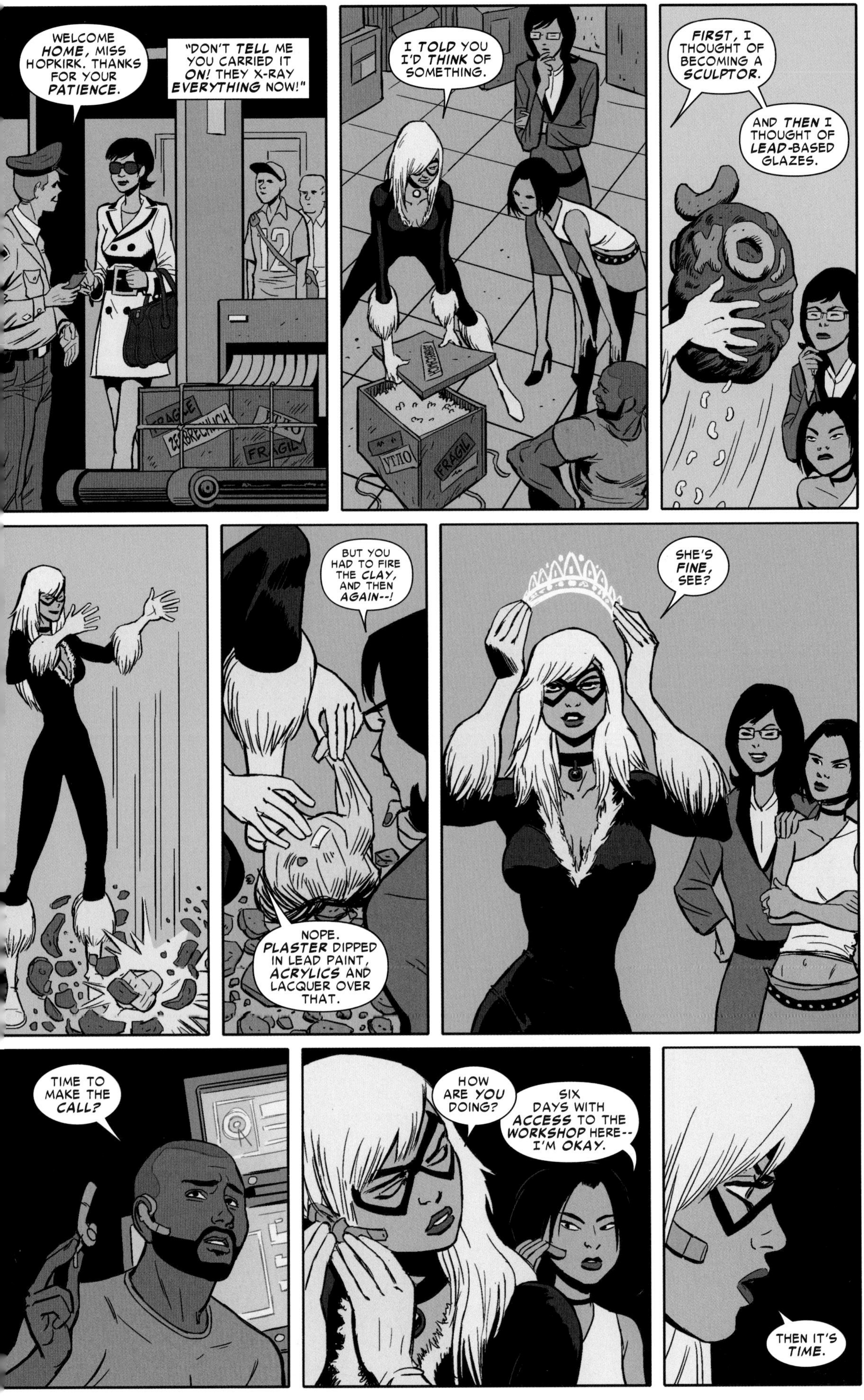
WELCOME HOME, MISS HOPKIRK. THANKS FOR YOUR PATIENCE.
"DON'T TELL ME YOU CARRIED IT ON! THEY X-RAY EVERYTHING NOW!"
FRAGILE
ZERBRECHLICH
FRAGIL
I TOLD YOU I'D THINK OF SOMETHING.
FRAGIL
FIRST, I THOUGHT OF BECOMING A SCULPTOR.
AND THEN I THOUGHT OF LEAD-BASED GLAZES.
BUT YOU HAD TO FIRE THE CLAY, AND THEN AGAIN--!
NOPE. PLASTER DIPPED IN LEAD PAINT, ACRYLICS AND LACQUER OVER THAT.
SHE'S FINE, SEE?
TIME TO MAKE THE CALL?
HOW ARE YOU DOING?
SIX DAYS WITH ACCESS TO THE WORKSHOP HERE-- I'M OKAY.
THEN IT'S TIME.

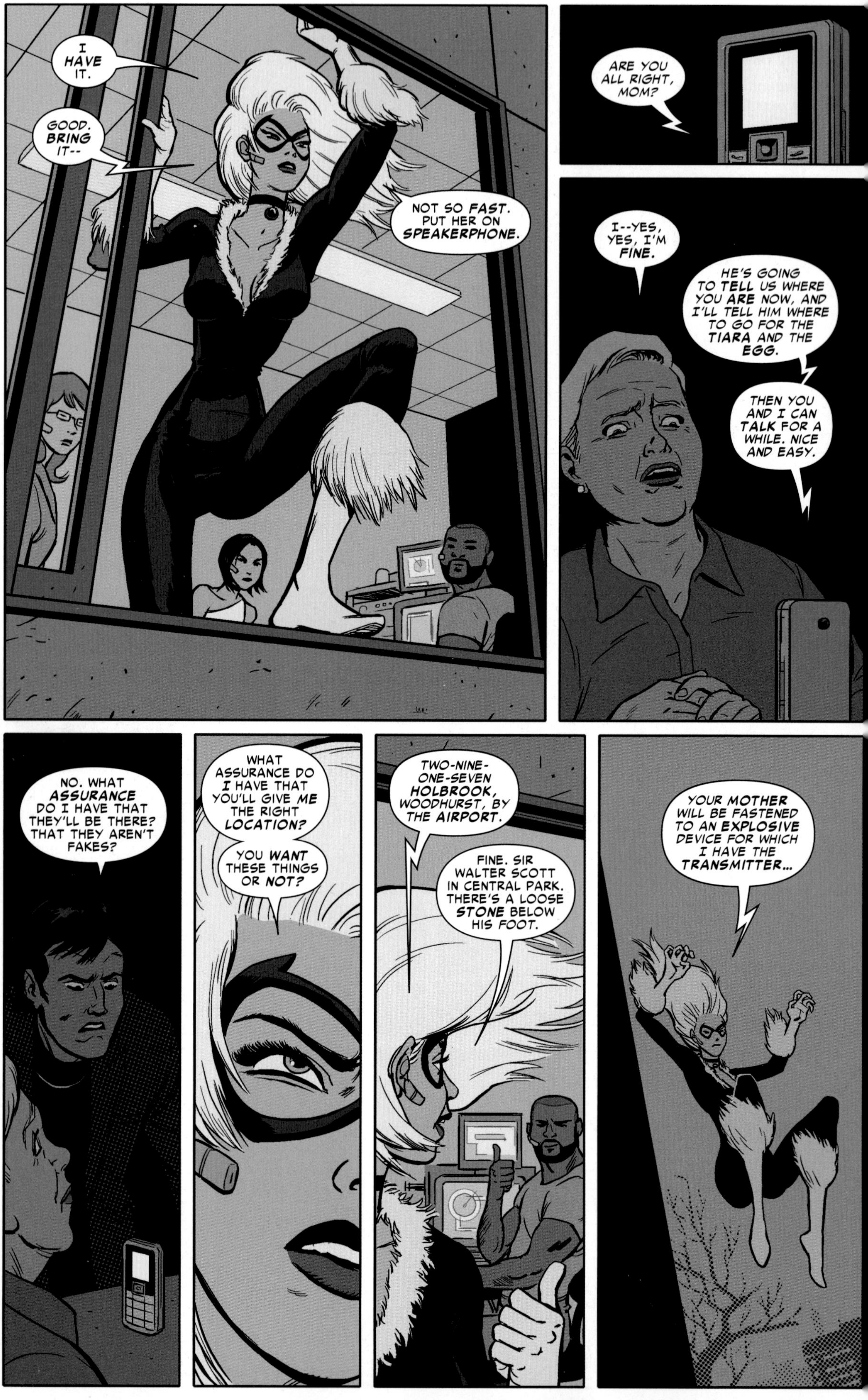
I HAVE IT.
GOOD. BRING IT--
NOT SO FAST. PUT HER ON SPEAKERPHONE.
ARE YOU ALL RIGHT, MOM?
I--YES, YES, I'M FINE.
HE'S GOING TO TELL US WHERE YOU ARE NOW, AND I'LL TELL HIM WHERE TO GO FOR THE TIARA AND THE EGG.
THEN YOU AND I CAN TALK FOR A WHILE. NICE AND EASY.
NO. WHAT ASSURANCE DO I HAVE THAT THEY'LL BE THERE? THAT THEY AREN'T FAKES?
WHAT ASSURANCE DO I HAVE THAT YOU'LL GIVE ME THE RIGHT LOCATION?
YOU WANT THESE THINGS OR NOT?
TWO-NINE-ONE-SEVEN HOLBROOK, WOODHURST, BY THE AIRPORT.
FINE. SIR WALTER SCOTT IN CENTRAL PARK. THERE'S A LOOSE STONE BELOW HIS FOOT.
YOUR MOTHER WILL BE FASTENED TO AN EXPLOSIVE DEVICE FOR WHICH I HAVE THE TRANSMITTER...

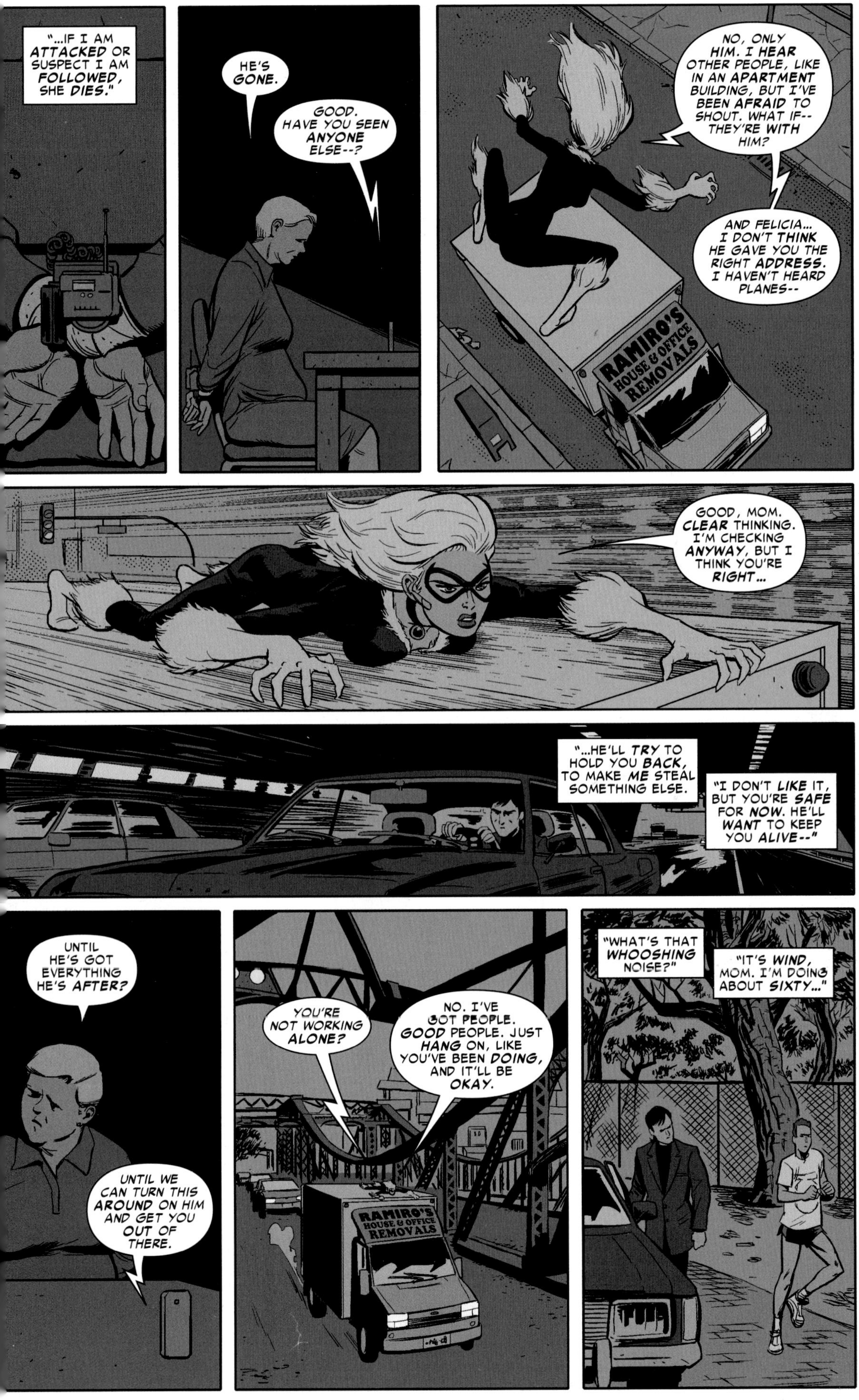
"...IF I AM ATTACKED OR SUSPECT I AM FOLLOWED, SHE DIES."
HE'S GONE.
GOOD. HAVE YOU SEEN ANYONE ELSE--?
NO, ONLY HIM. I HEAR OTHER PEOPLE, LIKE IN AN APARTMENT BUILDING, BUT I'VE BEEN AFRAID TO SHOUT. WHAT IF--THEY'RE WITH HIM?
AND FELICIA... I DON'T THINK HE GAVE YOU THE RIGHT ADDRESS. I HAVEN'T HEARD PLANES--
RAMIRO'S HOUSE & OFFICE REMOVALS
GOOD, MOM. CLEAR THINKING. I'M CHECKING ANYWAY, BUT I THINK YOU'RE RIGHT...
"...HE'LL TRY TO HOLD YOU BACK, TO MAKE ME STEAL SOMETHING ELSE.
"I DON'T LIKE IT, BUT YOU'RE SAFE FOR NOW. HE'LL WANT TO KEEP YOU ALIVE--"
UNTIL HE'S GOT EVERYTHING HE'S AFTER?
UNTIL WE CAN TURN THIS AROUND ON HIM AND GET YOU OUT OF THERE.
YOU'RE NOT WORKING ALONE?
NO. I'VE GOT PEOPLE. GOOD PEOPLE. JUST HANG ON, LIKE YOU'VE BEEN DOING, AND IT'LL BE OKAY.
RAMIRO'S HOUSE & OFFICE REMOVALS
"WHAT'S THAT WHOOSHING NOISE?"
"IT'S WIND, MOM. I'M DOING ABOUT SIXTY..."

...ON THE ROOF OF AN EASTBOUND SEMI.

THE *THINGS* YOU DO...I SEE YOU ON THE *NEWS* SOMETIMES.

LIKE WHEN YOU WERE *KISSING* THAT--THAT--

GUY, MOM. HE'S A *DECENT* GUY, IN A FUNNY SUIT, DOING WHAT HE *HAS* TO DO.

I THOUGHT THAT ABOUT YOUR FATHER...THAT IT WAS WHAT HE HAD TO DO.

YEAH?

BAD ADDY. HE PIK-UP?

BUT IT *WASN'T,* YOU KNOW. HE WAS A *SMART* MAN. AND WE DIDN'T LIVE ANY BETTER THAN WE WOULD HAVE ON REGULAR SALARY. HE STOLE...

"...BECAUSE HE *WANTED* TO. IT WAS A *SELFISH* PASSION."

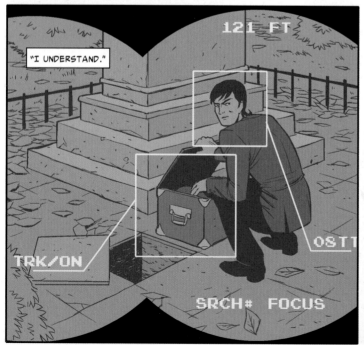

121 FT

"I UNDERSTAND."

TRK/ON

08T1

SRCH# FOCUS

ME? OR HIM?

HAS BOX. LVING NOW. DIDN'T SEE XMITTER.

BOTH. I UNDERSTAND HIS PASSION...

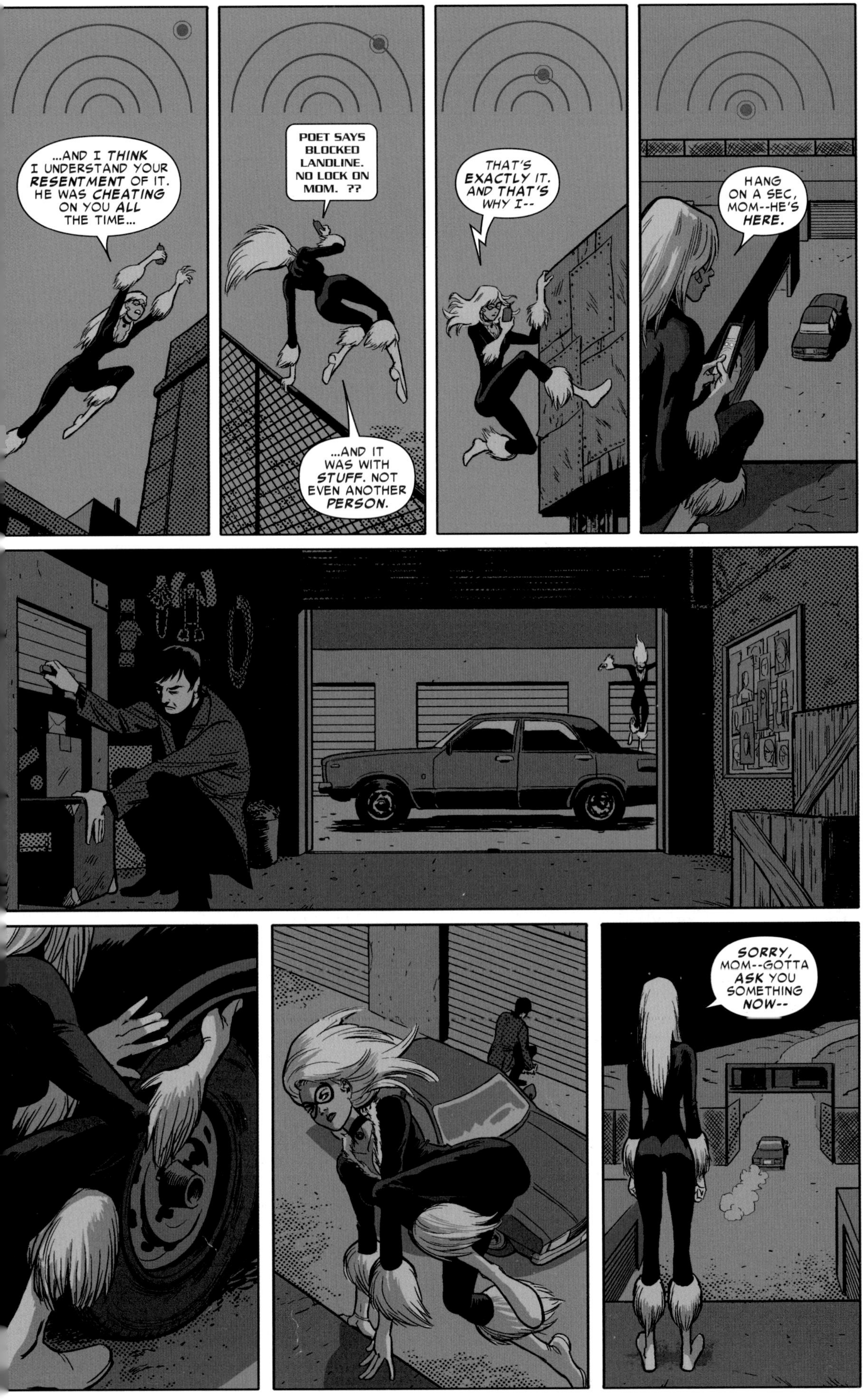
...AND I THINK I UNDERSTAND YOUR RESENTMENT OF IT. HE WAS CHEATING ON YOU ALL THE TIME...
POET SAYS BLOCKED LANDLINE. NO LOCK ON MOM. ??
...AND IT WAS WITH STUFF. NOT EVEN ANOTHER PERSON.
THAT'S EXACTLY IT. AND THAT'S WHY I--
HANG ON A SEC, MOM--HE'S HERE.
SORRY, MOM--GOTTA ASK YOU SOMETHING NOW--

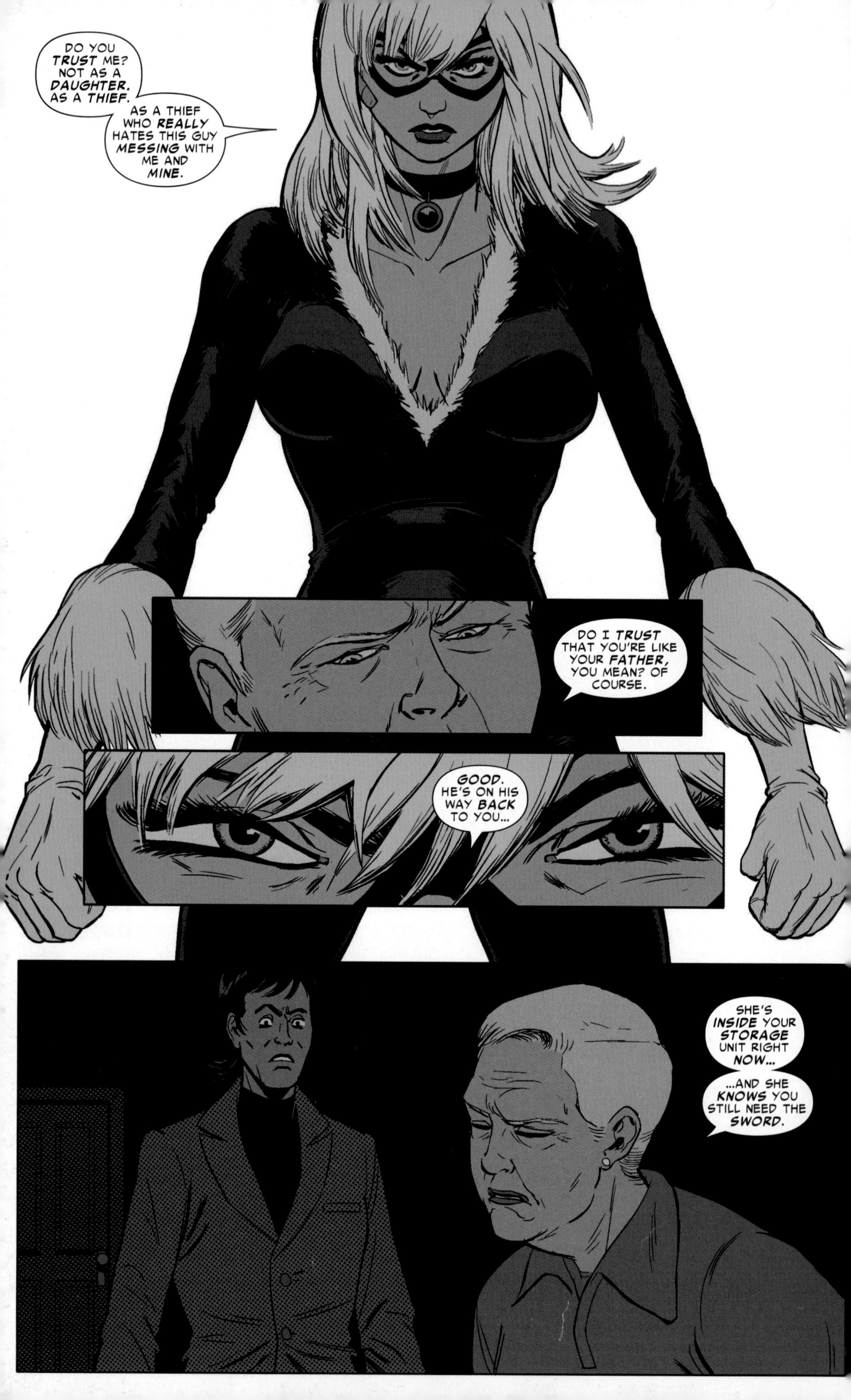
DO YOU TRUST ME? NOT AS A DAUGHTER. AS A THIEF.
AS A THIEF WHO REALLY HATES THIS GUY MESSING WITH ME AND MINE.
DO I TRUST THAT YOU'RE LIKE YOUR FATHER, YOU MEAN? OF COURSE.
GOOD. HE'S ON HIS WAY BACK TO YOU...
SHE'S INSIDE YOUR STORAGE UNIT RIGHT NOW...
...AND SHE KNOWS YOU STILL NEED THE SWORD.

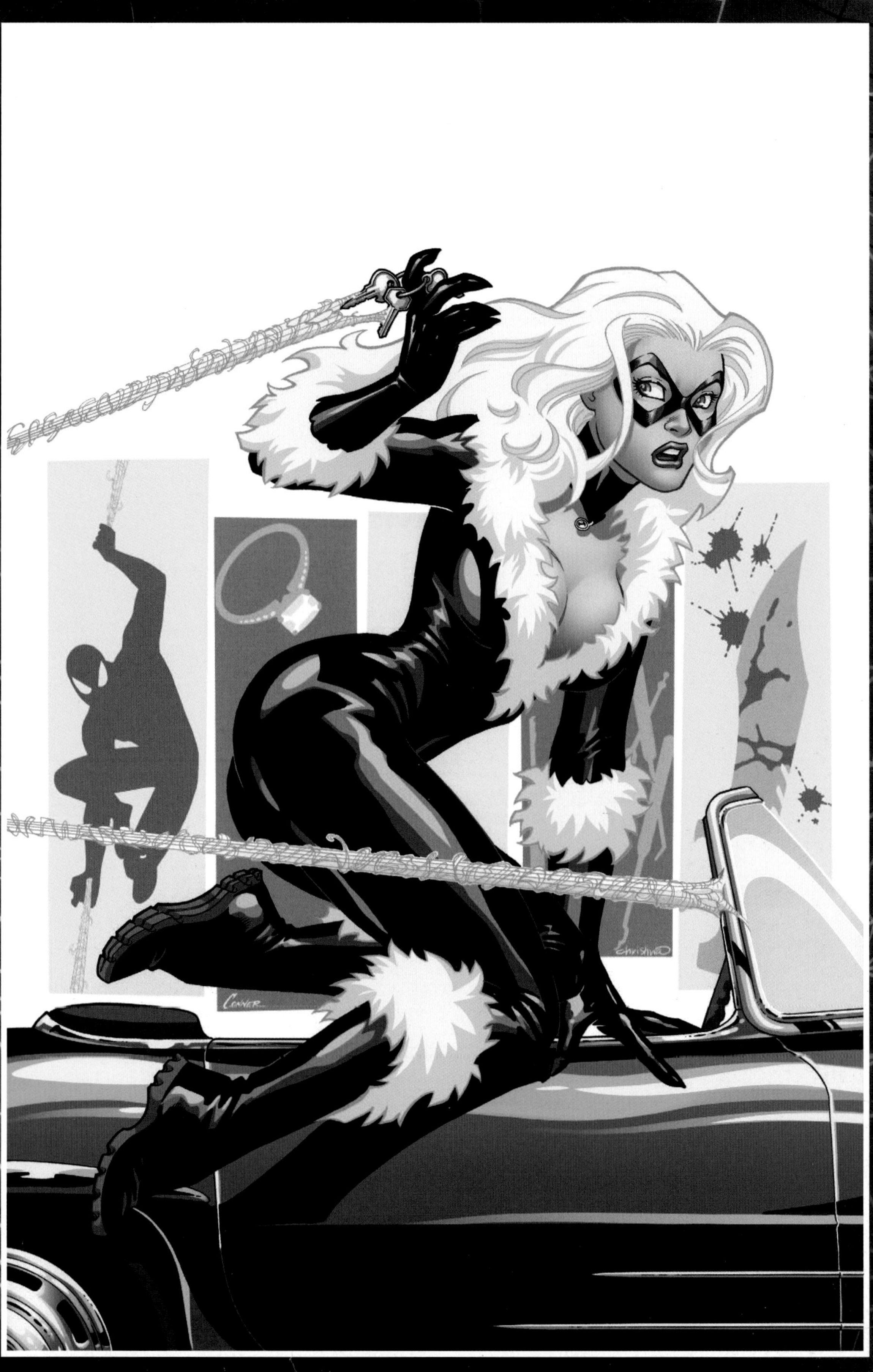

AMAZING SPIDER-MAN PRESENTS: BLACK CAT #3

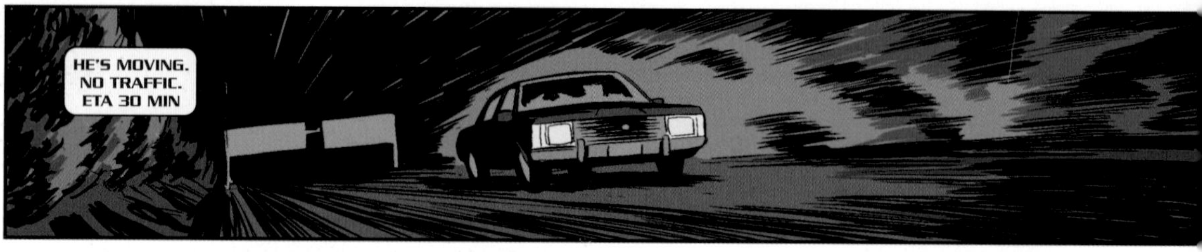
HE'S MOVING. NO TRAFFIC. ETA 30 MIN

MATT HOLLINGSWORTH
w/ JAVIER RODRIGUEZ, pgs. 11-18
COLOR ART

VC'S JOE CARAMAGNA
LETTERS

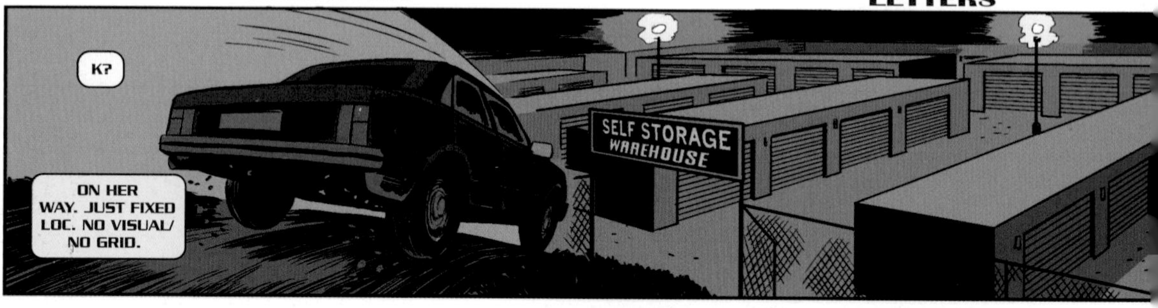
K?
SELF STORAGE WAREHOUSE
ON HER WAY. JUST FIXED LOC. NO VISUAL/ NO GRID.

JEN VAN METER
WRITER

JAVIER RODRIGUEZ
w/ JAVIER PULIDO, pgs. 18-22
ARTIST

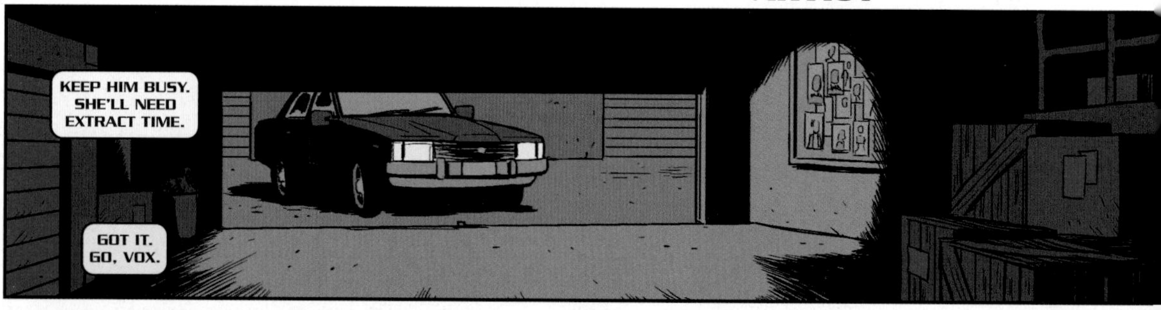
KEEP HIM BUSY. SHE'LL NEED EXTRACT TIME.
GOT IT. GO, VOX.

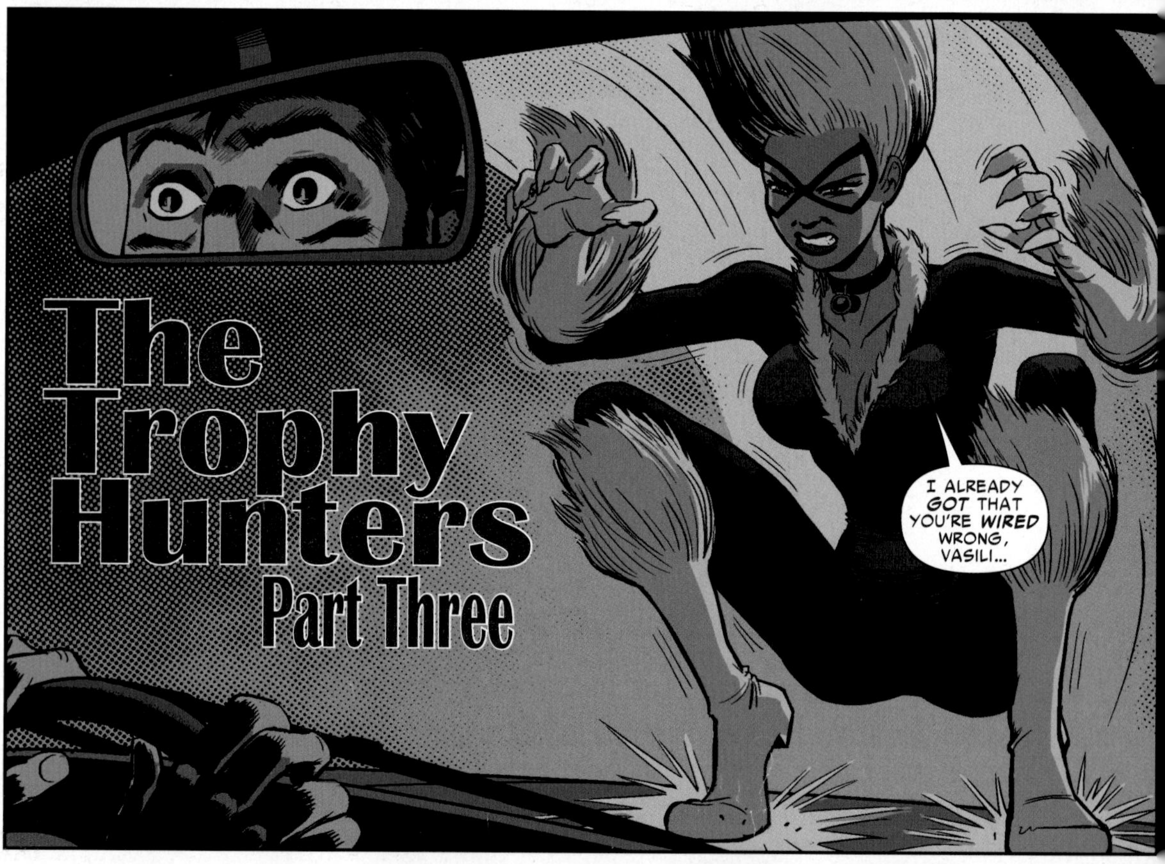
The Trophy Hunters
Part Three
I ALREADY *GOT* THAT YOU'RE *WIRED* WRONG, VASILI...

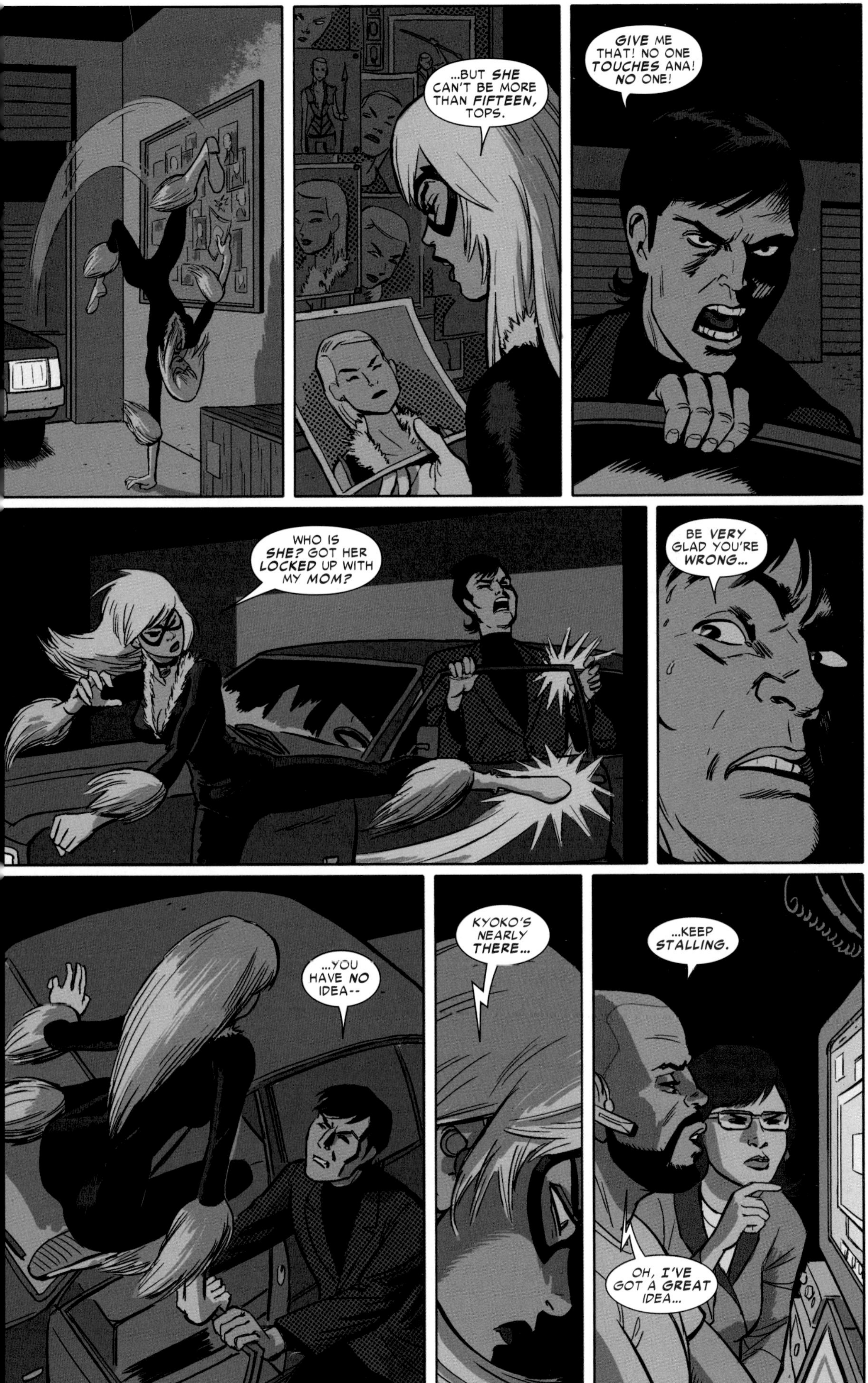
...BUT SHE CAN'T BE MORE THAN FIFTEEN, TOPS.
GIVE ME THAT! NO ONE TOUCHES ANA! NO ONE!
WHO IS SHE? GOT HER LOCKED UP WITH MY MOM?
BE VERY GLAD YOU'RE WRONG...
...YOU HAVE NO IDEA--
KYOKO'S NEARLY THERE...
...KEEP STALLING.
OH, I'VE GOT A GREAT IDEA...

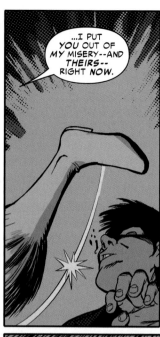

...I PUT YOU OUT OF MY MISERY--AND THEIRS-- RIGHT NOW.

WON'T TAKE ME LONG TO FIND MOM ONCE YOU'RE OUT OF THE WAY.

DON'T COME ANY CLOSER--IF YOU WANT YOUR MOTHER TO LIVE.

HAD YOU FORGOTTEN THIS?

NO, AND IT'S NICE...

...BUT WE'LL GET MORE FOR THE PAIR AT AUCTION.

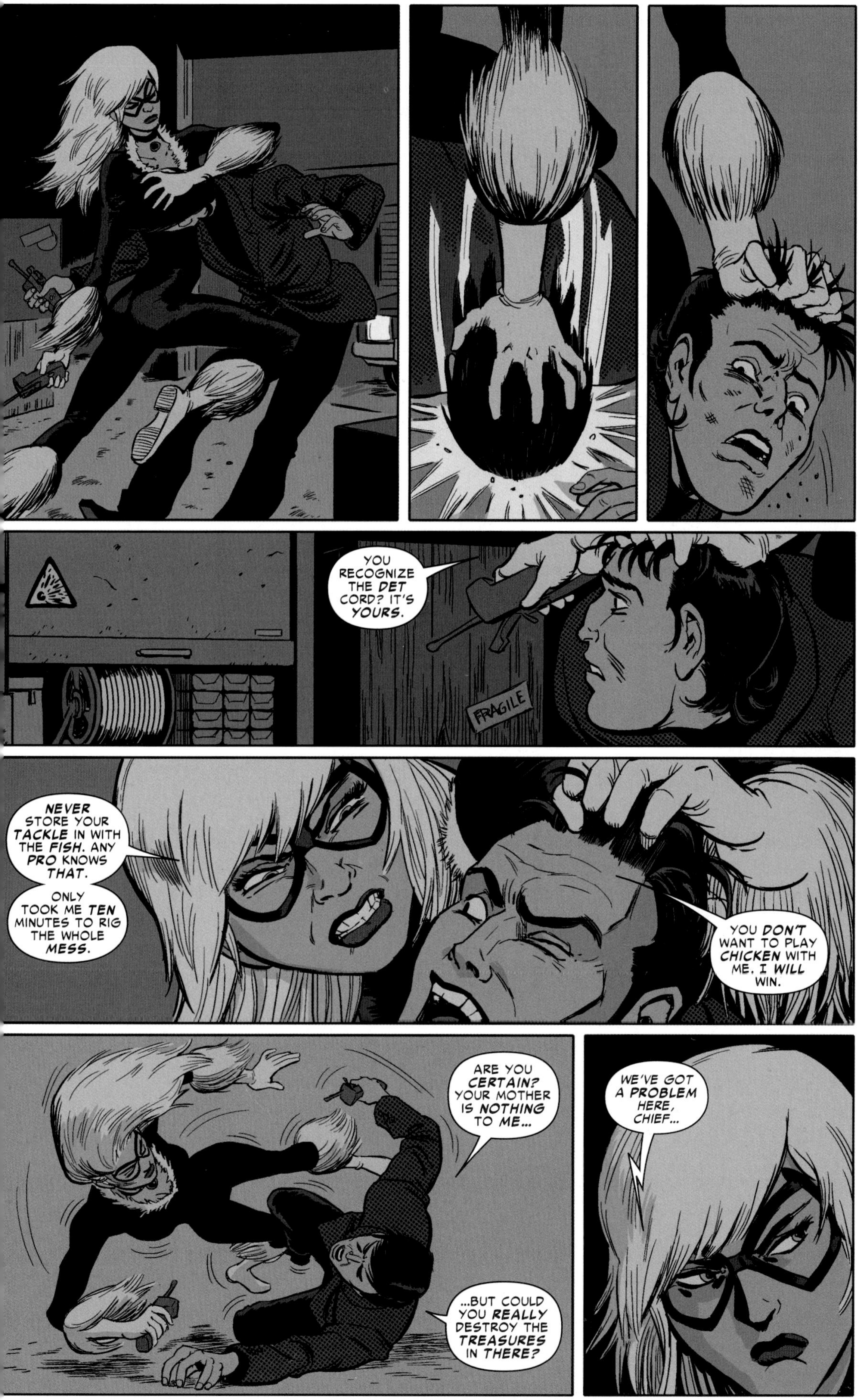
YOU RECOGNIZE THE DET CORD? IT'S YOURS.
FRAGILE
NEVER STORE YOUR TACKLE IN WITH THE FISH. ANY PRO KNOWS THAT.
ONLY TOOK ME TEN MINUTES TO RIG THE WHOLE MESS.
YOU DON'T WANT TO PLAY CHICKEN WITH ME. I WILL WIN.
ARE YOU CERTAIN? YOUR MOTHER IS NOTHING TO ME...
...BUT COULD YOU REALLY DESTROY THE TREASURES IN THERE?
WE'VE GOT A PROBLEM HERE, CHIEF...

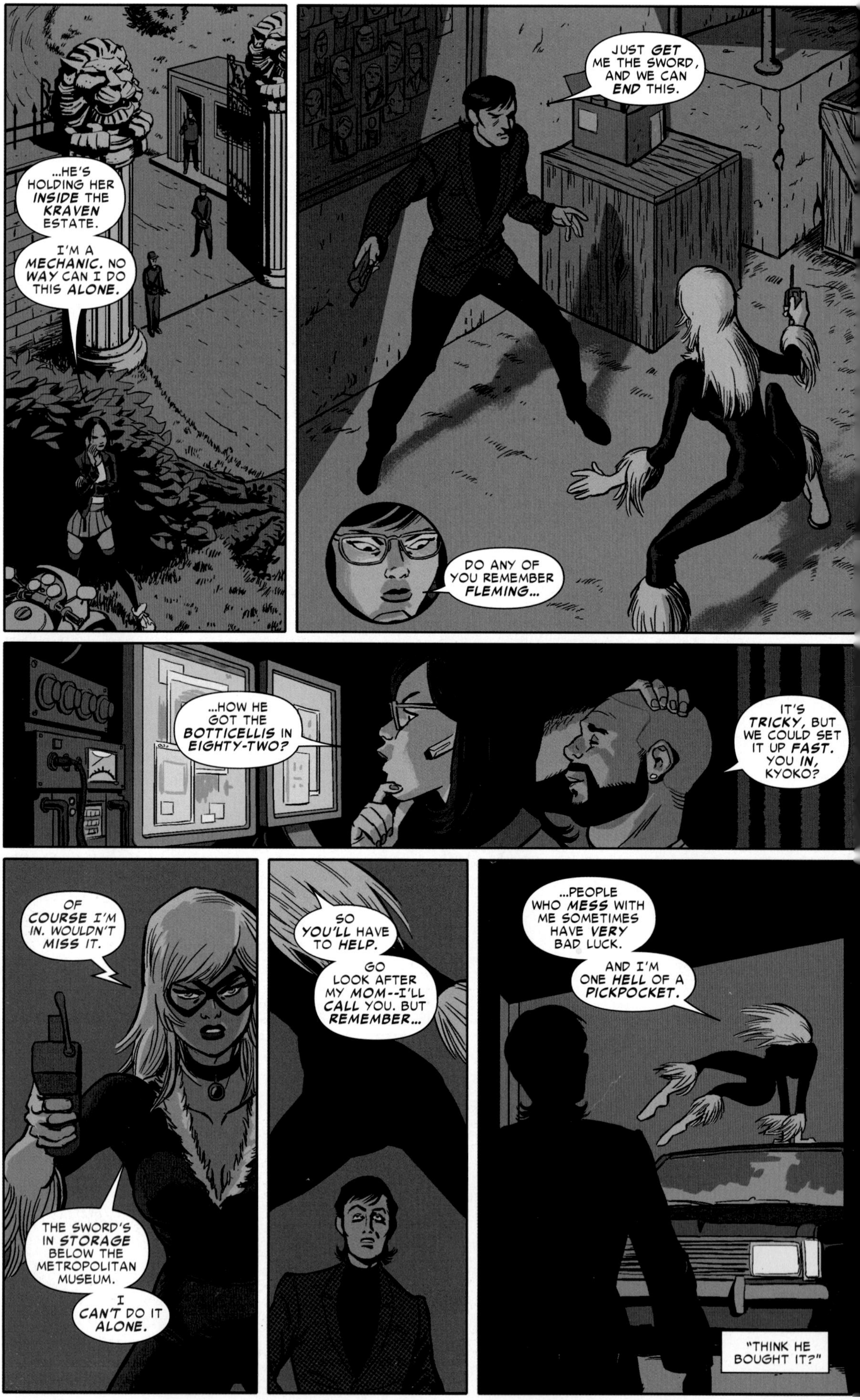
...HE'S HOLDING HER INSIDE THE KRAVEN ESTATE.
I'M A MECHANIC. NO WAY CAN I DO THIS ALONE.
JUST GET ME THE SWORD, AND WE CAN END THIS.
DO ANY OF YOU REMEMBER FLEMING...
...HOW HE GOT THE BOTTICELLIS IN EIGHTY-TWO?
IT'S TRICKY, BUT WE COULD SET IT UP FAST. YOU IN, KYOKO?
OF COURSE I'M IN. WOULDN'T MISS IT.
THE SWORD'S IN STORAGE BELOW THE METROPOLITAN MUSEUM.
I CAN'T DO IT ALONE.
SO YOU'LL HAVE TO HELP.
GO LOOK AFTER MY MOM--I'LL CALL YOU. BUT REMEMBER...
...PEOPLE WHO MESS WITH ME SOMETIMES HAVE VERY BAD LUCK.
AND I'M ONE HELL OF A PICKPOCKET.
"THINK HE BOUGHT IT?"

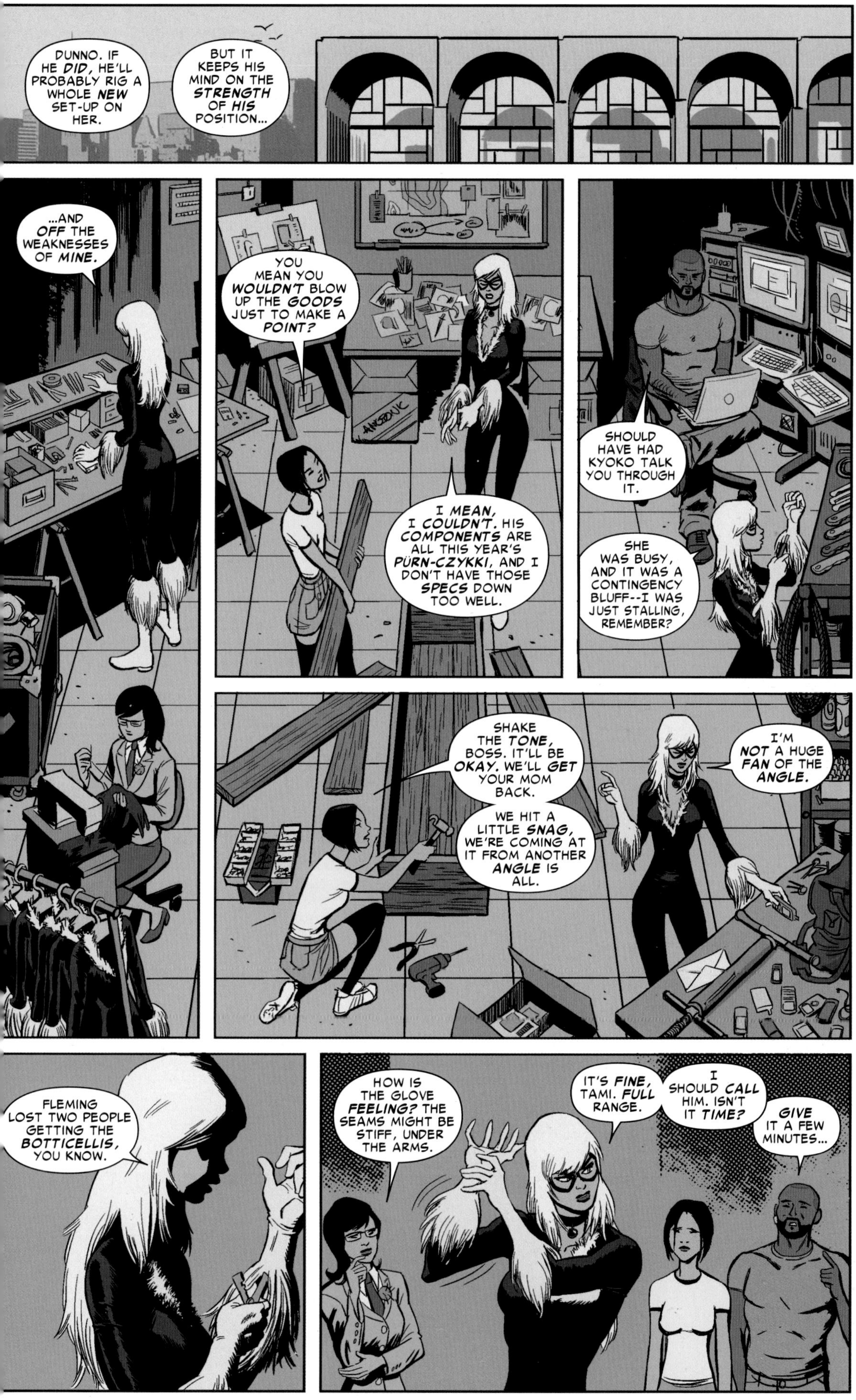

DUNNO. IF HE DID, HE'LL PROBABLY RIG A WHOLE NEW SET-UP ON HER.
BUT IT KEEPS HIS MIND ON THE STRENGTH OF HIS POSITION...
...AND OFF THE WEAKNESSES OF MINE.
YOU MEAN YOU WOULDN'T BLOW UP THE GOODS JUST TO MAKE A POINT?
I MEAN, I COULDN'T. HIS COMPONENTS ARE ALL THIS YEAR'S PÜRN-CZYKKI, AND I DON'T HAVE THOSE SPECS DOWN TOO WELL.
SHOULD HAVE HAD KYOKO TALK YOU THROUGH IT.
SHE WAS BUSY, AND IT WAS A CONTINGENCY BLUFF--I WAS JUST STALLING, REMEMBER?
SHAKE THE TONE, BOSS. IT'LL BE OKAY. WE'LL GET YOUR MOM BACK.
WE HIT A LITTLE SNAG, WE'RE COMING AT IT FROM ANOTHER ANGLE IS ALL.
I'M NOT A HUGE FAN OF THE ANGLE.
FLEMING LOST TWO PEOPLE GETTING THE BOTTICELLIS, YOU KNOW.
HOW IS THE GLOVE FEELING? THE SEAMS MIGHT BE STIFF, UNDER THE ARMS.
IT'S FINE, TAMI. FULL RANGE.
I SHOULD CALL HIM. ISN'T IT TIME?
GIVE IT A FEW MINUTES...

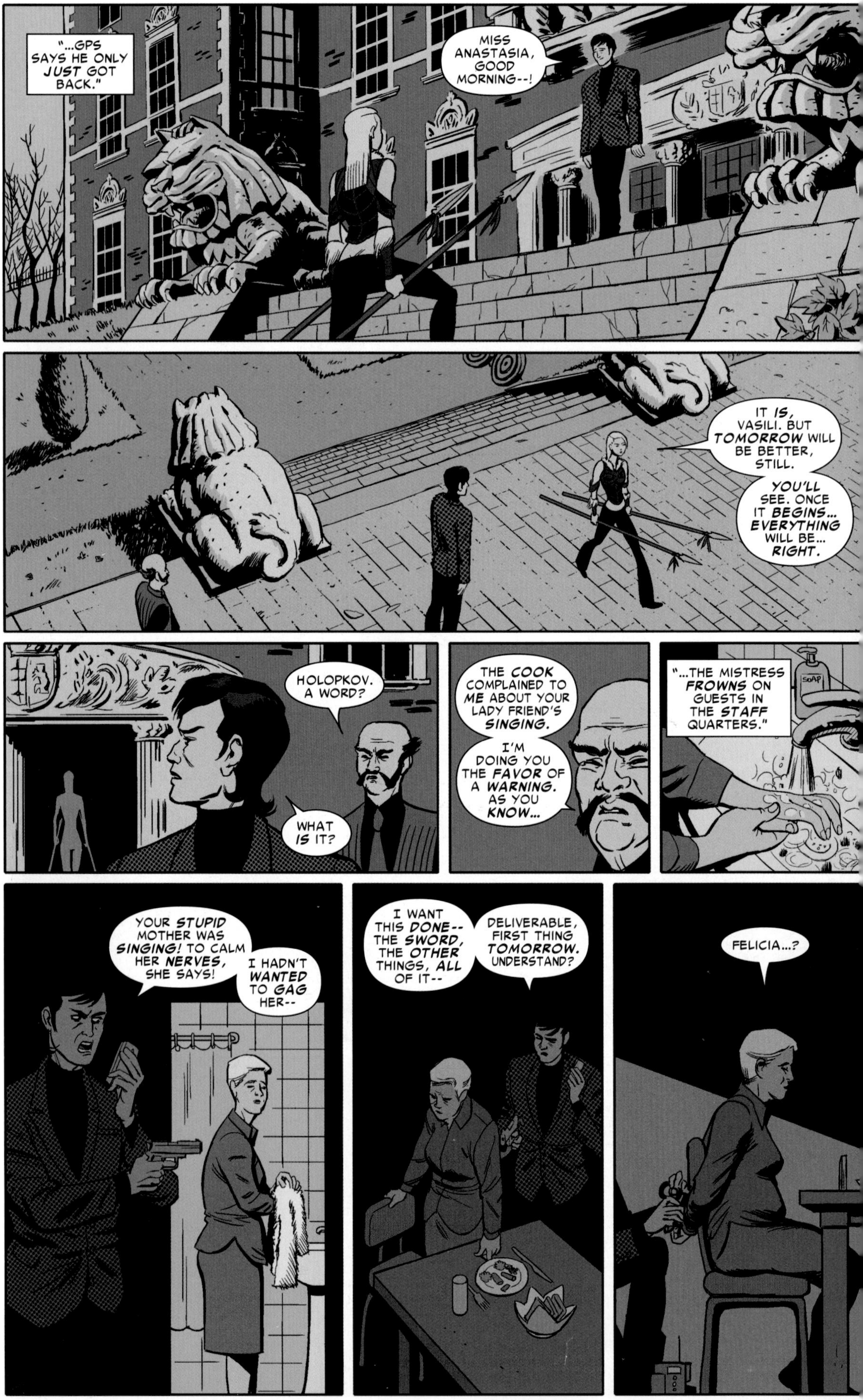
"...GPS SAYS HE ONLY JUST GOT BACK."
MISS ANASTASIA, GOOD MORNING--!
IT IS, VASILI. BUT TOMORROW WILL BE BETTER, STILL.
YOU'LL SEE. ONCE IT BEGINS... EVERYTHING WILL BE... RIGHT.
HOLOPKOV. A WORD?
WHAT IS IT?
THE COOK COMPLAINED TO ME ABOUT YOUR LADY FRIEND'S SINGING.
I'M DOING YOU THE FAVOR OF A WARNING. AS YOU KNOW...
"...THE MISTRESS FROWNS ON GUESTS IN THE STAFF QUARTERS."
SOAP
YOUR STUPID MOTHER WAS SINGING! TO CALM HER NERVES, SHE SAYS!
I HADN'T WANTED TO GAG HER--
I WANT THIS DONE-- THE SWORD, THE OTHER THINGS, ALL OF IT--
DELIVERABLE, FIRST THING TOMORROW. UNDERSTAND?
FELICIA...?

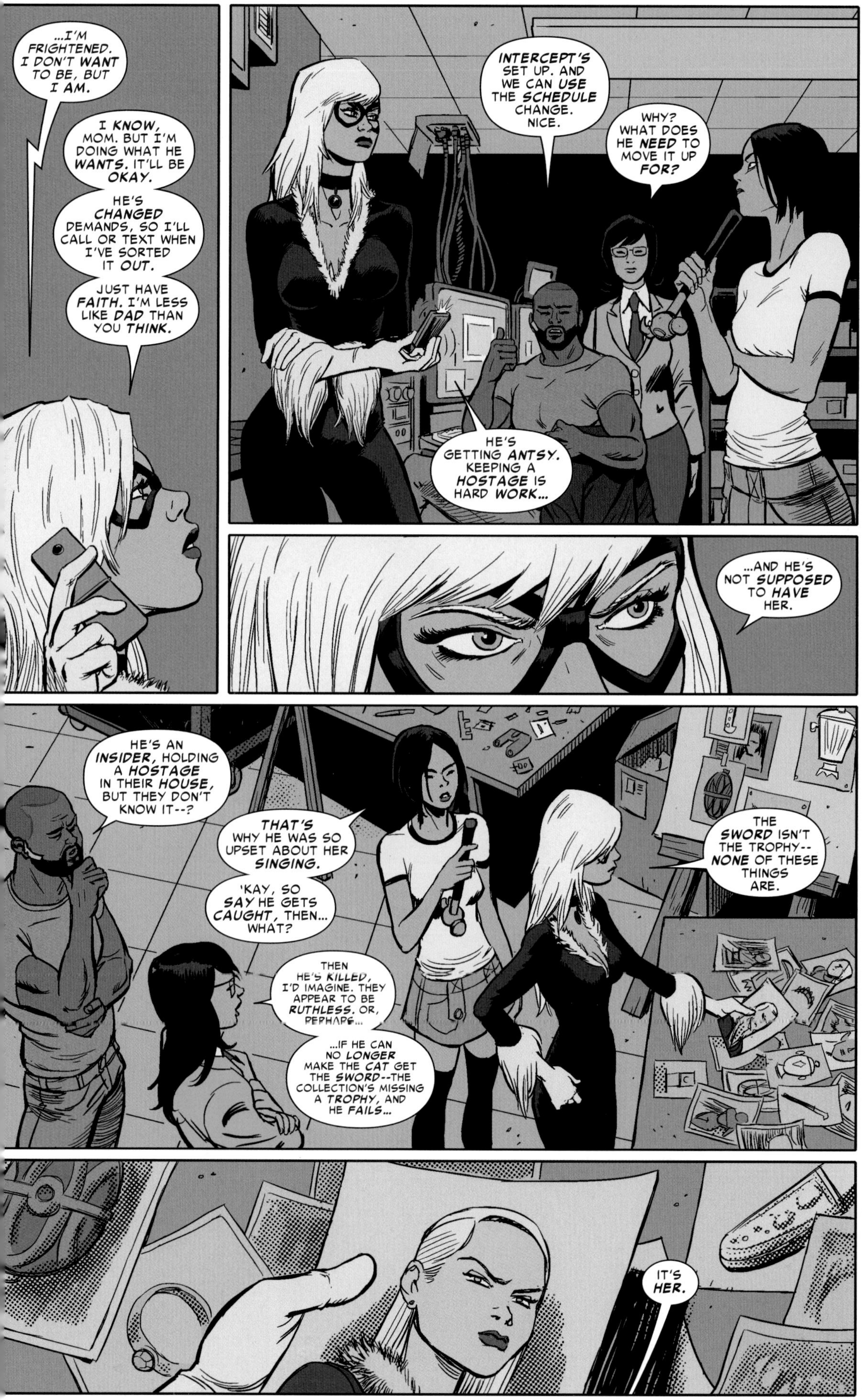
...I'M FRIGHTENED. I DON'T WANT TO BE, BUT I AM.
I KNOW, MOM. BUT I'M DOING WHAT HE WANTS. IT'LL BE OKAY.
HE'S CHANGED DEMANDS, SO I'LL CALL OR TEXT WHEN I'VE SORTED IT OUT.
JUST HAVE FAITH. I'M LESS LIKE DAD THAN YOU THINK.
INTERCEPT'S SET UP. AND WE CAN USE THE SCHEDULE CHANGE. NICE.
WHY? WHAT DOES HE NEED TO MOVE IT UP FOR?
HE'S GETTING ANTSY. KEEPING A HOSTAGE IS HARD WORK...
...AND HE'S NOT SUPPOSED TO HAVE HER.
HE'S AN INSIDER, HOLDING A HOSTAGE IN THEIR HOUSE, BUT THEY DON'T KNOW IT--?
THAT'S WHY HE WAS SO UPSET ABOUT HER SINGING.
'KAY, SO SAY HE GETS CAUGHT, THEN... WHAT?
THEN HE'S KILLED, I'D IMAGINE. THEY APPEAR TO BE RUTHLESS. OR, PERHAPS...
...IF HE CAN NO LONGER MAKE THE CAT GET THE SWORD--THE COLLECTION'S MISSING A TROPHY, AND HE FAILS...
THE SWORD ISN'T THE TROPHY-- NONE OF THESE THINGS ARE.
IT'S HER.

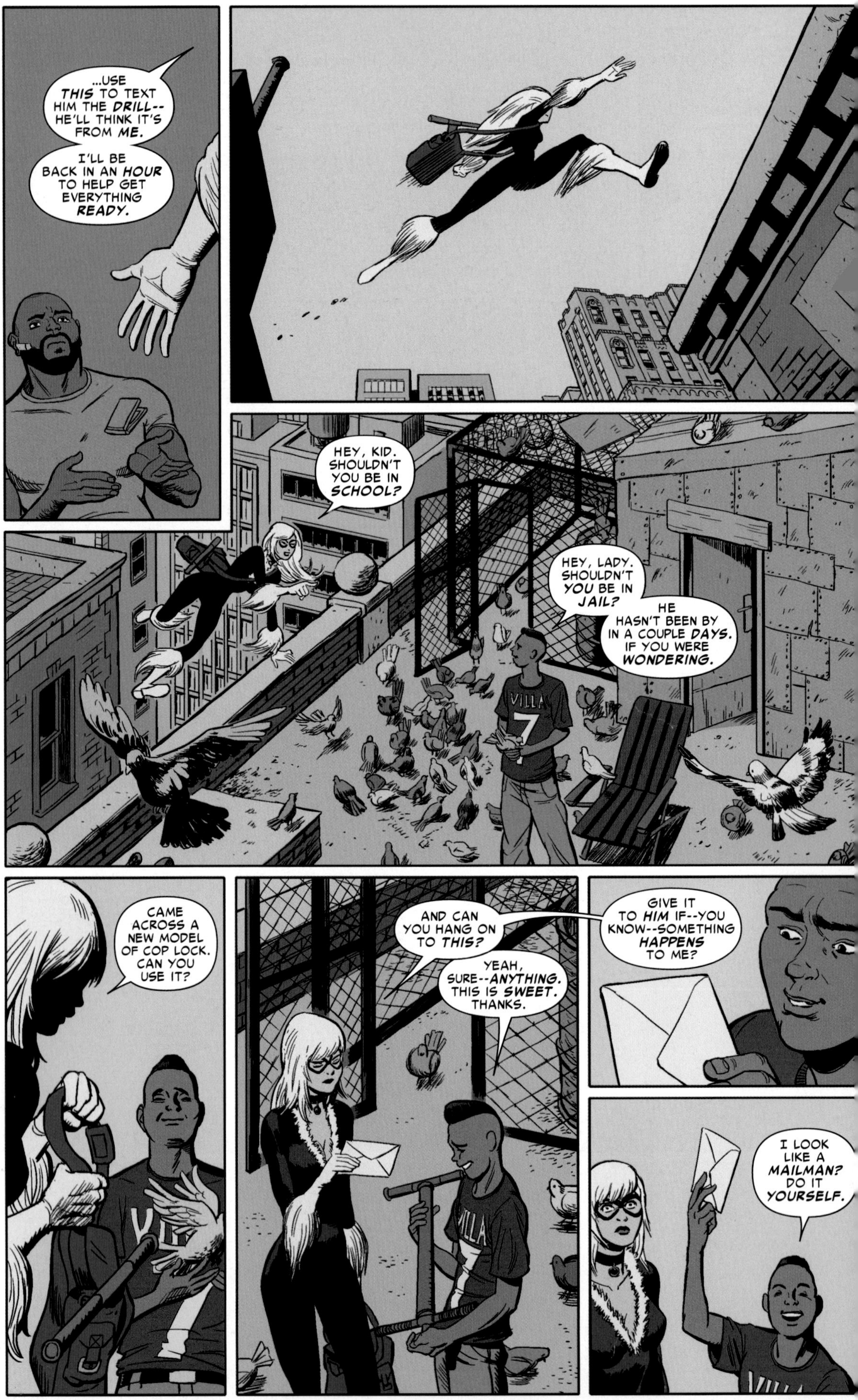
...USE THIS TO TEXT HIM THE DRILL--HE'LL THINK IT'S FROM ME.
I'LL BE BACK IN AN HOUR TO HELP GET EVERYTHING READY.
HEY, KID. SHOULDN'T YOU BE IN SCHOOL?
HEY, LADY. SHOULDN'T YOU BE IN JAIL?
HE HASN'T BEEN BY IN A COUPLE DAYS. IF YOU WERE WONDERING.
VILLA 7
CAME ACROSS A NEW MODEL OF COP LOCK. CAN YOU USE IT?
AND CAN YOU HANG ON TO THIS?
YEAH, SURE--ANYTHING. THIS IS SWEET. THANKS.
GIVE IT TO HIM IF--YOU KNOW--SOMETHING HAPPENS TO ME?
I LOOK LIKE A MAILMAN? DO IT YOURSELF.

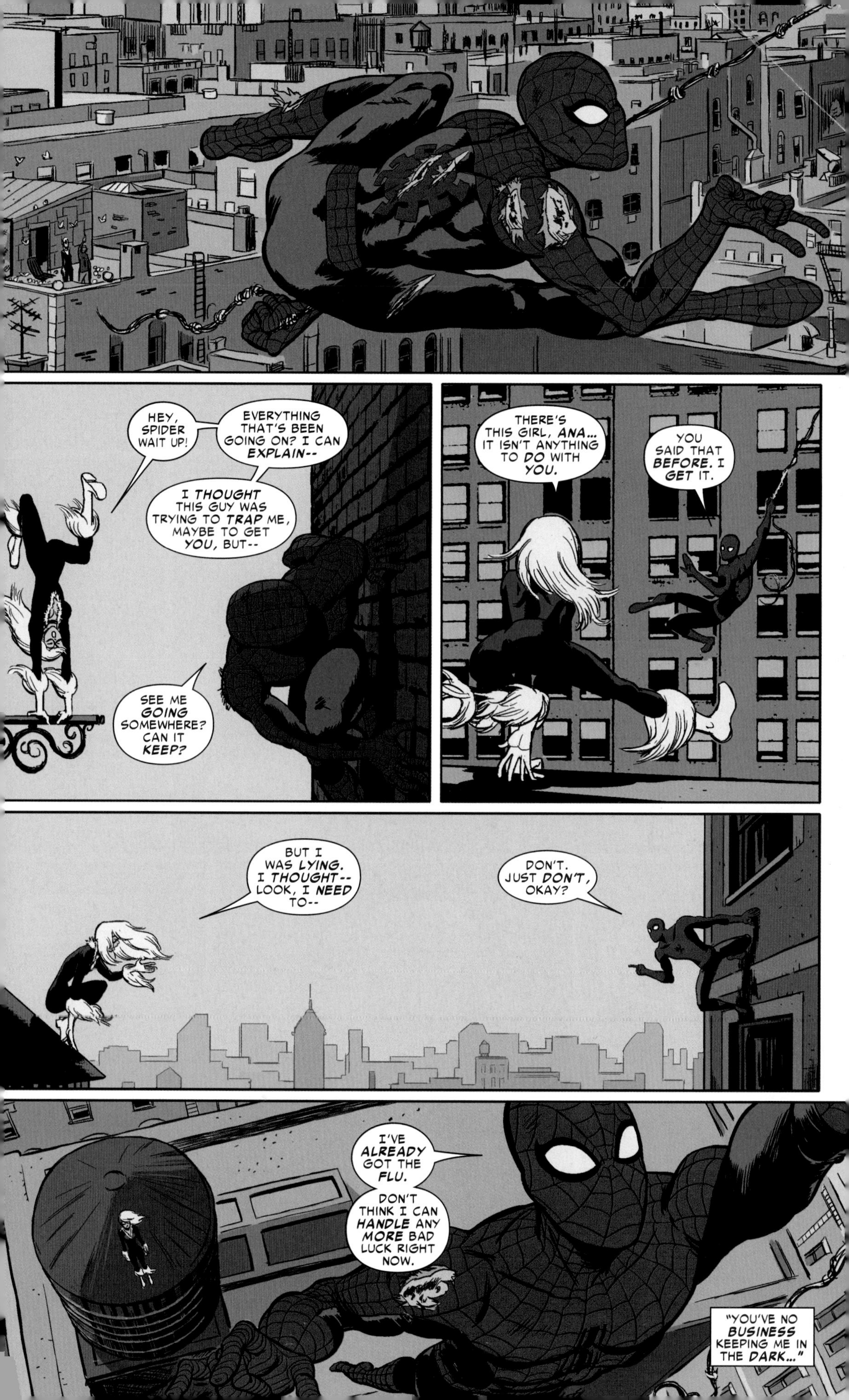
HEY, SPIDER WAIT UP!
EVERYTHING THAT'S BEEN GOING ON? I CAN EXPLAIN--
I THOUGHT THIS GUY WAS TRYING TO TRAP ME, MAYBE TO GET YOU, BUT--
SEE ME GOING SOMEWHERE? CAN IT KEEP?
THERE'S THIS GIRL, ANA... IT ISN'T ANYTHING TO DO WITH YOU.
YOU SAID THAT BEFORE. I GET IT.
BUT I WAS LYING. I THOUGHT-- LOOK, I NEED TO--
DON'T. JUST DON'T, OKAY?
I'VE ALREADY GOT THE FLU.
DON'T THINK I CAN HANDLE ANY MORE BAD LUCK RIGHT NOW.
"YOU'VE NO BUSINESS KEEPING ME IN THE DARK..."

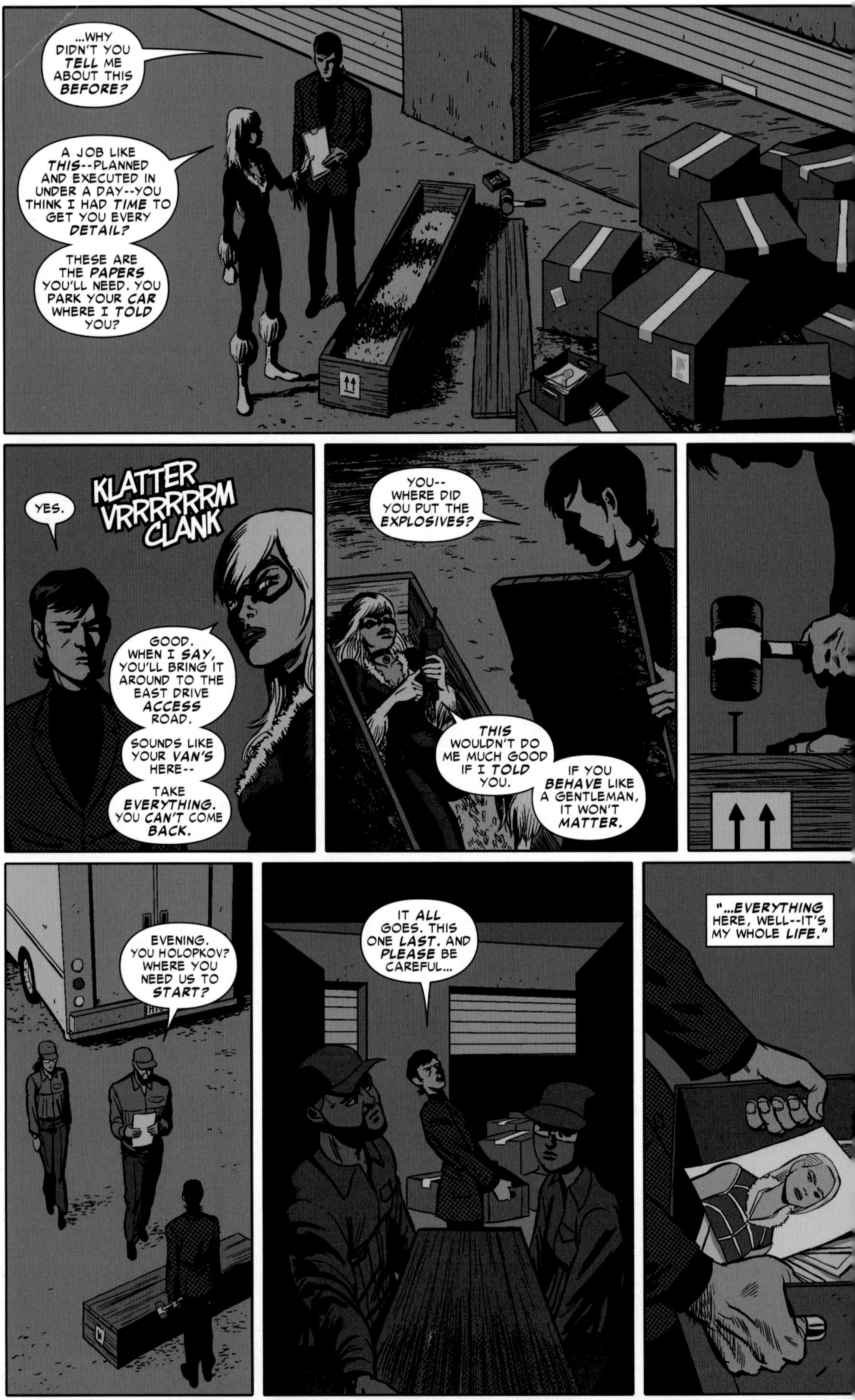
...WHY DIDN'T YOU TELL ME ABOUT THIS BEFORE?
A JOB LIKE THIS--PLANNED AND EXECUTED IN UNDER A DAY--YOU THINK I HAD TIME TO GET YOU EVERY DETAIL?
THESE ARE THE PAPERS YOU'LL NEED. YOU PARK YOUR CAR WHERE I TOLD YOU?
YES.
KLATTER VRRRRRRM CLANK
GOOD. WHEN I SAY, YOU'LL BRING IT AROUND TO THE EAST DRIVE ACCESS ROAD.
SOUNDS LIKE YOUR VAN'S HERE--
TAKE EVERYTHING. YOU CAN'T COME BACK.
YOU--WHERE DID YOU PUT THE EXPLOSIVES?
THIS WOULDN'T DO ME MUCH GOOD IF I TOLD YOU.
IF YOU BEHAVE LIKE A GENTLEMAN, IT WON'T MATTER.
EVENING. YOU HOLOPKOV? WHERE YOU NEED US TO START?
IT ALL GOES. THIS ONE LAST. AND PLEASE BE CAREFUL...
"...EVERYTHING HERE, WELL--IT'S MY WHOLE LIFE."

KID, NEXT TIME THERE'S A DELAY, YOU GOTTA CALL AHEAD. NOT MANY OF US NIGHT GUYS HERE AT THE MUSEUM ARE CLEARED FOR RECEIVABLES.

LOOKS LIKE EVERYTHING'S IN ORDER, THOUGH--

HAVE A GOOD ONE!

PARK AT THIS ADDRESS AND WAIT. IT MAY BE A WHILE.

I'LL CALL YOU WHEN I'M READY.

WHATEVER YOU SAY, MAN. YOU'RE PAYING BY THE HOUR.

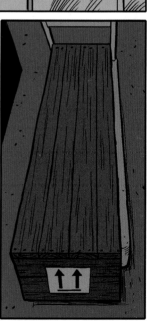

FLOC

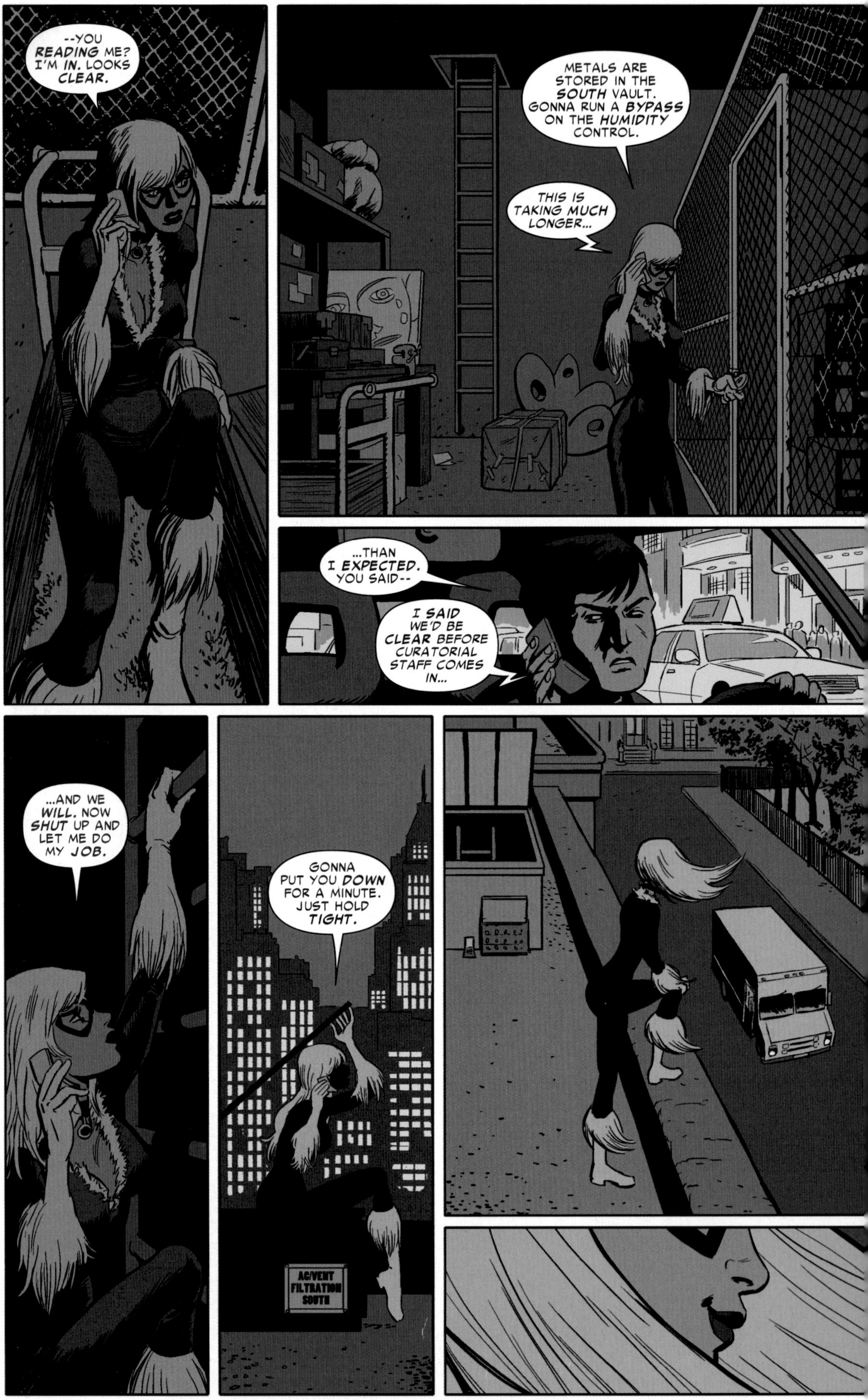
--YOU READING ME? I'M IN. LOOKS CLEAR.
METALS ARE STORED IN THE SOUTH VAULT. GONNA RUN A BYPASS ON THE HUMIDITY CONTROL.
THIS IS TAKING MUCH LONGER...
...THAN I EXPECTED. YOU SAID--
I SAID WE'D BE CLEAR BEFORE CURATORIAL STAFF COMES IN...
...AND WE WILL. NOW SHUT UP AND LET ME DO MY JOB.
GONNA PUT YOU DOWN FOR A MINUTE. JUST HOLD TIGHT.
AC/VENT FILTRATION SOUTH

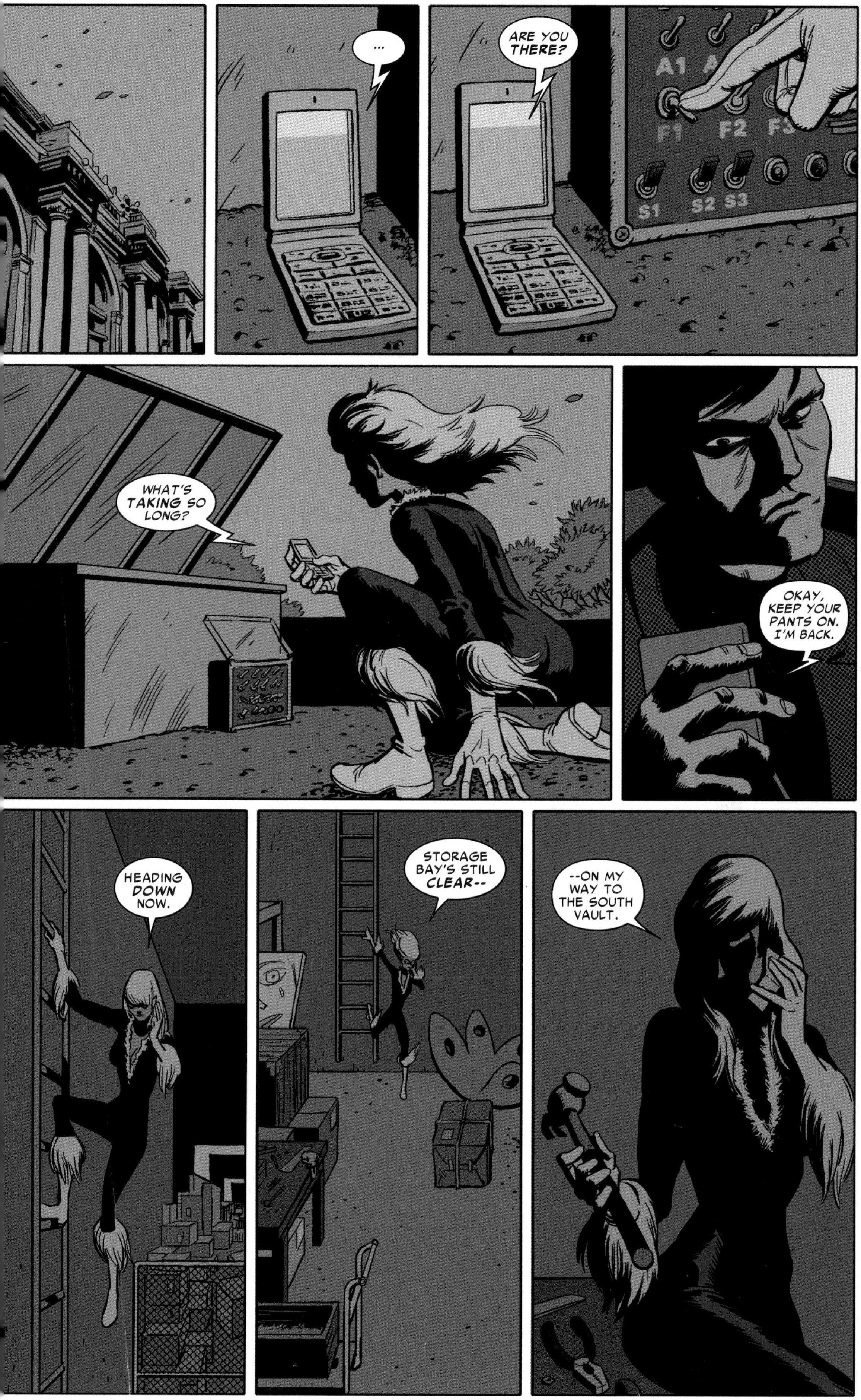
...
ARE YOU THERE?
A1
F1
F2
F3
S1
S2
S3
WHAT'S TAKING SO LONG?
OKAY, KEEP YOUR PANTS ON. I'M BACK.
HEADING DOWN NOW.
STORAGE BAY'S STILL CLEAR--
--ON MY WAY TO THE SOUTH VAULT.

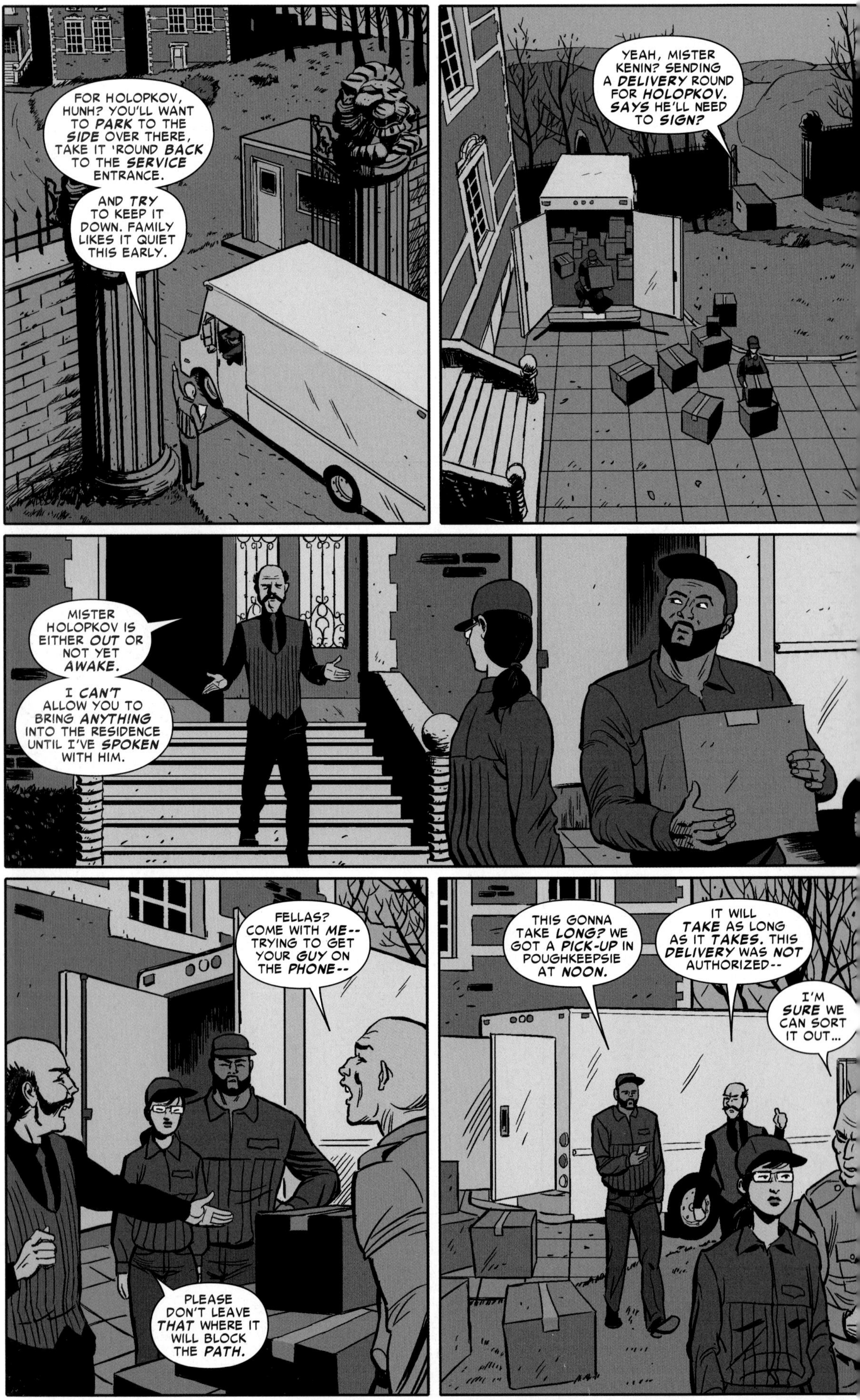
FOR HOLOPKOV, HUNH? YOU'LL WANT TO PARK TO THE SIDE OVER THERE, TAKE IT 'ROUND BACK TO THE SERVICE ENTRANCE.
AND TRY TO KEEP IT DOWN. FAMILY LIKES IT QUIET THIS EARLY.
YEAH, MISTER KENIN? SENDING A DELIVERY ROUND FOR HOLOPKOV. SAYS HE'LL NEED TO SIGN?
MISTER HOLOPKOV IS EITHER OUT OR NOT YET AWAKE.
I CAN'T ALLOW YOU TO BRING ANYTHING INTO THE RESIDENCE UNTIL I'VE SPOKEN WITH HIM.
FELLAS? COME WITH ME-- TRYING TO GET YOUR GUY ON THE PHONE--
PLEASE DON'T LEAVE THAT WHERE IT WILL BLOCK THE PATH.
THIS GONNA TAKE LONG? WE GOT A PICK-UP IN POUGHKEEPSIE AT NOON.
IT WILL TAKE AS LONG AS IT TAKES. THIS DELIVERY WAS NOT AUTHORIZED--
I'M SURE WE CAN SORT IT OUT...

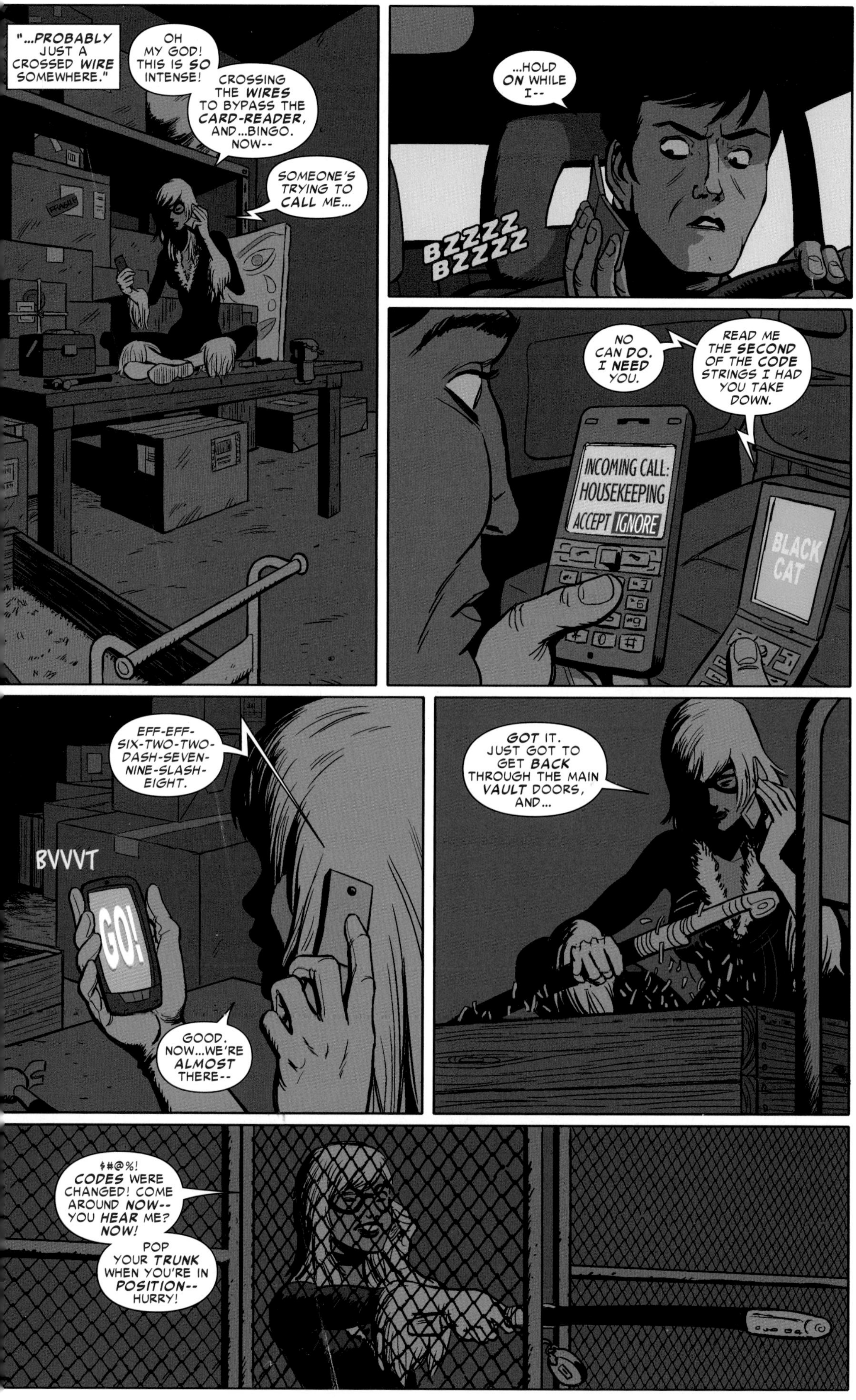
"...PROBABLY JUST A CROSSED WIRE SOMEWHERE."
OH MY GOD! THIS IS SO INTENSE!
CROSSING THE WIRES TO BYPASS THE CARD-READER, AND...BINGO. NOW--
SOMEONE'S TRYING TO CALL ME...
...HOLD ON WHILE I--
BZZZZ BZZZZ
NO CAN DO. I NEED YOU.
READ ME THE SECOND OF THE CODE STRINGS I HAD YOU TAKE DOWN.
INCOMING CALL: HOUSEKEEPING
ACCEPT IGNORE
BLACK CAT
EFF-EFF-SIX-TWO-TWO-DASH-SEVEN-NINE-SLASH-EIGHT.
BVVVT
GO!
GOOD. NOW...WE'RE ALMOST THERE--
GOT IT. JUST GOT TO GET BACK THROUGH THE MAIN VAULT DOORS, AND...
$#@%! CODES WERE CHANGED! COME AROUND NOW-- YOU HEAR ME? NOW!
POP YOUR TRUNK WHEN YOU'RE IN POSITION-- HURRY!

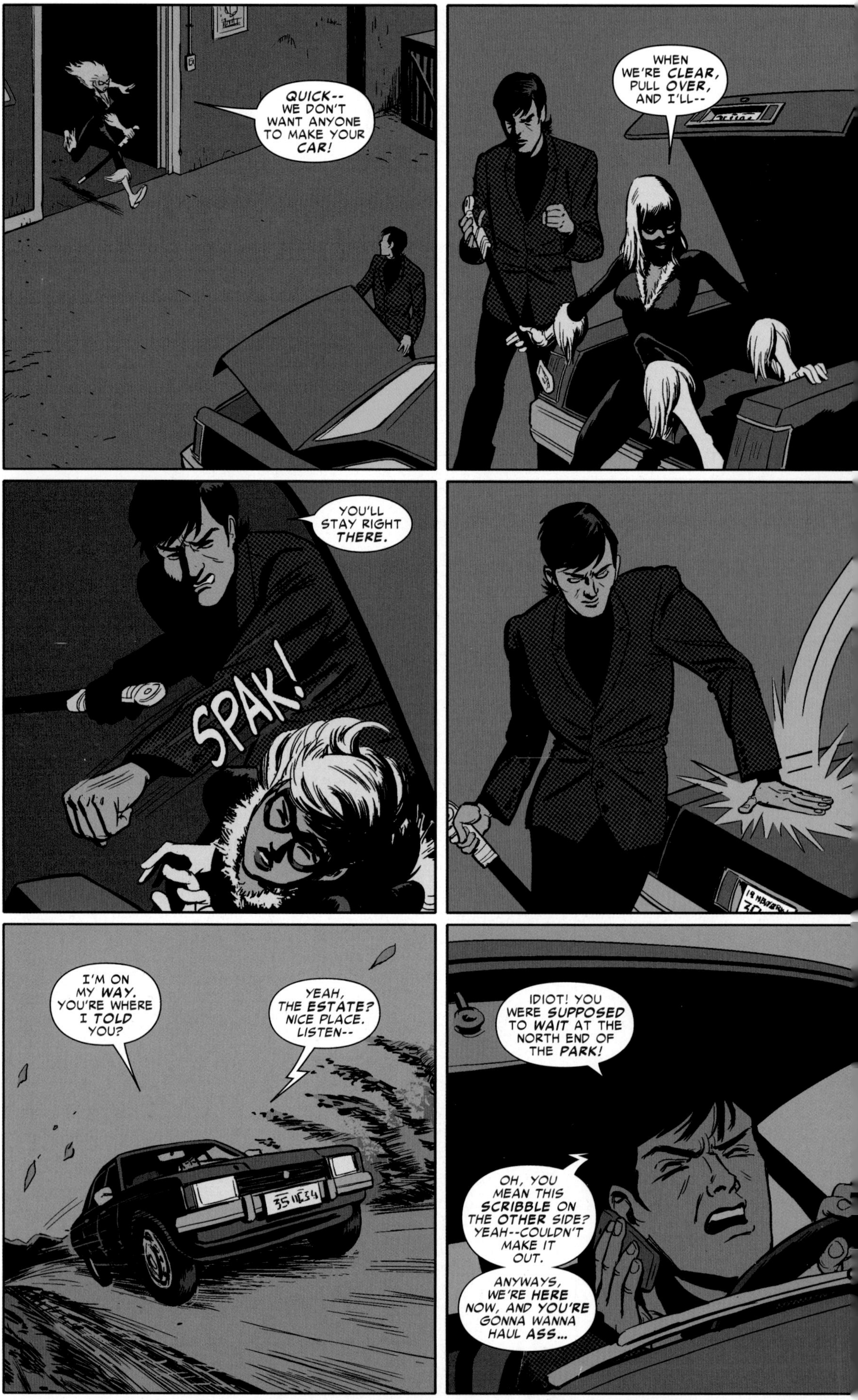
QUICK--
WE DON'T WANT ANYONE TO MAKE YOUR CAR!
WHEN WE'RE CLEAR, PULL OVER, AND I'LL--
YOU'LL STAY RIGHT THERE.
SPAK!
I'M ON MY WAY. YOU'RE WHERE I TOLD YOU?
YEAH, THE ESTATE? NICE PLACE. LISTEN--
IDIOT! YOU WERE SUPPOSED TO WAIT AT THE NORTH END OF THE PARK!
OH, YOU MEAN THIS SCRIBBLE ON THE OTHER SIDE? YEAH--COULDN'T MAKE IT OUT.
ANYWAYS, WE'RE HERE NOW, AND YOU'RE GONNA WANNA HAUL ASS...

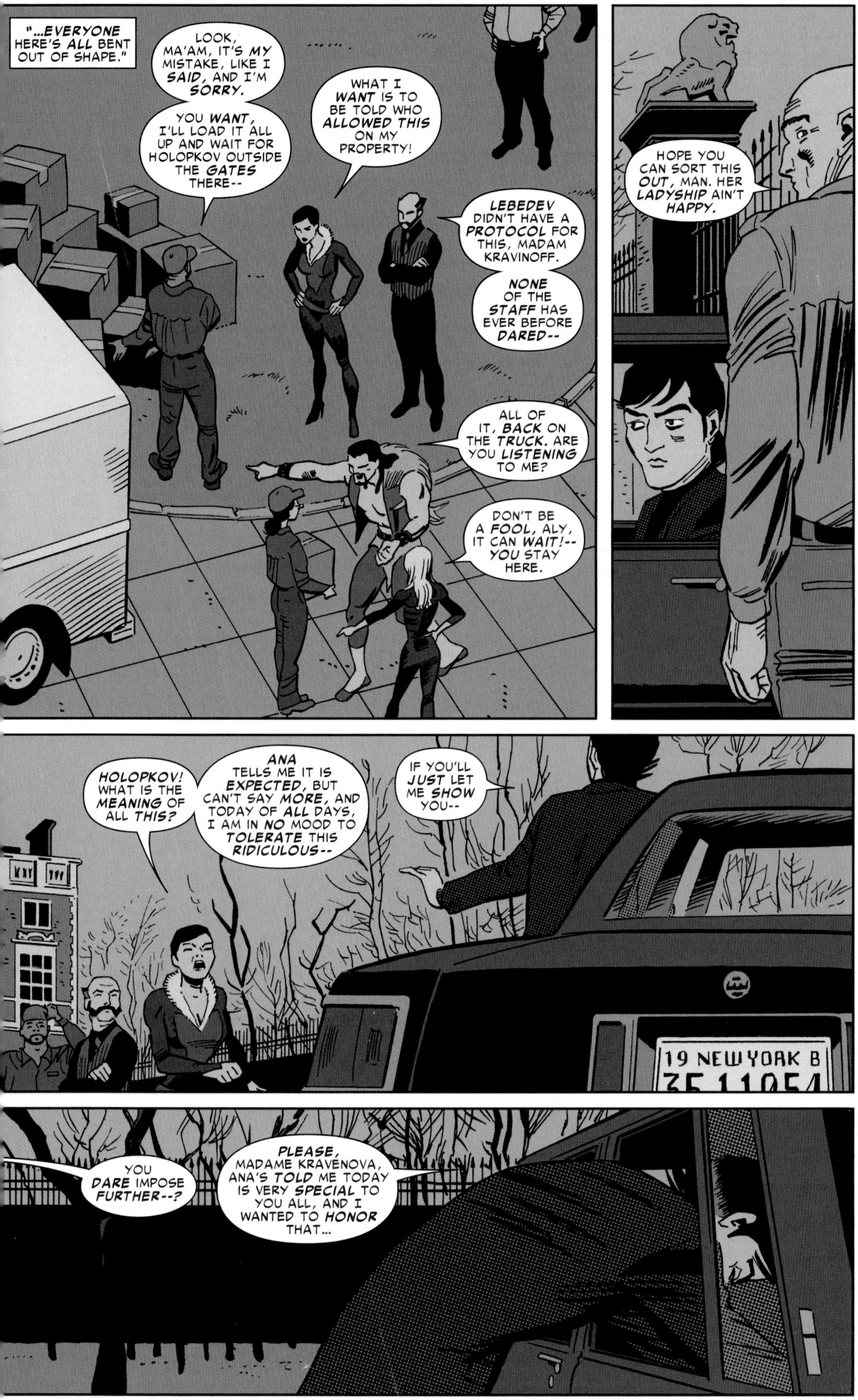
"...EVERYONE HERE'S ALL BENT OUT OF SHAPE."
LOOK, MA'AM, IT'S MY MISTAKE, LIKE I SAID, AND I'M SORRY.
YOU WANT, I'LL LOAD IT ALL UP AND WAIT FOR HOLOPKOV OUTSIDE THE GATES THERE--
WHAT I WANT IS TO BE TOLD WHO ALLOWED THIS ON MY PROPERTY!
LEBEDEV DIDN'T HAVE A PROTOCOL FOR THIS, MADAM KRAVINOFF.
NONE OF THE STAFF HAS EVER BEFORE DARED--
ALL OF IT, BACK ON THE TRUCK. ARE YOU LISTENING TO ME?
DON'T BE A FOOL, ALY, IT CAN WAIT!-- YOU STAY HERE.
HOPE YOU CAN SORT THIS OUT, MAN. HER LADYSHIP AIN'T HAPPY.
HOLOPKOV! WHAT IS THE MEANING OF ALL THIS?
ANA TELLS ME IT IS EXPECTED, BUT CAN'T SAY MORE, AND TODAY OF ALL DAYS, I AM IN NO MOOD TO TOLERATE THIS RIDICULOUS--
IF YOU'LL JUST LET ME SHOW YOU--
19 NEW YORK B
YOU DARE IMPOSE FURTHER--?
PLEASE, MADAME KRAVENOVA, ANA'S TOLD ME TODAY IS VERY SPECIAL TO YOU ALL, AND I WANTED TO HONOR THAT...

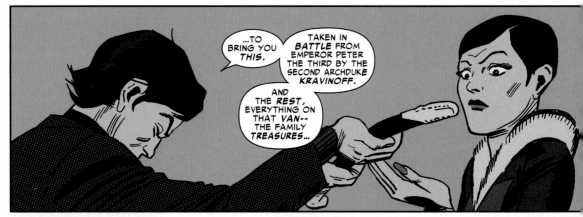

...TO BRING YOU *THIS.*

TAKEN IN *BATTLE* FROM EMPEROR PETER THE THIRD BY THE SECOND ARCHDUKE *KRAVINOFF.*

AND THE *REST,* EVERYTHING ON THAT *VAN*-- THE FAMILY *TREASURES...*

...EVERYTHING FROM MY GRANDMOTHER'S *LEDGER,* RESTORED AT *LAST...*

...JUST AS *YOU* ONCE WISHED.

AND THERE'S ONE THING *MORE.*

IT'S NO *SECRET* HOW *DEEPLY* YOU DESPISE THE *SPIDER-MAN,* MADAME, SO WHEN I SAW THE *OPPORTUNITY...*

...I GOT *THIS* FOR YOU AS WELL.

AN... INTERESTING GIFT. I IMAGINE IT *WOULD* CAUSE HIM *PAIN* TO SEE HER *SUFFER.*

HEY, NOW! EVERYONE HOLD ON JUST *ONE DAMN SECOND!* I AM *NOT*--

SMACK!

CURIOUS. I WONDER WHAT IT *IS* HE *SEES* IN YOU...?

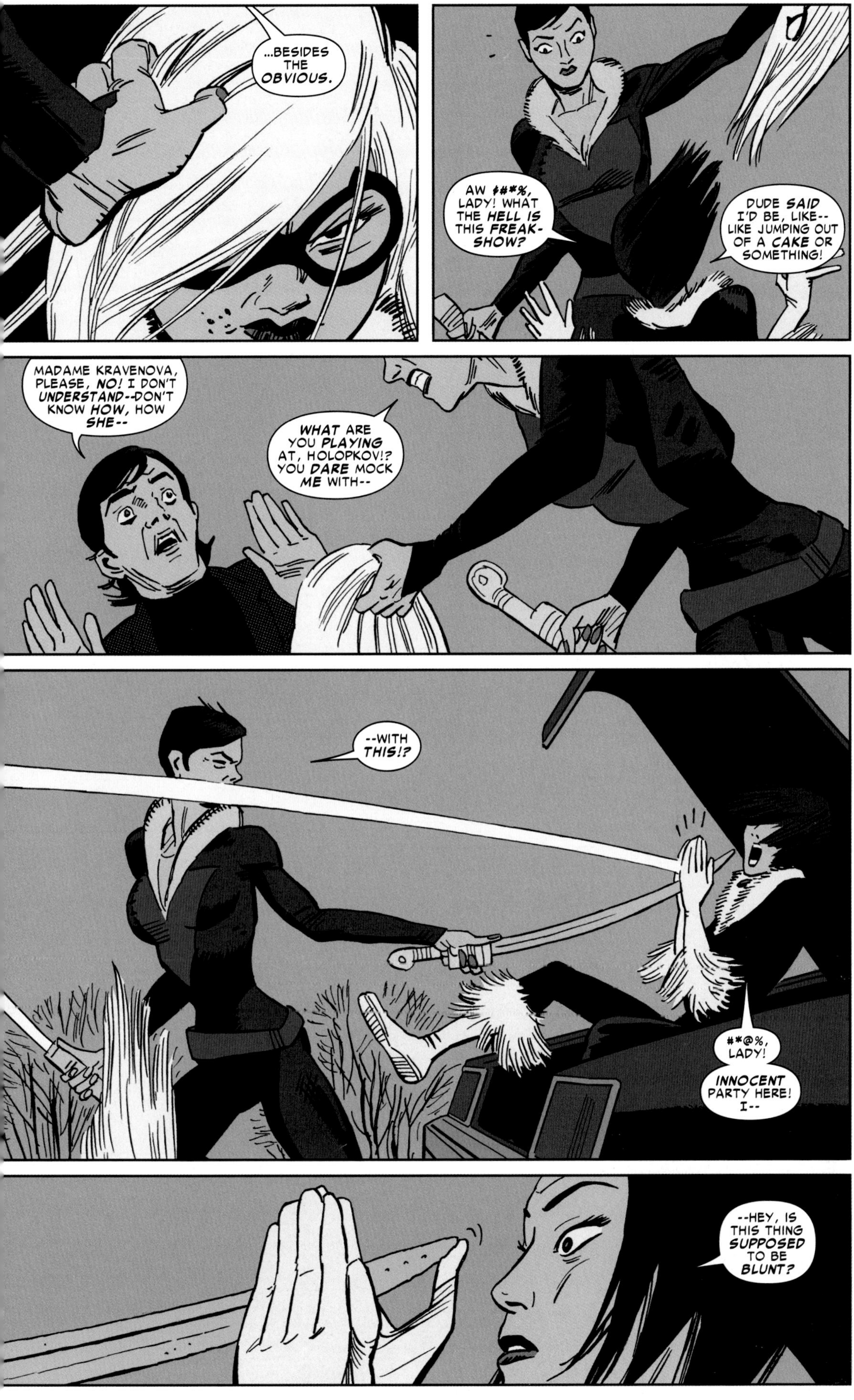
...BESIDES THE OBVIOUS.
AW $#*%, LADY! WHAT THE HELL IS THIS FREAK-SHOW?
DUDE SAID I'D BE, LIKE-- LIKE JUMPING OUT OF A CAKE OR SOMETHING!
MADAME KRAVENOVA, PLEASE, NO! I DON'T UNDERSTAND--DON'T KNOW HOW, HOW SHE--
WHAT ARE YOU PLAYING AT, HOLOPKOV!? YOU DARE MOCK ME WITH--
--WITH THIS!?
#*@%, LADY!
INNOCENT PARTY HERE! I--
--HEY, IS THIS THING SUPPOSED TO BE BLUNT?

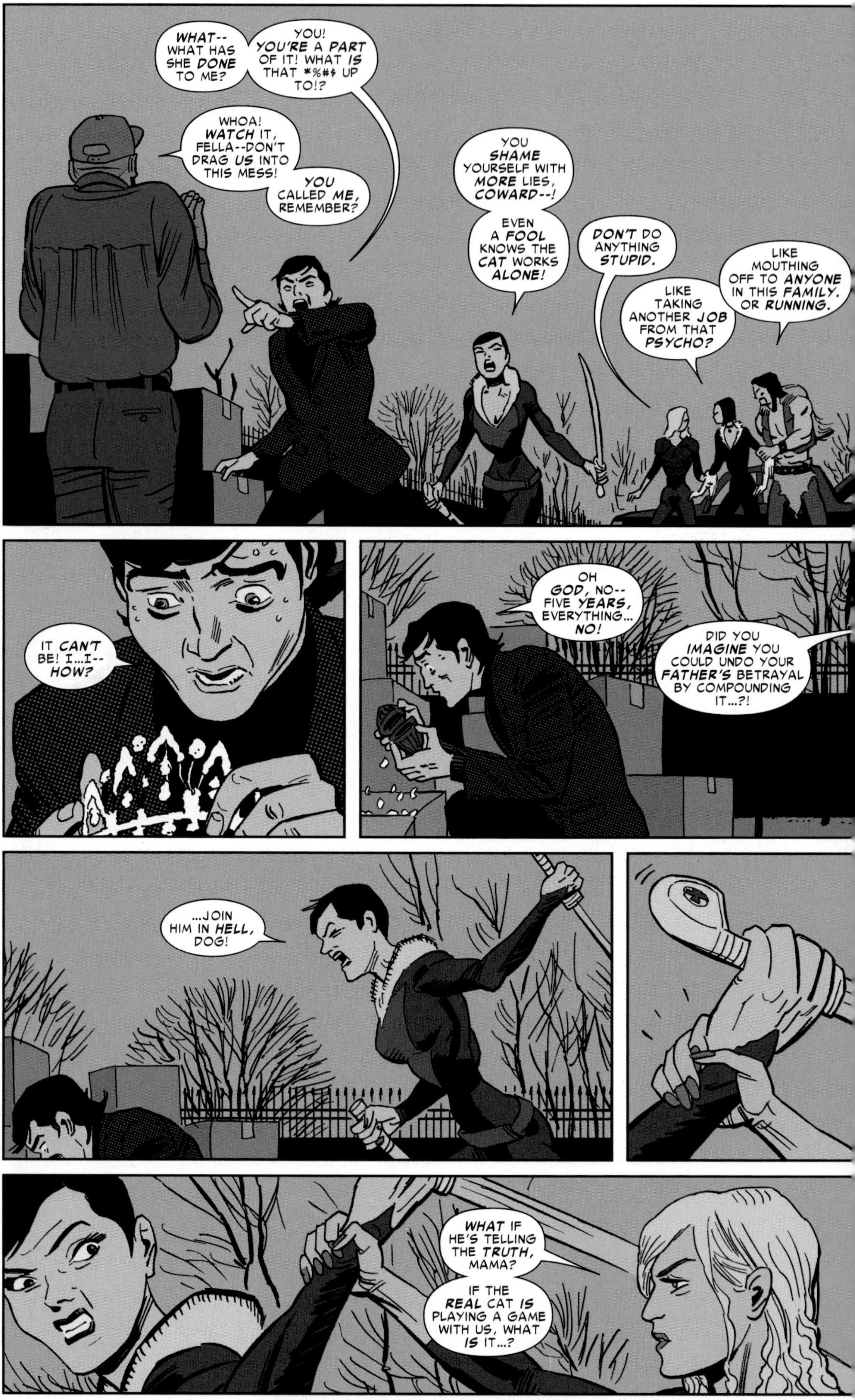
WHAT-- WHAT HAS SHE DONE TO ME?
YOU! YOU'RE A PART OF IT! WHAT IS THAT *%#$ UP TO!?
WHOA! WATCH IT, FELLA--DON'T DRAG US INTO THIS MESS!
YOU CALLED ME, REMEMBER?
YOU SHAME YOURSELF WITH MORE LIES, COWARD--!
EVEN A FOOL KNOWS THE CAT WORKS ALONE!
DON'T DO ANYTHING STUPID.
LIKE TAKING ANOTHER JOB FROM THAT PSYCHO?
LIKE MOUTHING OFF TO ANYONE IN THIS FAMILY. OR RUNNING.
IT CAN'T BE! I...I-- HOW?
OH GOD, NO-- FIVE YEARS, EVERYTHING... NO!
DID YOU IMAGINE YOU COULD UNDO YOUR FATHER'S BETRAYAL BY COMPOUNDING IT...?!
...JOIN HIM IN HELL, DOG!
WHAT IF HE'S TELLING THE TRUTH, MAMA?
IF THE REAL CAT IS PLAYING A GAME WITH US, WHAT IS IT...?

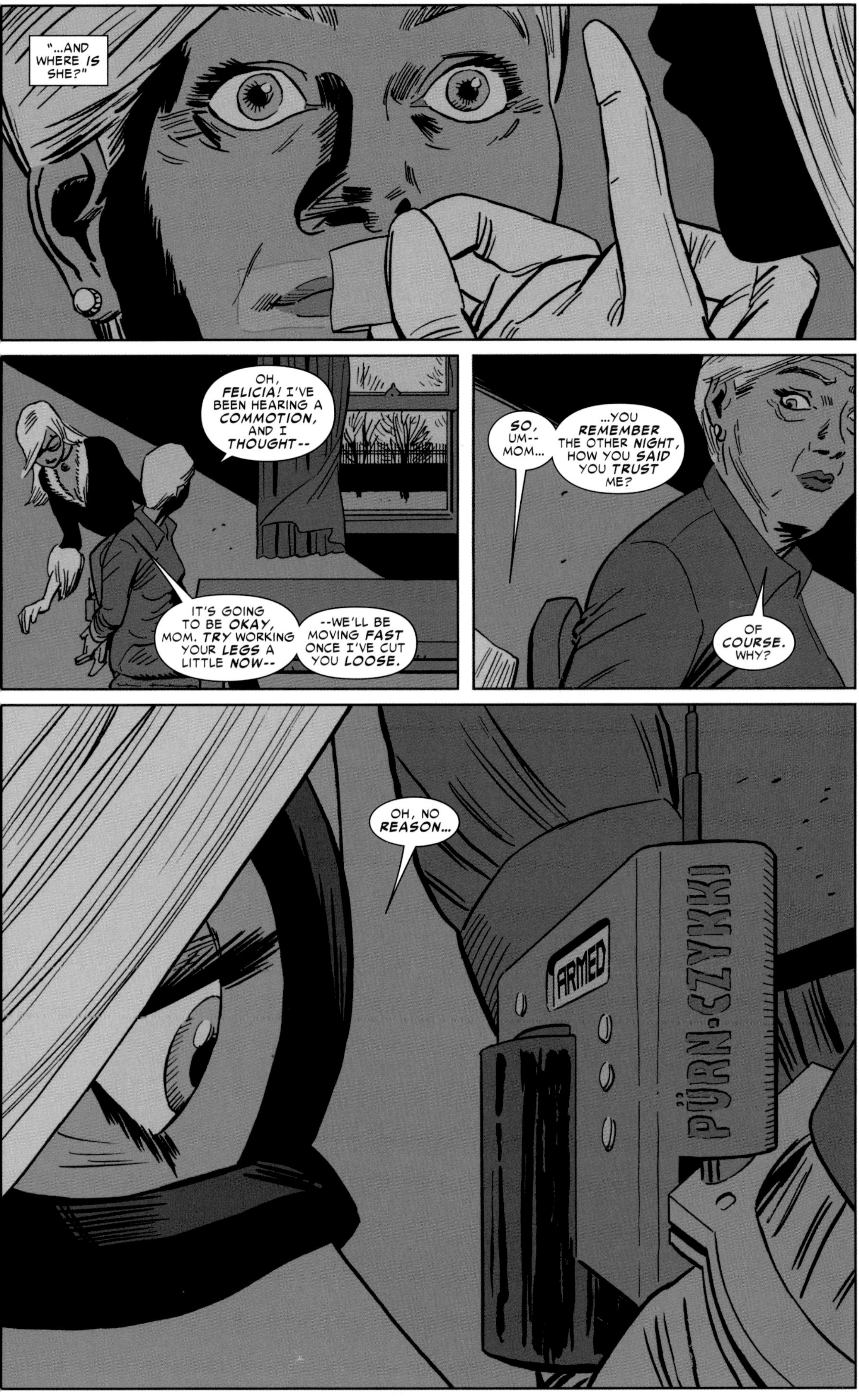
"...AND WHERE *IS* SHE?"
OH, *FELICIA!* I'VE BEEN HEARING A *COMMOTION,* AND I *THOUGHT*--
IT'S GOING TO BE *OKAY,* MOM. *TRY* WORKING YOUR *LEGS* A LITTLE *NOW*--
--WE'LL BE MOVING *FAST* ONCE I'VE CUT YOU *LOOSE.*
SO, UM-- MOM...
...YOU *REMEMBER* THE OTHER *NIGHT,* HOW YOU *SAID* YOU *TRUST* ME?
OF *COURSE.* WHY?
OH, NO *REASON*...
ARMED
PÜRN-CZYKKI

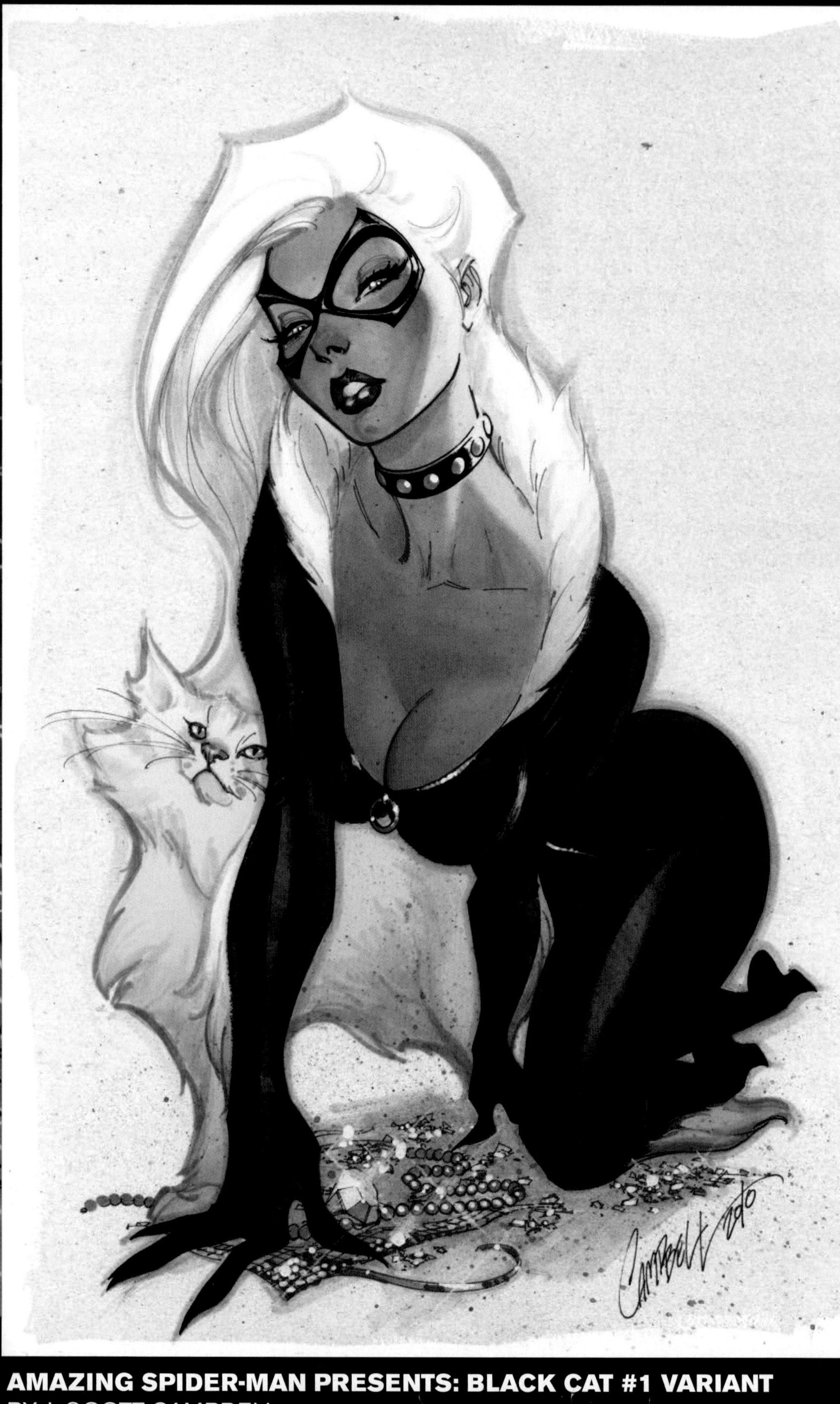

AMAZING SPIDER-MAN PRESENTS: BLACK CAT #1 VARIANT
BY J. SCOTT CAMPBELL

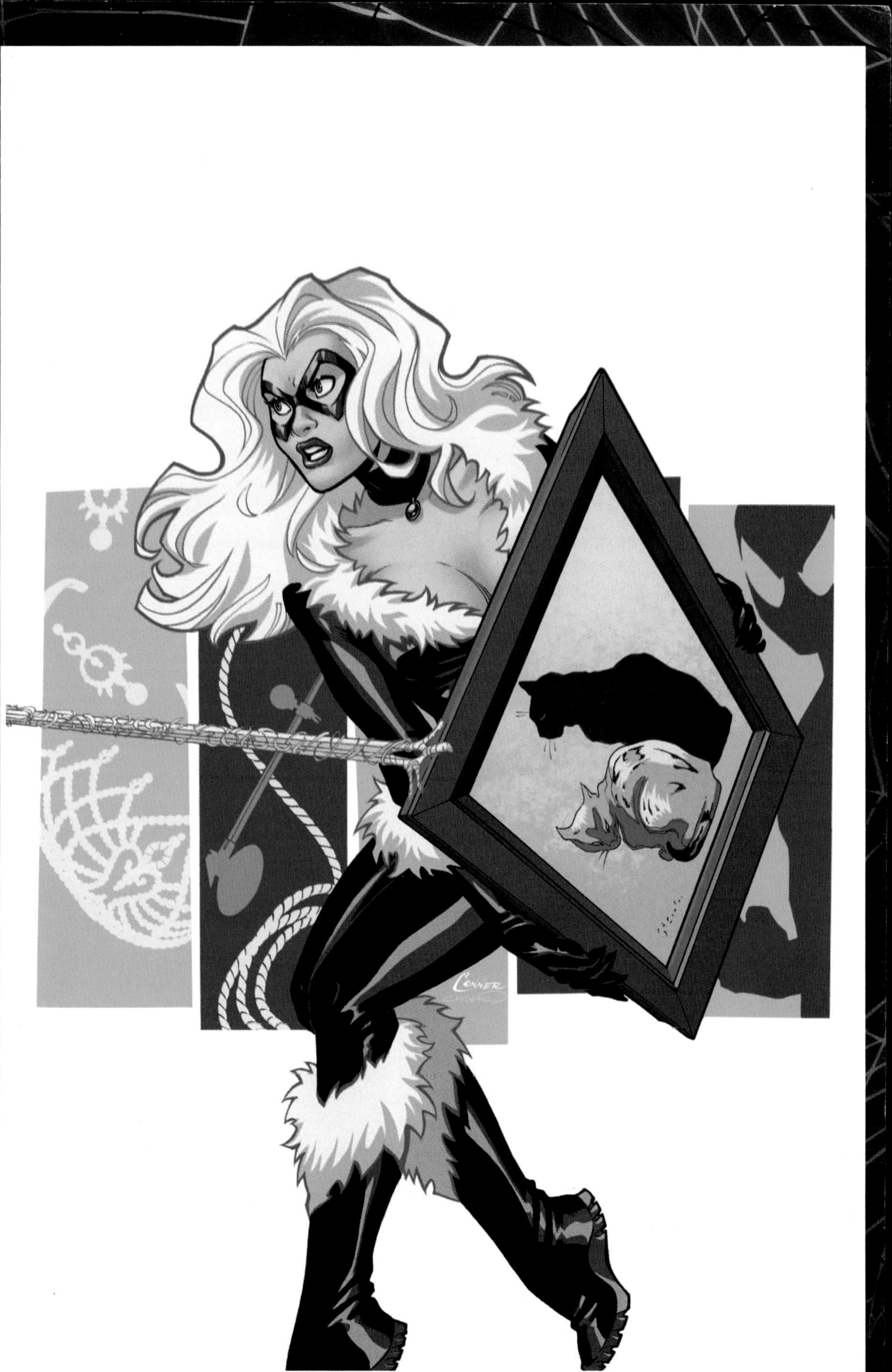
CONNER

AMAZING SPIDER-MAN PRESENTS: BLACK CAT #4

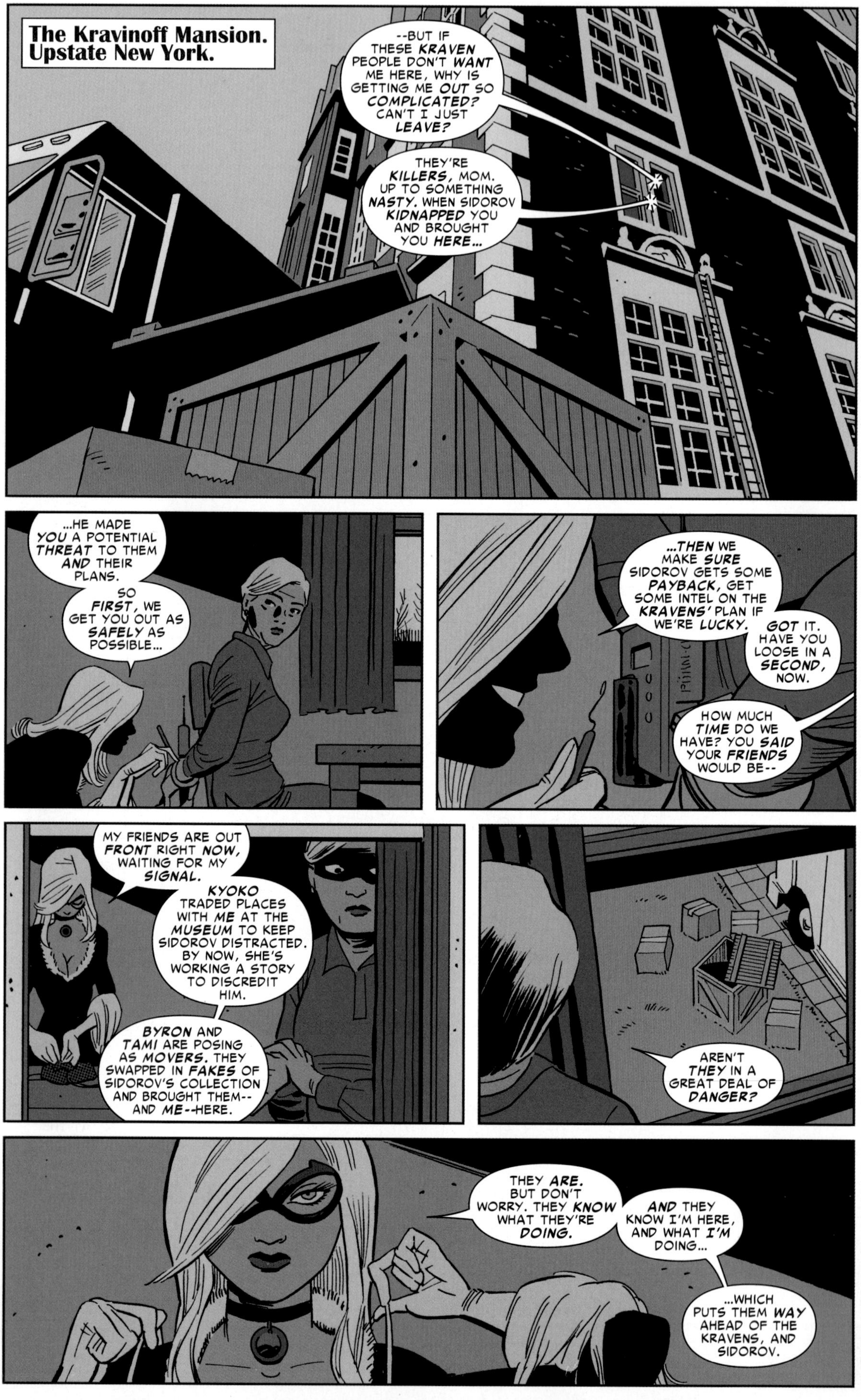
The Kravinoff Mansion. Upstate New York.
--BUT IF THESE KRAVEN PEOPLE DON'T WANT ME HERE, WHY IS GETTING ME OUT SO COMPLICATED? CAN'T I JUST LEAVE?
THEY'RE KILLERS, MOM. UP TO SOMETHING NASTY. WHEN SIDOROV KIDNAPPED YOU AND BROUGHT YOU HERE...
...HE MADE YOU A POTENTIAL THREAT TO THEM AND THEIR PLANS.
SO FIRST, WE GET YOU OUT AS SAFELY AS POSSIBLE...
...THEN WE MAKE SURE SIDOROV GETS SOME PAYBACK, GET SOME INTEL ON THE KRAVENS' PLAN IF WE'RE LUCKY.
GOT IT. HAVE YOU LOOSE IN A SECOND, NOW.
HOW MUCH TIME DO WE HAVE? YOU SAID YOUR FRIENDS WOULD BE--
MY FRIENDS ARE OUT FRONT RIGHT NOW, WAITING FOR MY SIGNAL.
KYOKO TRADED PLACES WITH ME AT THE MUSEUM TO KEEP SIDOROV DISTRACTED. BY NOW, SHE'S WORKING A STORY TO DISCREDIT HIM.
BYRON AND TAMI ARE POSING AS MOVERS. THEY SWAPPED IN FAKES OF SIDOROV'S COLLECTION AND BROUGHT THEM-- AND ME--HERE.
AREN'T THEY IN A GREAT DEAL OF DANGER?
THEY ARE. BUT DON'T WORRY. THEY KNOW WHAT THEY'RE DOING.
AND THEY KNOW I'M HERE, AND WHAT I'M DOING...
...WHICH PUTS THEM WAY AHEAD OF THE KRAVENS, AND SIDOROV.

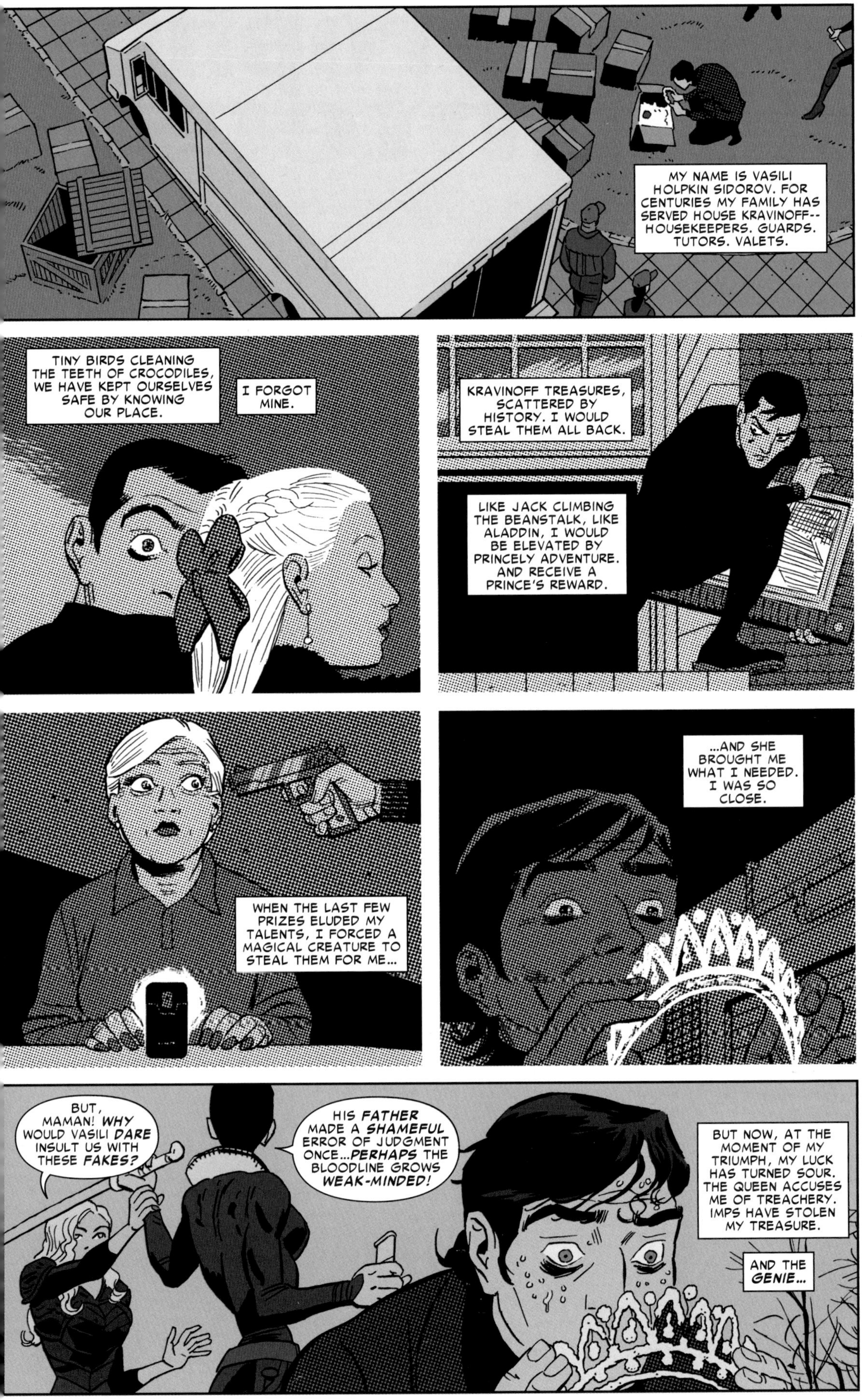
MY NAME IS VASILI HOLPKIN SIDOROV. FOR CENTURIES MY FAMILY HAS SERVED HOUSE KRAVINOFF-- HOUSEKEEPERS. GUARDS. TUTORS. VALETS.
TINY BIRDS CLEANING THE TEETH OF CROCODILES, WE HAVE KEPT OURSELVES SAFE BY KNOWING OUR PLACE.
I FORGOT MINE.
KRAVINOFF TREASURES, SCATTERED BY HISTORY. I WOULD STEAL THEM ALL BACK.
LIKE JACK CLIMBING THE BEANSTALK, LIKE ALADDIN, I WOULD BE ELEVATED BY PRINCELY ADVENTURE. AND RECEIVE A PRINCE'S REWARD.
WHEN THE LAST FEW PRIZES ELUDED MY TALENTS, I FORCED A MAGICAL CREATURE TO STEAL THEM FOR ME...
...AND SHE BROUGHT ME WHAT I NEEDED. I WAS SO CLOSE.
BUT, MAMAN! WHY WOULD VASILI DARE INSULT US WITH THESE FAKES?
HIS FATHER MADE A SHAMEFUL ERROR OF JUDGMENT ONCE...PERHAPS THE BLOODLINE GROWS WEAK-MINDED!
BUT NOW, AT THE MOMENT OF MY TRIUMPH, MY LUCK HAS TURNED SOUR. THE QUEEN ACCUSES ME OF TREACHERY. IMPS HAVE STOLEN MY TREASURE.
AND THE GENIE...

Black Cat: The Trophy Hunters Part Four

JEN VAN METER WRITER

JAVIER PULIDO ARTIST

MATT HOLLINGSWORTH COLOR ART

VC'S JOE CARAMAGNA LETTERS

TOM BRENNAN ASST. EDITOR

STEPHEN WACKER EDITOR

TOM BREVOORT EXEC. EDITOR

JOE QUESADA EDITOR IN CHIEF

DAN BUCKLEY PUBLISHER

ALAN FINE EXEC. PRODUCER

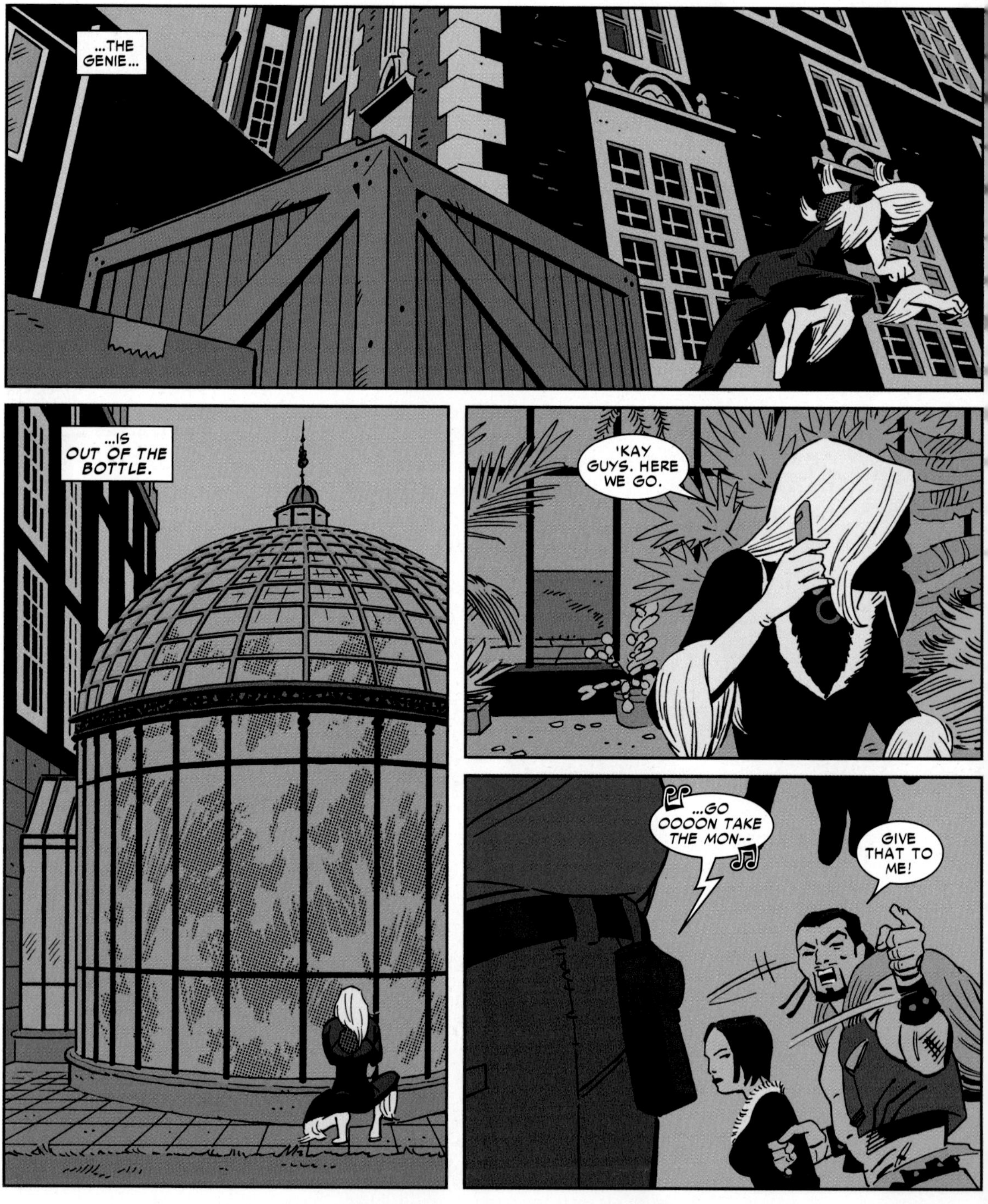
...THE GENIE...
...IS OUT OF THE BOTTLE.
'KAY GUYS. HERE WE GO.
...GO OOOON TAKE THE MON--
GIVE THAT TO ME!

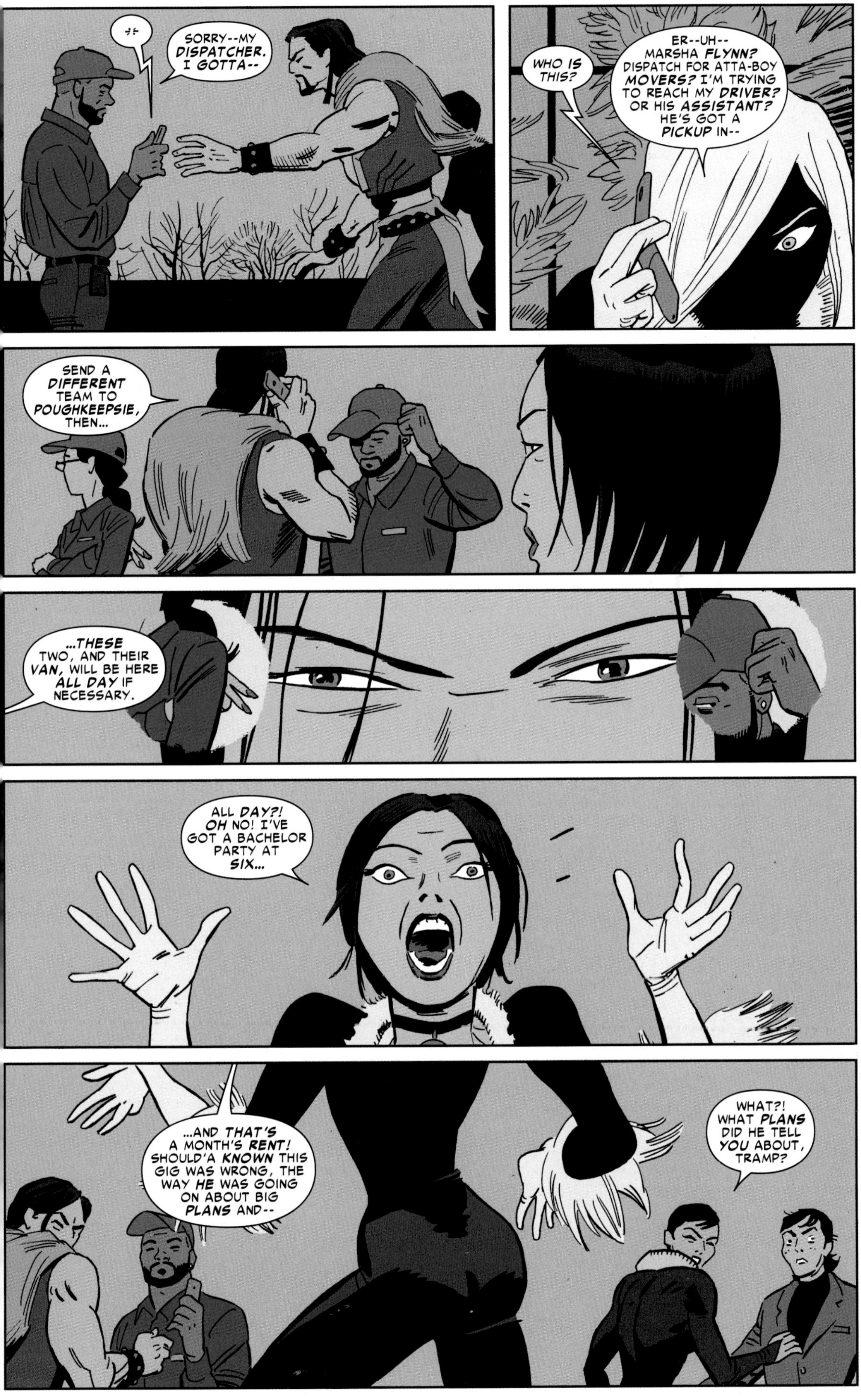

SORRY--MY DISPATCHER. I GOTTA--
WHO IS THIS?
ER--UH-- MARSHA FLYNN? DISPATCH FOR ATTA-BOY MOVERS? I'M TRYING TO REACH MY DRIVER? OR HIS ASSISTANT? HE'S GOT A PICKUP IN--
SEND A DIFFERENT TEAM TO POUGHKEEPSIE, THEN...
...THESE TWO, AND THEIR VAN, WILL BE HERE ALL DAY IF NECESSARY.
ALL DAY?! OH NO! I'VE GOT A BACHELOR PARTY AT SIX...
...AND THAT'S A MONTH'S RENT! SHOULD'A KNOWN THIS GIG WAS WRONG, THE WAY HE WAS GOING ON ABOUT BIG PLANS AND--
WHAT?! WHAT PLANS DID HE TELL YOU ABOUT, TRAMP?

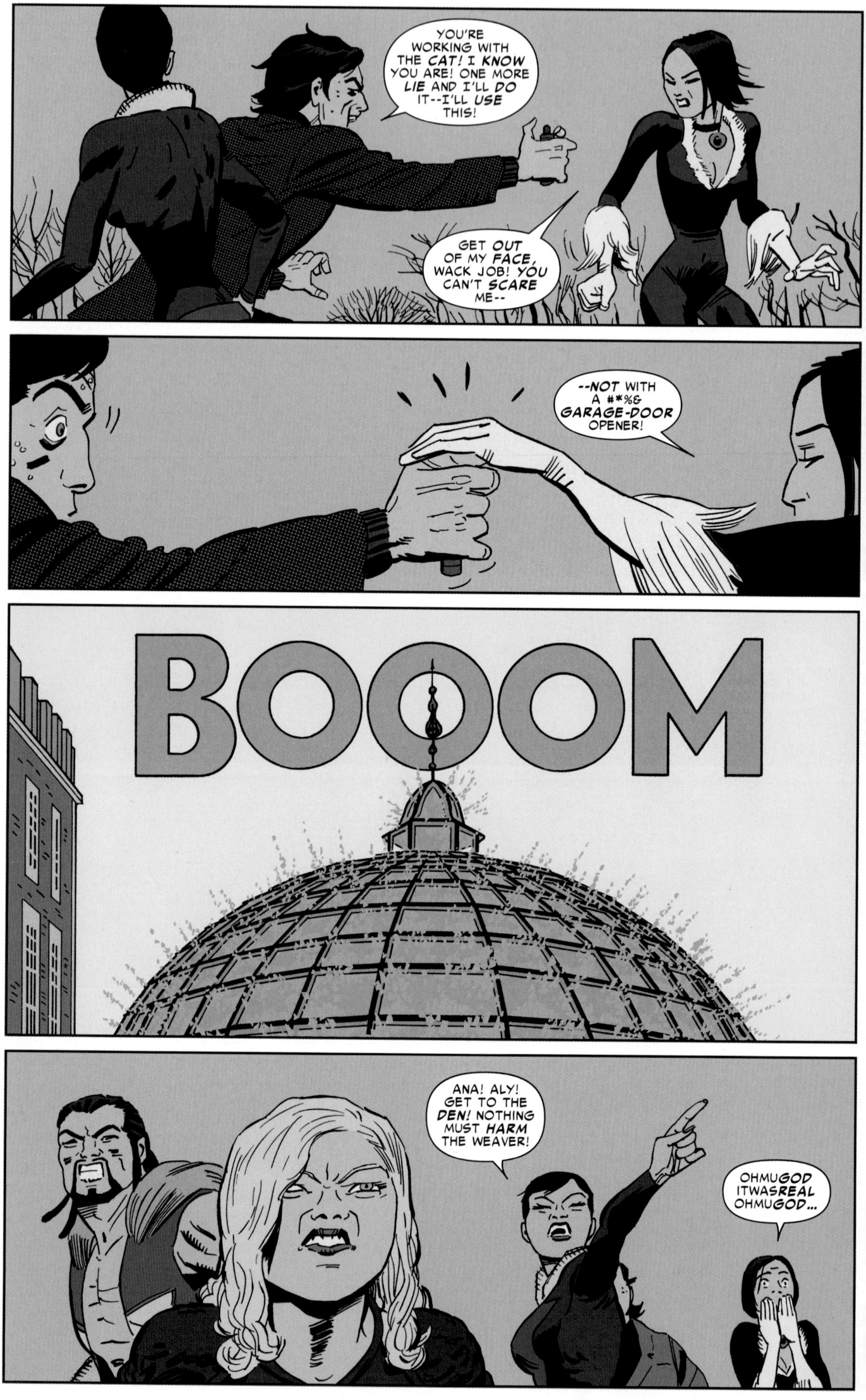
YOU'RE WORKING WITH THE CAT! I KNOW YOU ARE! ONE MORE LIE AND I'LL DO IT--I'LL USE THIS!
GET OUT OF MY FACE, WACK JOB! YOU CAN'T SCARE ME--
--NOT WITH A #*%& GARAGE-DOOR OPENER!
BOOOM
ANA! ALY! GET TO THE DEN! NOTHING MUST HARM THE WEAVER!
OHMUGOD ITWASREAL OHMUGOD...

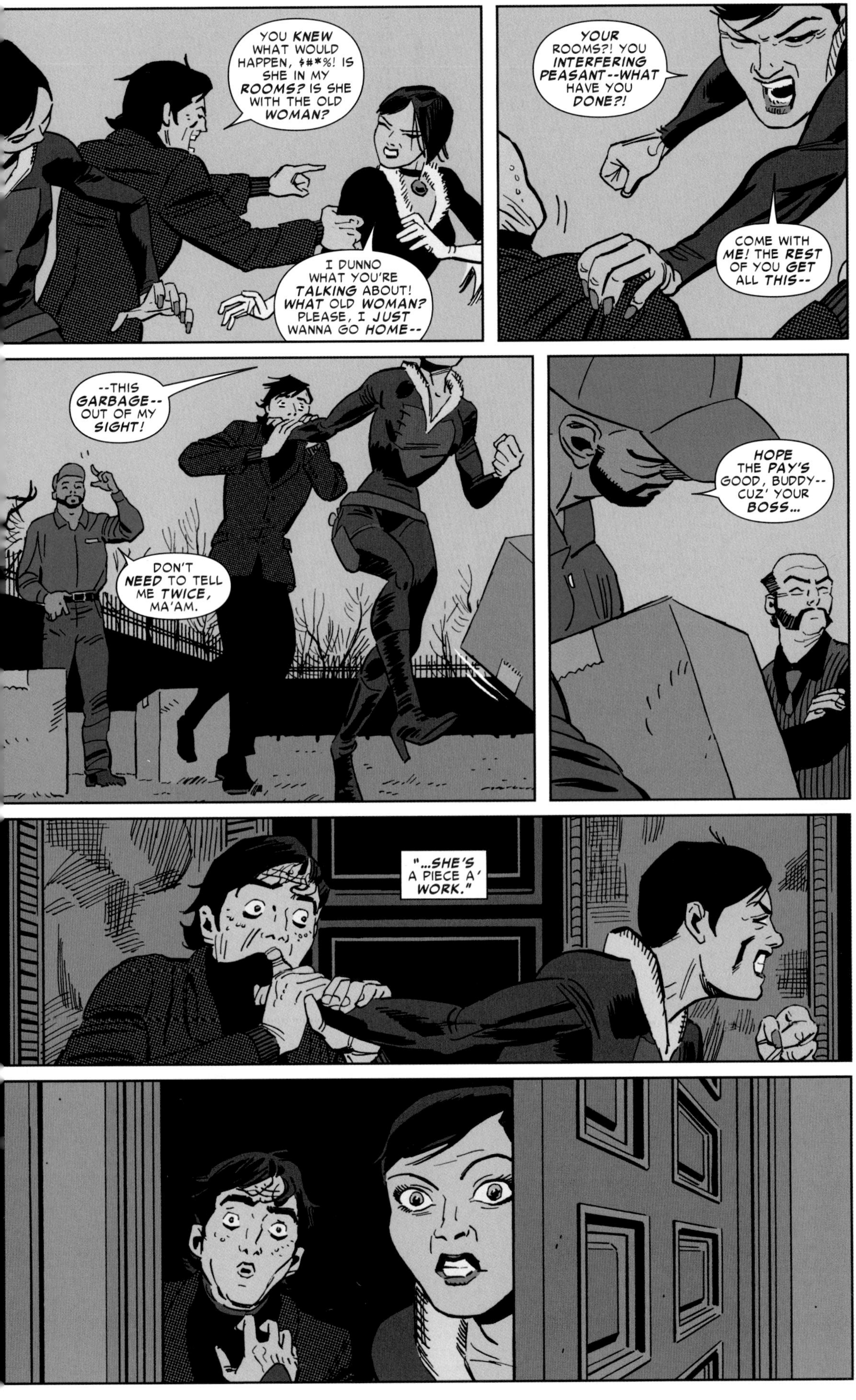
YOU KNEW WHAT WOULD HAPPEN, $#*%! IS SHE IN MY ROOMS? IS SHE WITH THE OLD WOMAN?
I DUNNO WHAT YOU'RE TALKING ABOUT! WHAT OLD WOMAN? PLEASE, I JUST WANNA GO HOME--
YOUR ROOMS?! YOU INTERFERING PEASANT--WHAT HAVE YOU DONE?!
COME WITH ME! THE REST OF YOU GET ALL THIS--
--THIS GARBAGE--OUT OF MY SIGHT!
DON'T NEED TO TELL ME TWICE, MA'AM.
HOPE THE PAY'S GOOD, BUDDY--CUZ' YOUR BOSS...
"...SHE'S A PIECE A' WORK."

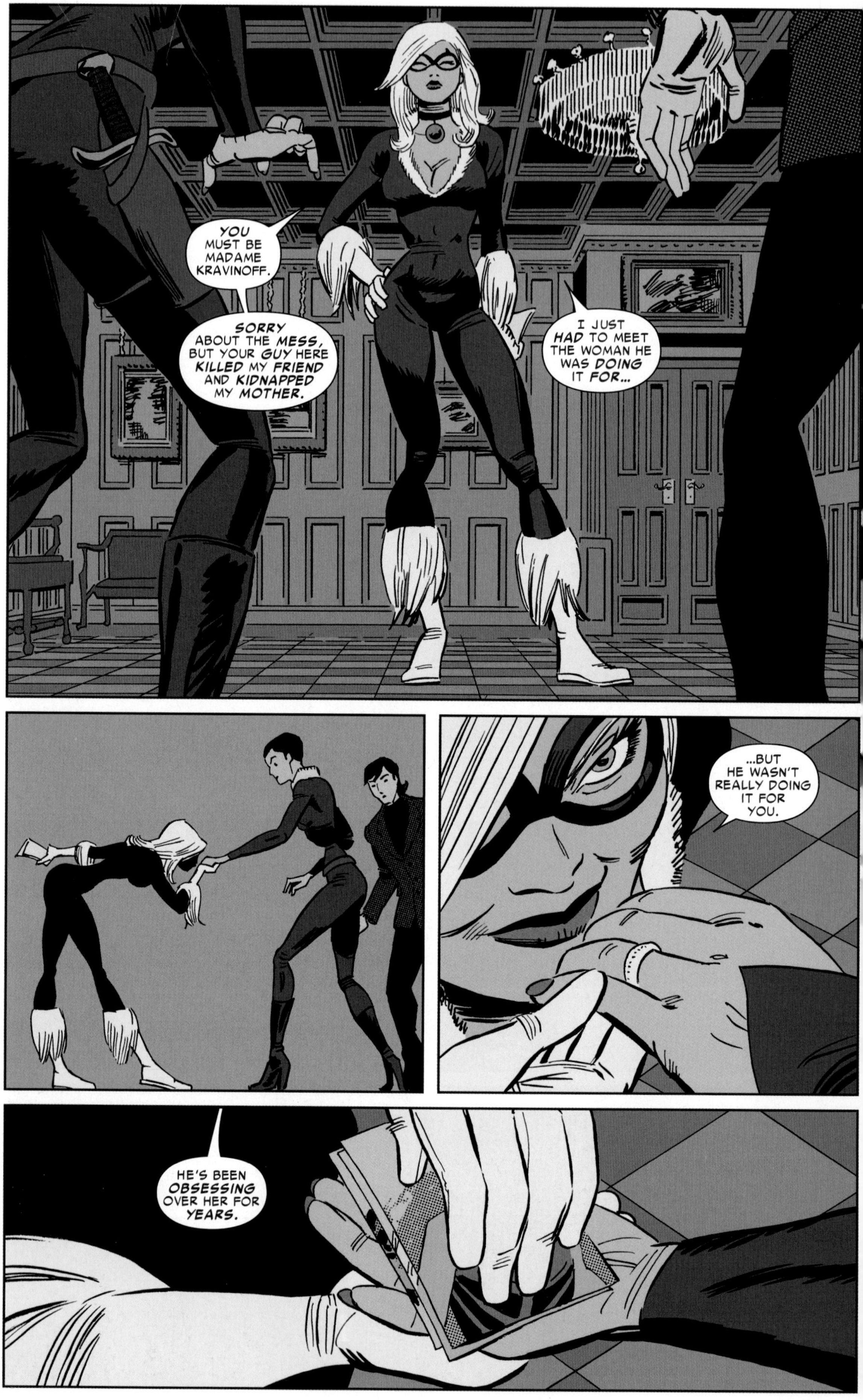
YOU MUST BE MADAME KRAVINOFF.
SORRY ABOUT THE MESS, BUT YOUR GUY HERE KILLED MY FRIEND AND KIDNAPPED MY MOTHER.
I JUST HAD TO MEET THE WOMAN HE WAS DOING IT FOR...
...BUT HE WASN'T REALLY DOING IT FOR YOU.
HE'S BEEN OBSESSING OVER HER FOR YEARS.

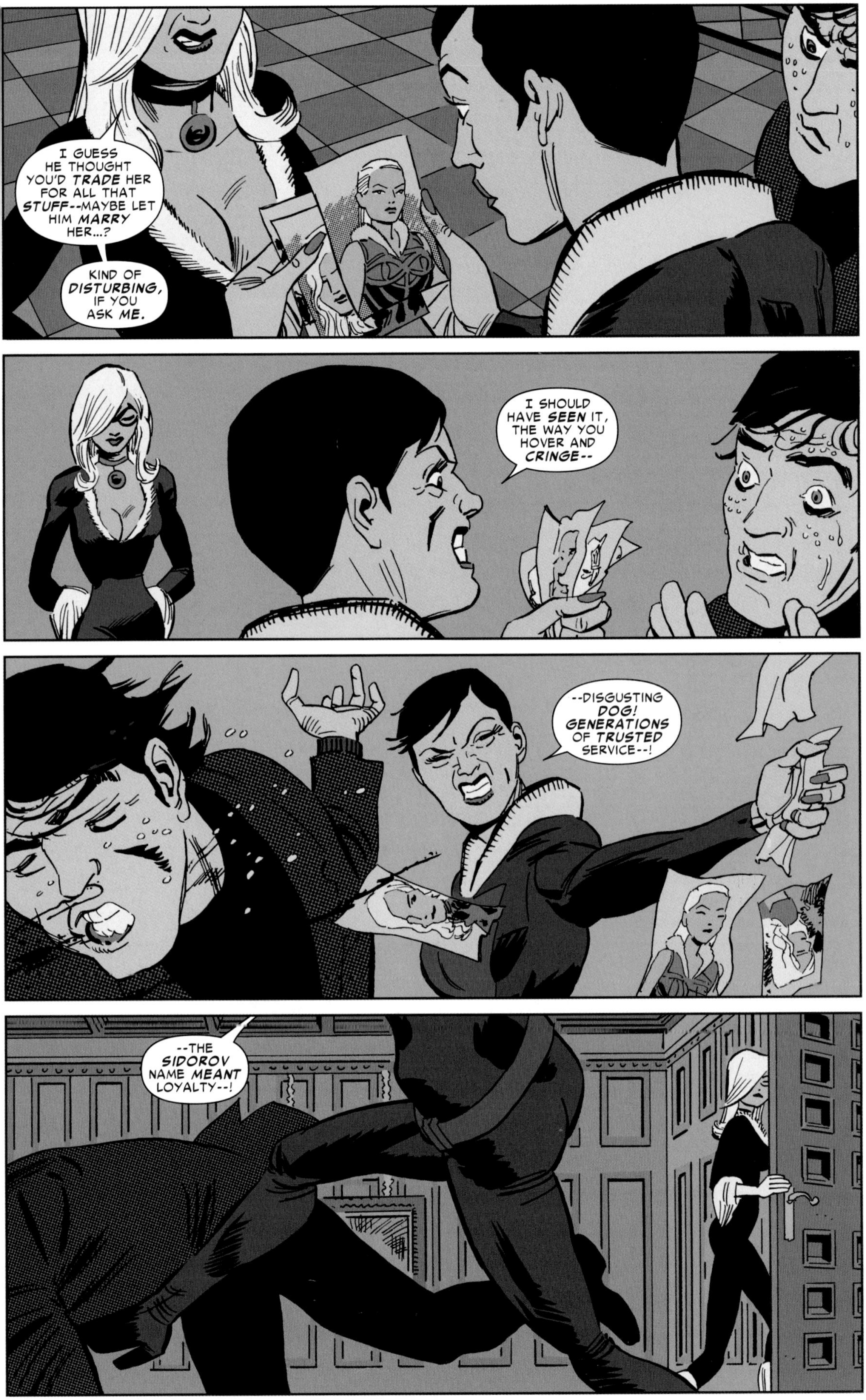
I GUESS HE THOUGHT YOU'D TRADE HER FOR ALL THAT STUFF--MAYBE LET HIM MARRY HER...?
KIND OF DISTURBING, IF YOU ASK ME.
I SHOULD HAVE SEEN IT, THE WAY YOU HOVER AND CRINGE--
--DISGUSTING DOG! GENERATIONS OF TRUSTED SERVICE--!
--THE SIDOROV NAME MEANT LOYALTY--!

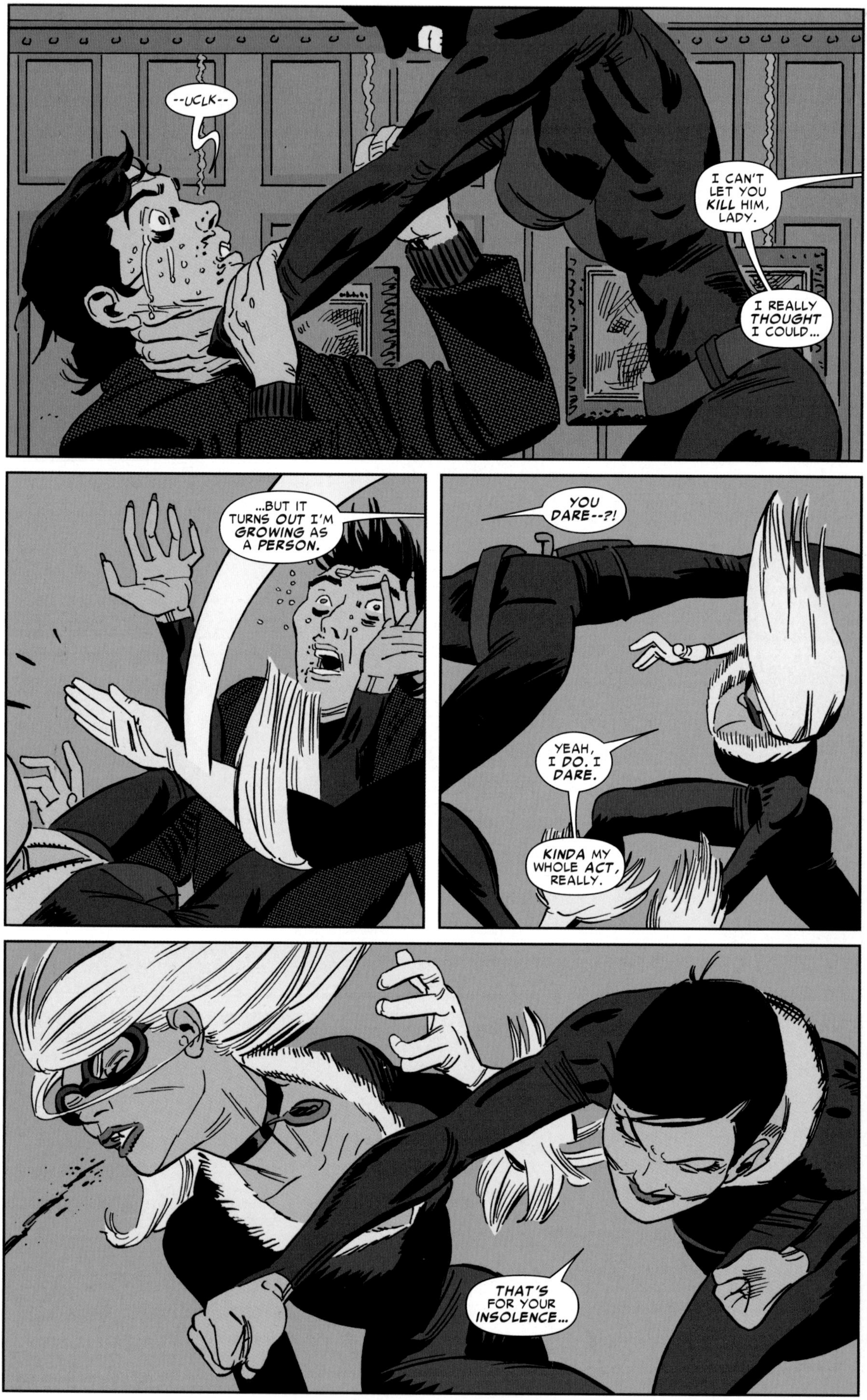
--UCLK--
I CAN'T LET YOU KILL HIM, LADY.
I REALLY THOUGHT I COULD...
...BUT IT TURNS OUT I'M GROWING AS A PERSON.
YOU DARE--?!
YEAH, I DO. I DARE.
KINDA MY WHOLE ACT, REALLY.
THAT'S FOR YOUR INSOLENCE...

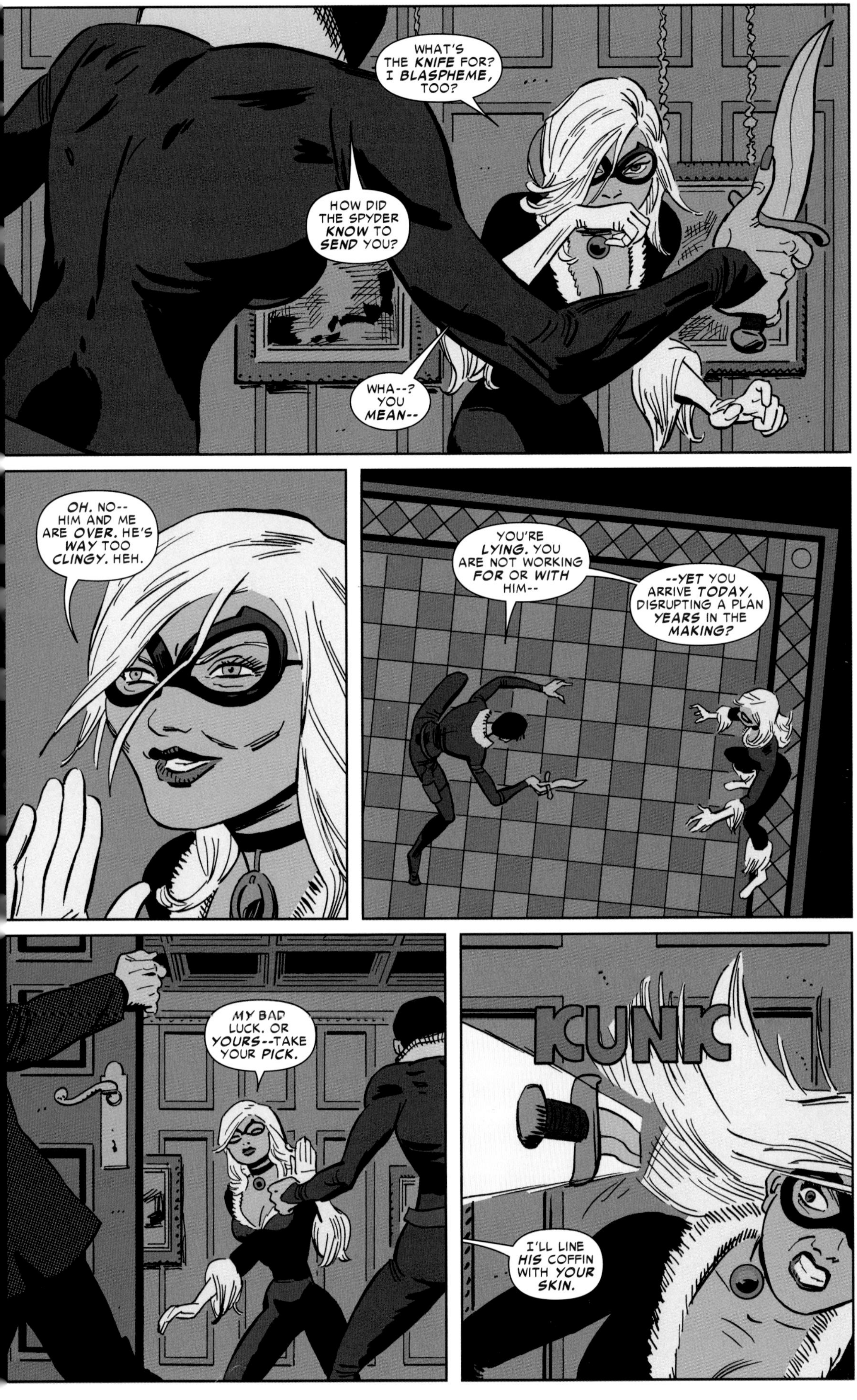
WHAT'S THE KNIFE FOR? I BLASPHEME, TOO?
HOW DID THE SPYDER KNOW TO SEND YOU?
WHA--? YOU MEAN--
OH. NO-- HIM AND ME ARE OVER. HE'S WAY TOO CLINGY. HEH.
YOU'RE LYING. YOU ARE NOT WORKING FOR OR WITH HIM--
--YET YOU ARRIVE TODAY, DISRUPTING A PLAN YEARS IN THE MAKING?
MY BAD LUCK. OR YOURS--TAKE YOUR PICK.
KUNK
I'LL LINE HIS COFFIN WITH YOUR SKIN.

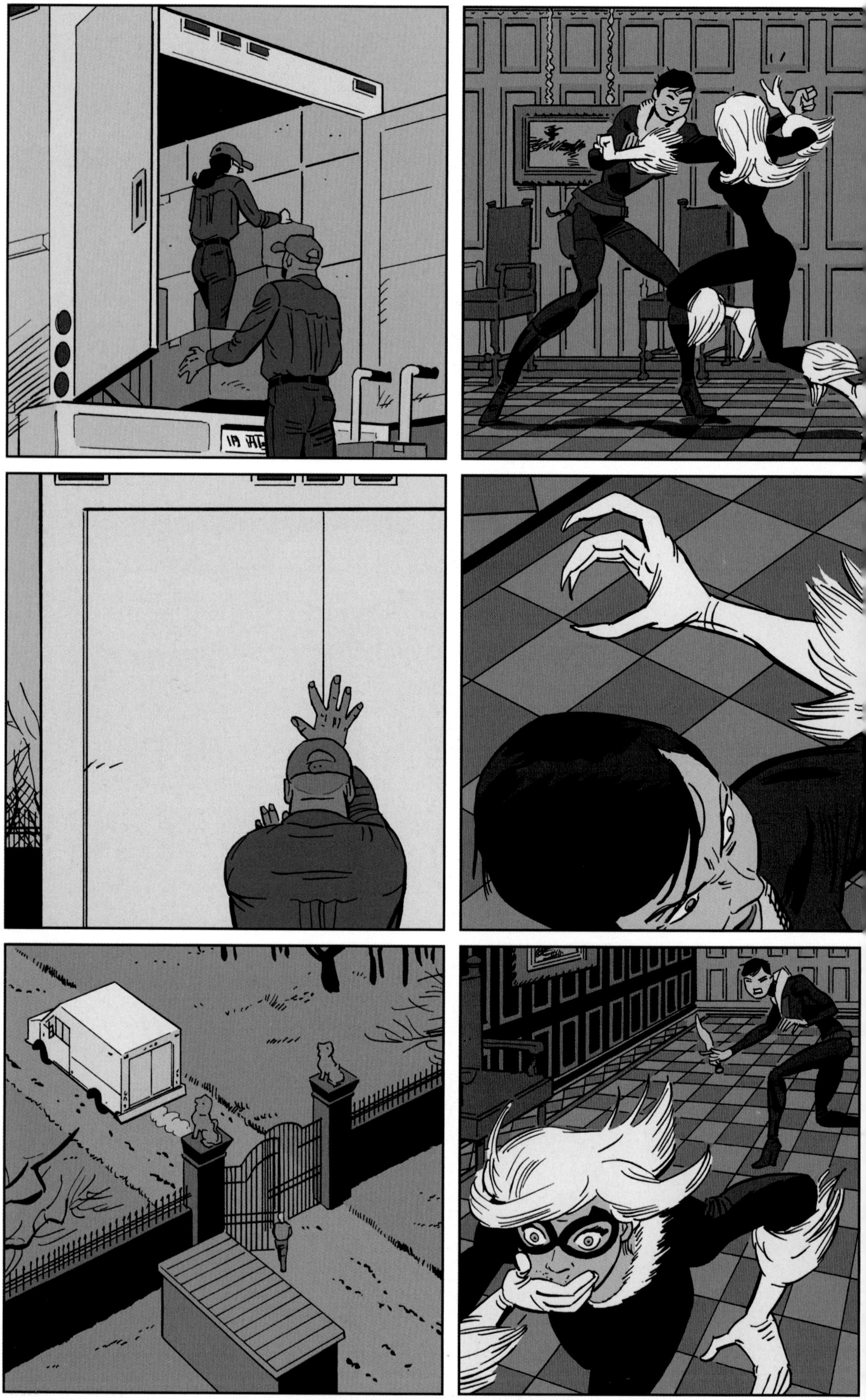

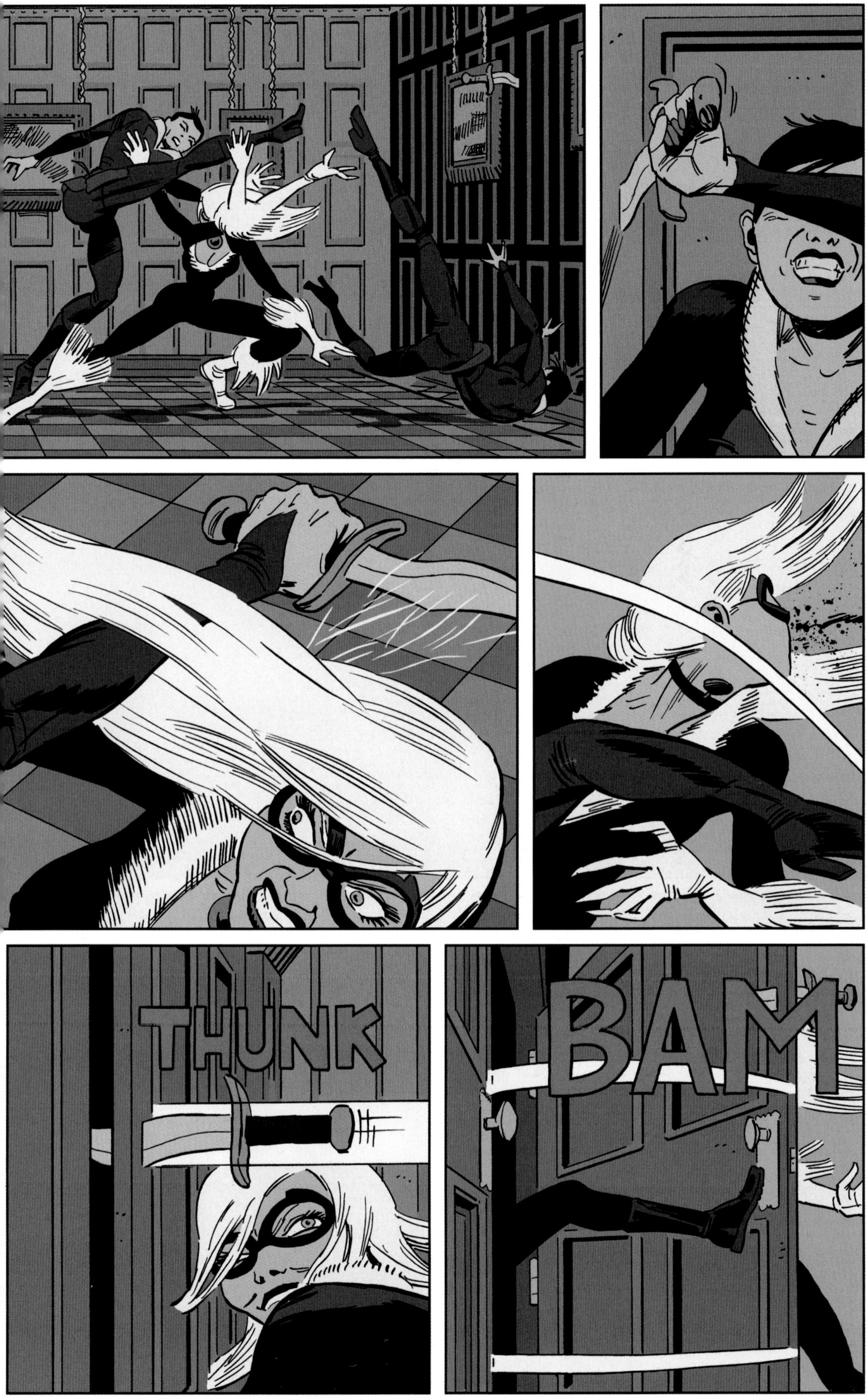
THUNK
BAM

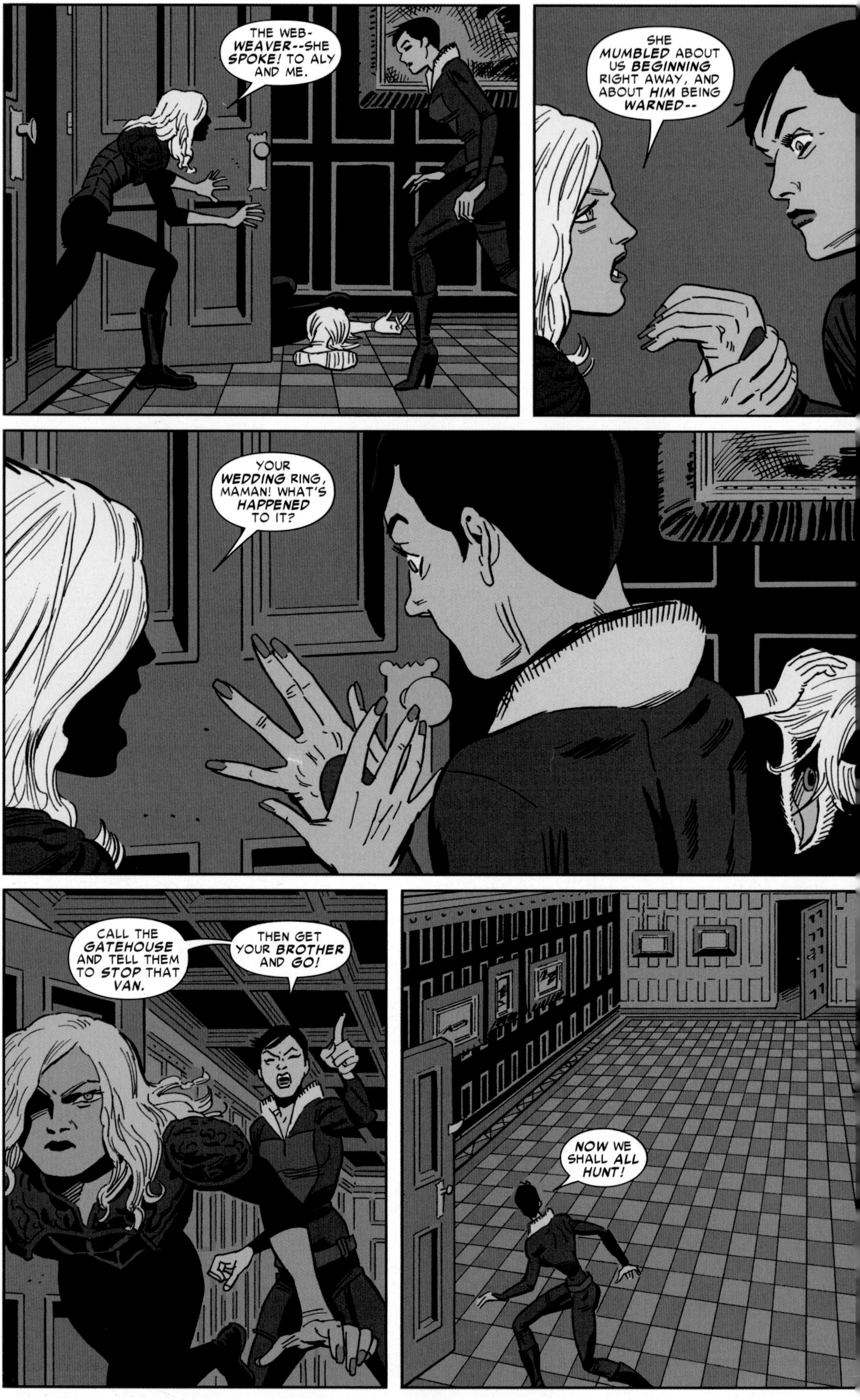
THE WEB-WEAVER--SHE SPOKE! TO ALY AND ME.
SHE MUMBLED ABOUT US BEGINNING RIGHT AWAY, AND ABOUT HIM BEING WARNED--
YOUR WEDDING RING, MAMAN! WHAT'S HAPPENED TO IT?
CALL THE GATEHOUSE AND TELL THEM TO STOP THAT VAN.
THEN GET YOUR BROTHER AND GO!
NOW WE SHALL ALL HUNT!

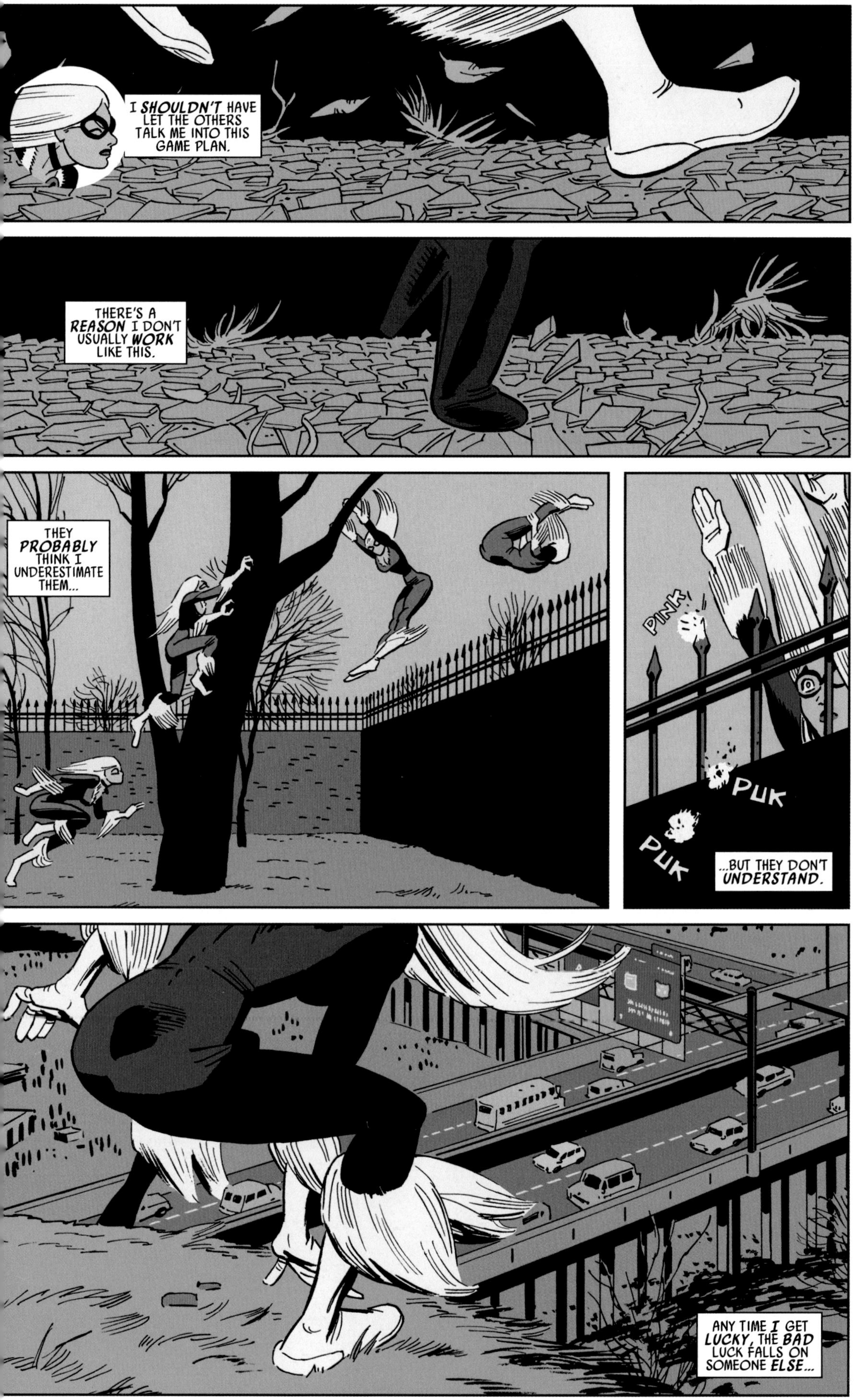
I SHOULDN'T HAVE LET THE OTHERS TALK ME INTO THIS GAME PLAN.
THERE'S A REASON I DON'T USUALLY WORK LIKE THIS.
THEY PROBABLY THINK I UNDERESTIMATE THEM...
PINK
PUK
PUK
...BUT THEY DON'T UNDERSTAND.
ANY TIME I GET LUCKY, THE BAD LUCK FALLS ON SOMEONE ELSE...

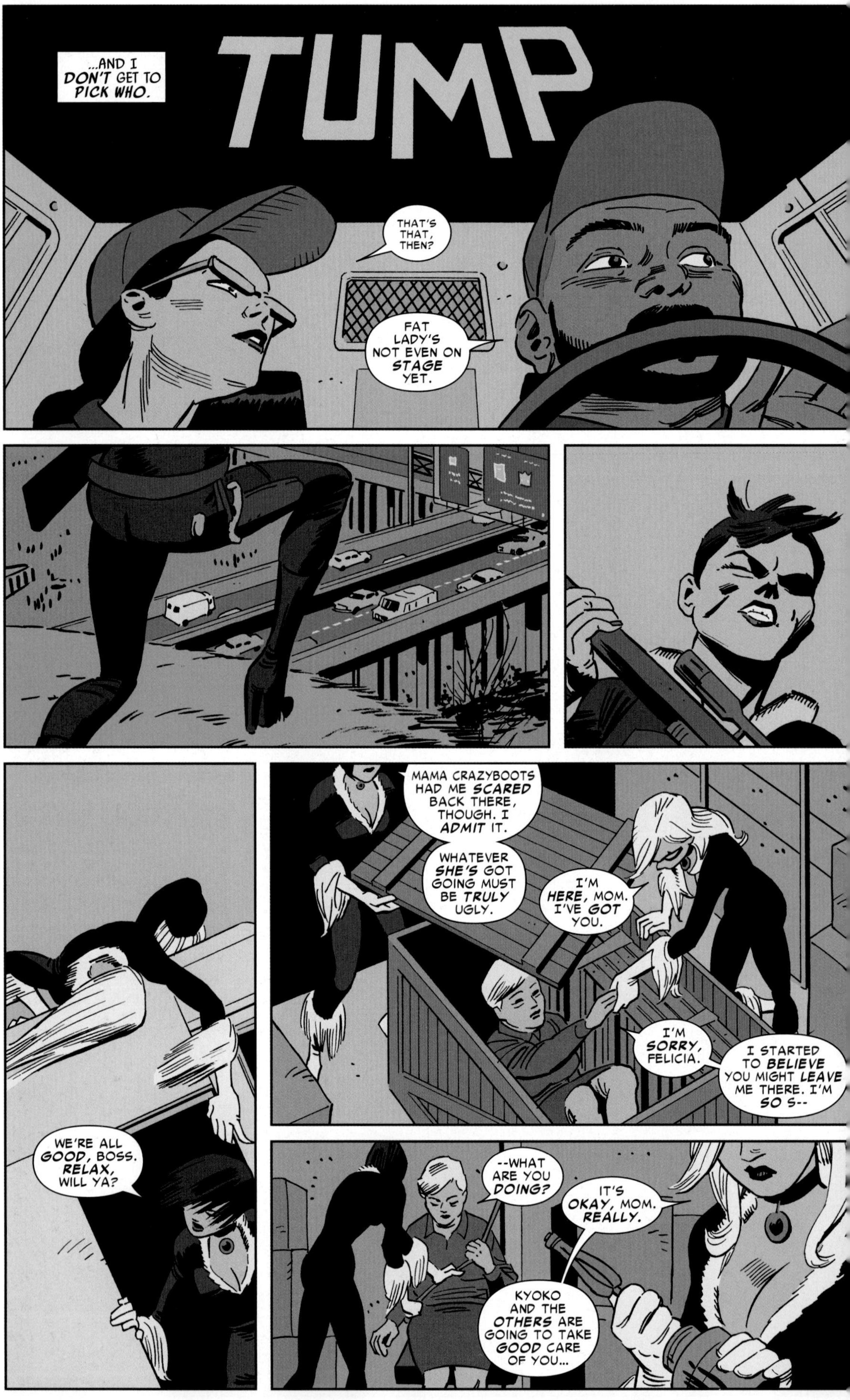
...AND I DON'T GET TO PICK WHO.
TUMP
THAT'S THAT, THEN?
FAT LADY'S NOT EVEN ON STAGE YET.
MAMA CRAZYBOOTS HAD ME SCARED BACK THERE, THOUGH. I ADMIT IT.
WHATEVER SHE'S GOT GOING MUST BE TRULY UGLY.
I'M HERE, MOM. I'VE GOT YOU.
I'M SORRY, FELICIA.
I STARTED TO BELIEVE YOU MIGHT LEAVE ME THERE. I'M SO S--
WE'RE ALL GOOD, BOSS. RELAX, WILL YA?
--WHAT ARE YOU DOING?
IT'S OKAY, MOM. REALLY.
KYOKO AND THE OTHERS ARE GOING TO TAKE GOOD CARE OF YOU...

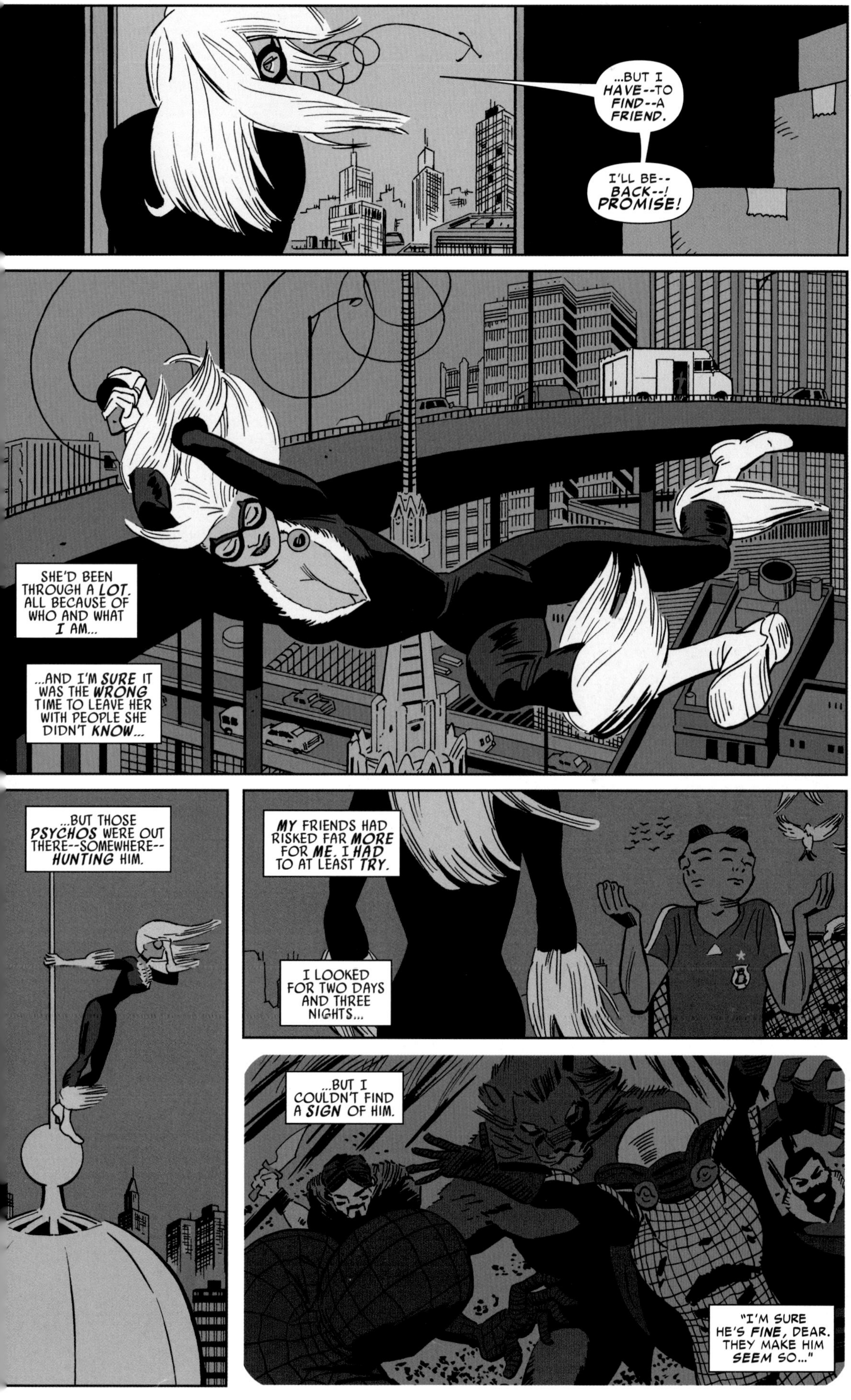
...BUT I HAVE--TO FIND--A FRIEND.
I'LL BE--BACK--! PROMISE!
SHE'D BEEN THROUGH A LOT. ALL BECAUSE OF WHO AND WHAT I AM...
...AND I'M SURE IT WAS THE WRONG TIME TO LEAVE HER WITH PEOPLE SHE DIDN'T KNOW...
...BUT THOSE PSYCHOS WERE OUT THERE--SOMEWHERE--HUNTING HIM.
MY FRIENDS HAD RISKED FAR MORE FOR ME. I HAD TO AT LEAST TRY.
I LOOKED FOR TWO DAYS AND THREE NIGHTS...
...BUT I COULDN'T FIND A SIGN OF HIM.
"I'M SURE HE'S FINE, DEAR. THEY MAKE HIM SEEM SO..."

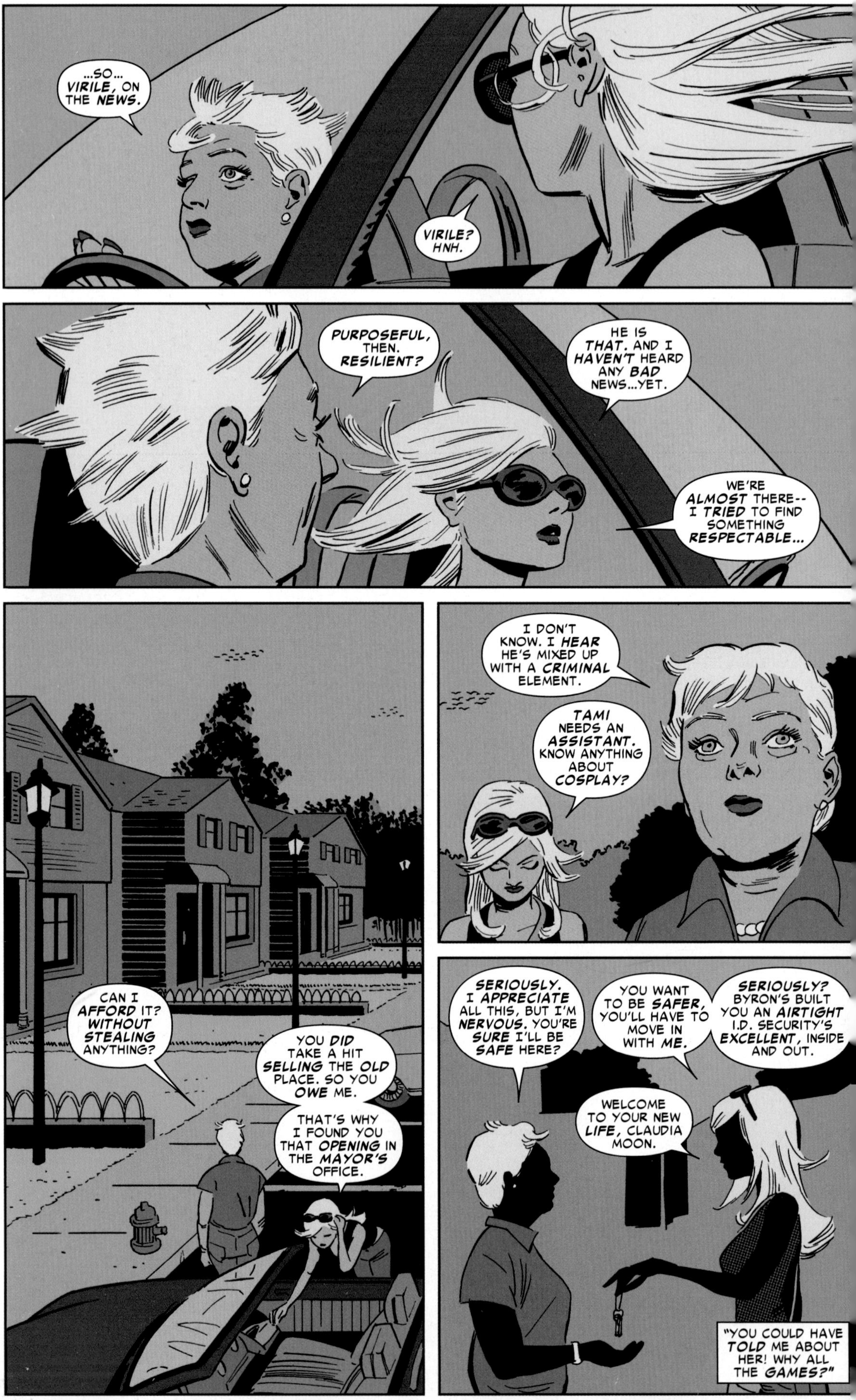
...SO... VIRILE, ON THE NEWS.
VIRILE? HNH.
PURPOSEFUL, THEN. RESILIENT?
HE IS THAT. AND I HAVEN'T HEARD ANY BAD NEWS...YET.
WE'RE ALMOST THERE-- I TRIED TO FIND SOMETHING RESPECTABLE...
CAN I AFFORD IT? WITHOUT STEALING ANYTHING?
YOU DID TAKE A HIT SELLING THE OLD PLACE. SO YOU OWE ME.
THAT'S WHY I FOUND YOU THAT OPENING IN THE MAYOR'S OFFICE.
I DON'T KNOW. I HEAR HE'S MIXED UP WITH A CRIMINAL ELEMENT.
TAMI NEEDS AN ASSISTANT. KNOW ANYTHING ABOUT COSPLAY?
SERIOUSLY. I APPRECIATE ALL THIS, BUT I'M NERVOUS. YOU'RE SURE I'LL BE SAFE HERE?
YOU WANT TO BE SAFER, YOU'LL HAVE TO MOVE IN WITH ME.
SERIOUSLY? BYRON'S BUILT YOU AN AIRTIGHT I.D. SECURITY'S EXCELLENT, INSIDE AND OUT.
WELCOME TO YOUR NEW LIFE, CLAUDIA MOON.
"YOU COULD HAVE TOLD ME ABOUT HER! WHY ALL THE GAMES?"

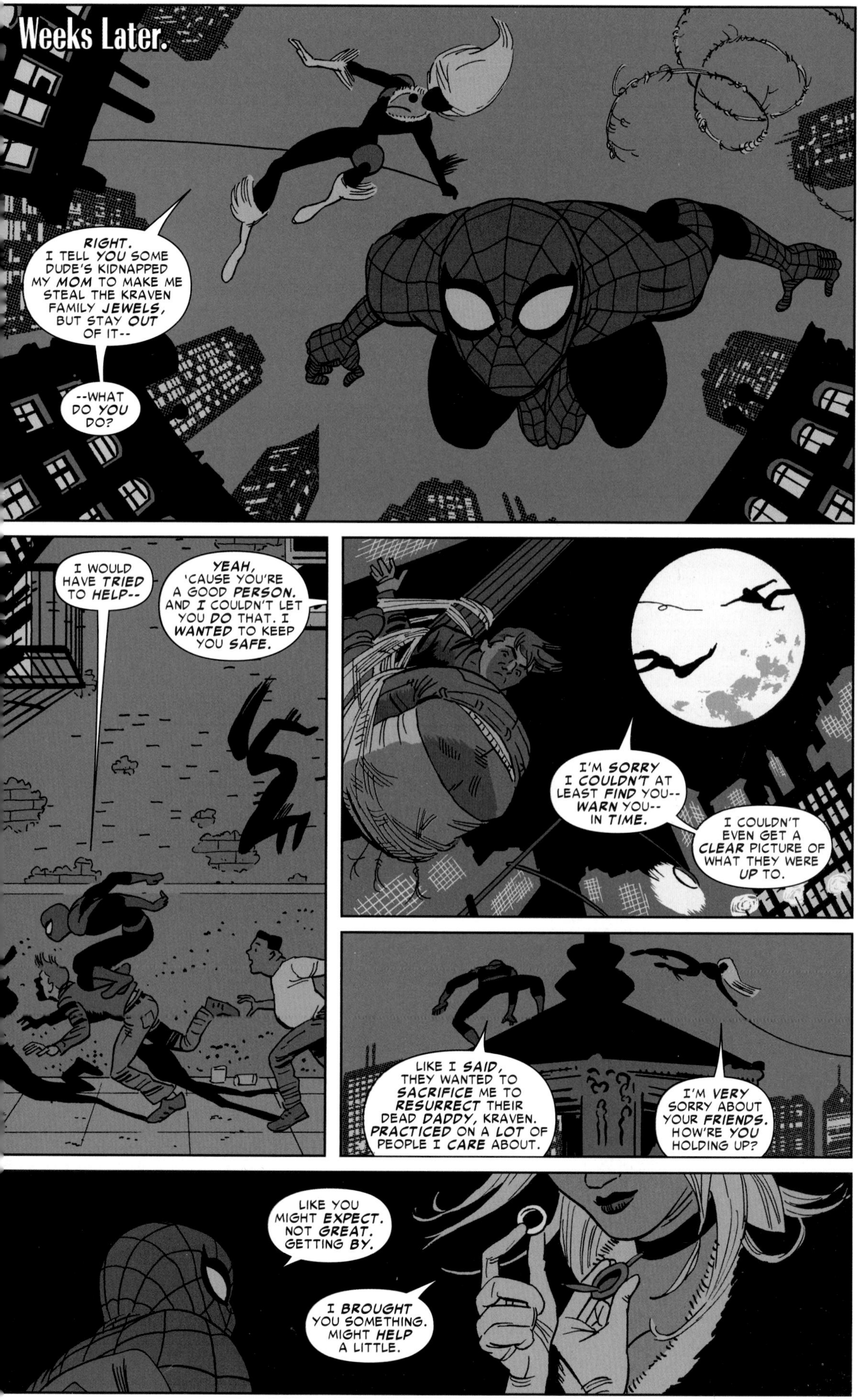
Weeks Later.
RIGHT. I TELL YOU SOME DUDE'S KIDNAPPED MY MOM TO MAKE ME STEAL THE KRAVEN FAMILY JEWELS, BUT STAY OUT OF IT--
--WHAT DO YOU DO?
I WOULD HAVE TRIED TO HELP--
YEAH, 'CAUSE YOU'RE A GOOD PERSON. AND I COULDN'T LET YOU DO THAT. I WANTED TO KEEP YOU SAFE.
I'M SORRY I COULDN'T AT LEAST FIND YOU-- WARN YOU-- IN TIME.
I COULDN'T EVEN GET A CLEAR PICTURE OF WHAT THEY WERE UP TO.
LIKE I SAID, THEY WANTED TO SACRIFICE ME TO RESURRECT THEIR DEAD DADDY, KRAVEN. PRACTICED ON A LOT OF PEOPLE I CARE ABOUT.
I'M VERY SORRY ABOUT YOUR FRIENDS. HOW'RE YOU HOLDING UP?
LIKE YOU MIGHT EXPECT. NOT GREAT. GETTING BY.
I BROUGHT YOU SOMETHING. MIGHT HELP A LITTLE.

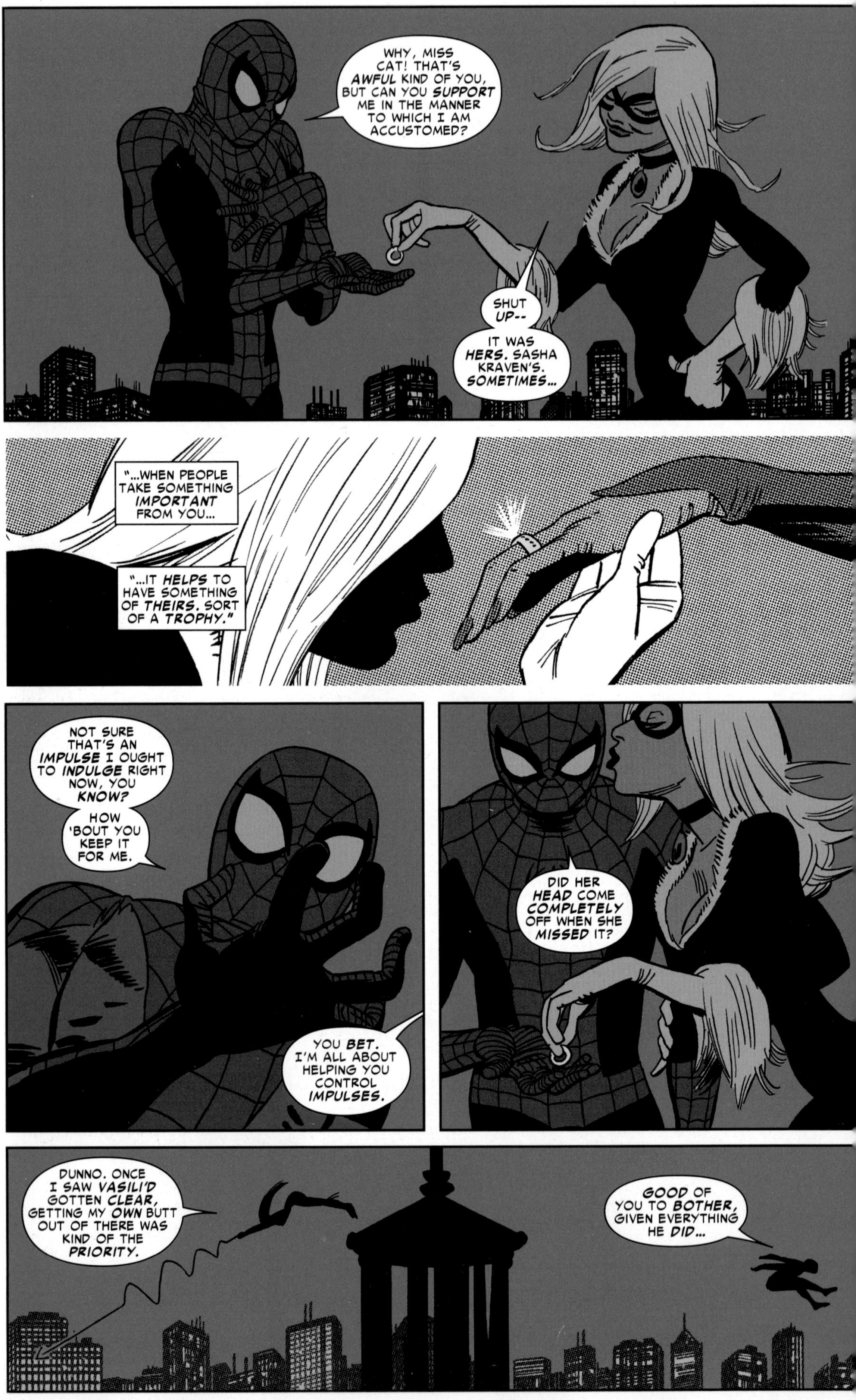
WHY, MISS CAT! THAT'S AWFUL KIND OF YOU, BUT CAN YOU SUPPORT ME IN THE MANNER TO WHICH I AM ACCUSTOMED?
SHUT UP--
IT WAS HERS. SASHA KRAVEN'S. SOMETIMES...
"...WHEN PEOPLE TAKE SOMETHING IMPORTANT FROM YOU...
"...IT HELPS TO HAVE SOMETHING OF THEIRS. SORT OF A TROPHY."
NOT SURE THAT'S AN IMPULSE I OUGHT TO INDULGE RIGHT NOW, YOU KNOW?
HOW 'BOUT YOU KEEP IT FOR ME.
YOU BET. I'M ALL ABOUT HELPING YOU CONTROL IMPULSES.
DID HER HEAD COME COMPLETELY OFF WHEN SHE MISSED IT?
DUNNO. ONCE I SAW VASILI'D GOTTEN CLEAR, GETTING MY OWN BUTT OUT OF THERE WAS KIND OF THE PRIORITY.
GOOD OF YOU TO BOTHER, GIVEN EVERYTHING HE DID...

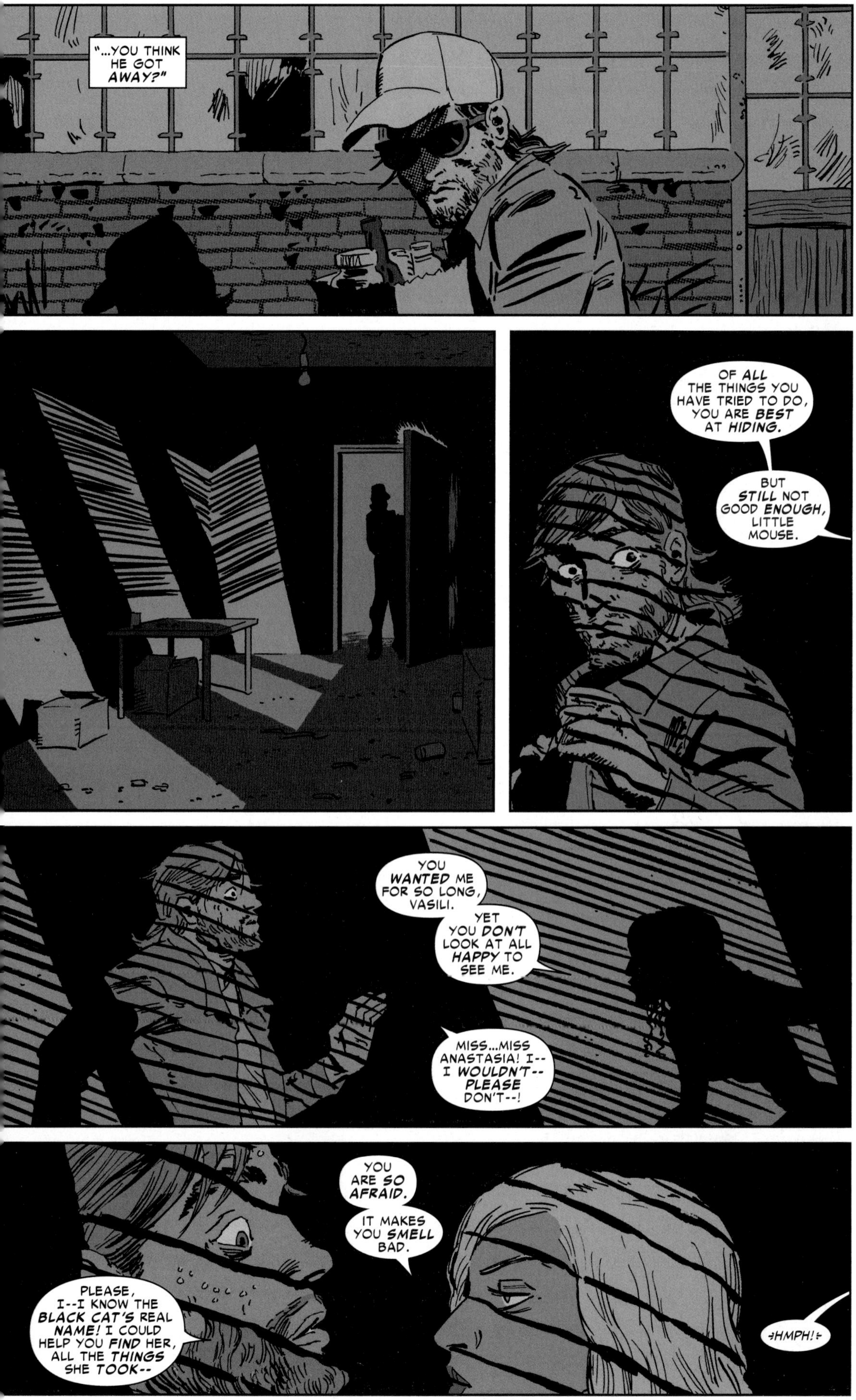
"...YOU THINK HE GOT AWAY?"
OF ALL THE THINGS YOU HAVE TRIED TO DO, YOU ARE BEST AT HIDING.
BUT STILL NOT GOOD ENOUGH, LITTLE MOUSE.
YOU WANTED ME FOR SO LONG, VASILI.
YET YOU DON'T LOOK AT ALL HAPPY TO SEE ME.
MISS...MISS ANASTASIA! I--I WOULDN'T--PLEASE DON'T--!
YOU ARE SO AFRAID.
IT MAKES YOU SMELL BAD.
PLEASE, I--I KNOW THE BLACK CAT'S REAL NAME! I COULD HELP YOU FIND HER, ALL THE THINGS SHE TOOK--
HMPH!

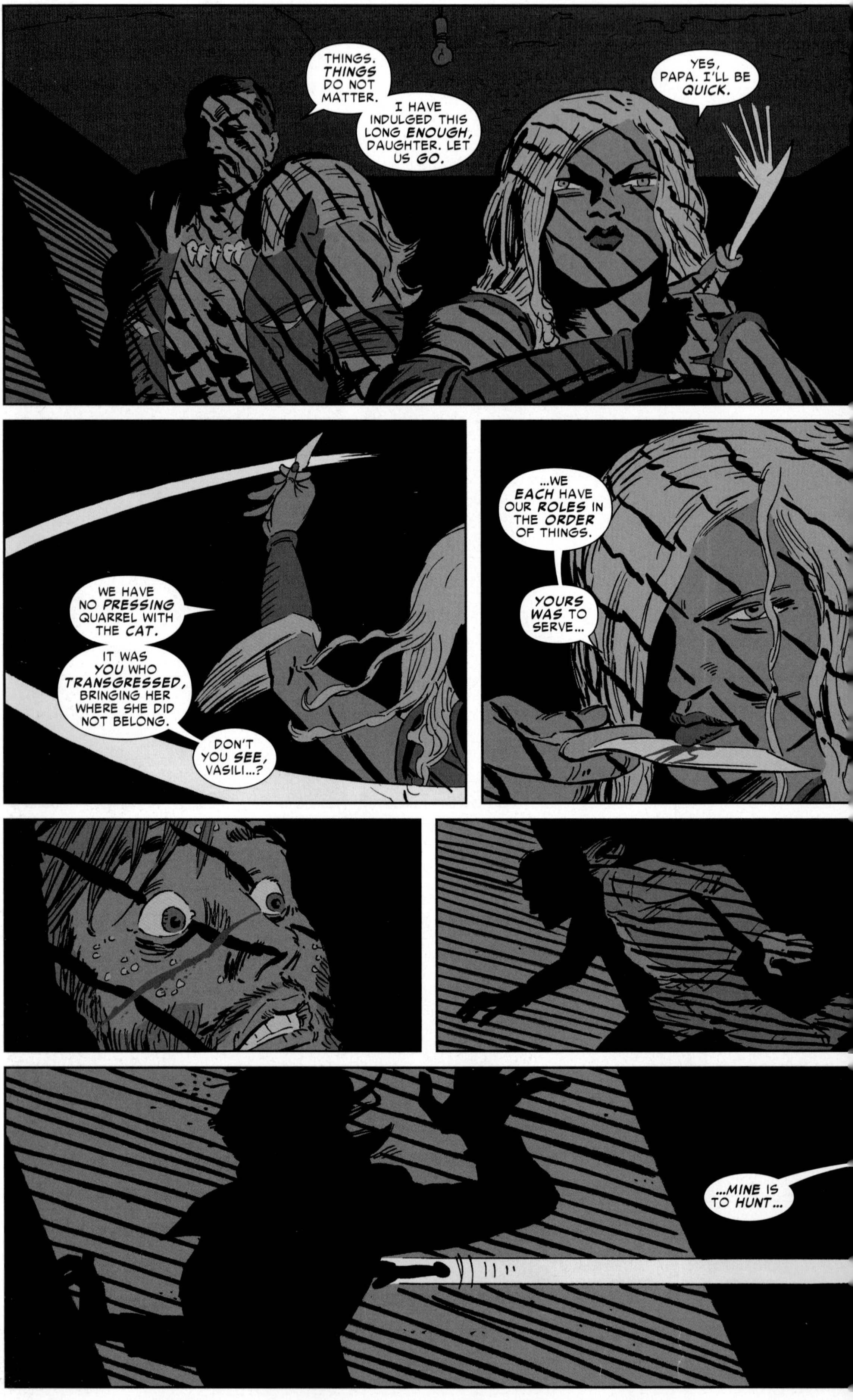
THINGS. THINGS DO NOT MATTER.
I HAVE INDULGED THIS LONG ENOUGH, DAUGHTER. LET US GO.
YES, PAPA. I'LL BE QUICK.
WE HAVE NO PRESSING QUARREL WITH THE CAT.
IT WAS YOU WHO TRANSGRESSED, BRINGING HER WHERE SHE DID NOT BELONG.
DON'T YOU SEE, VASILI...?
...WE EACH HAVE OUR ROLES IN THE ORDER OF THINGS.
YOURS WAS TO SERVE...
...MINE IS TO HUNT...

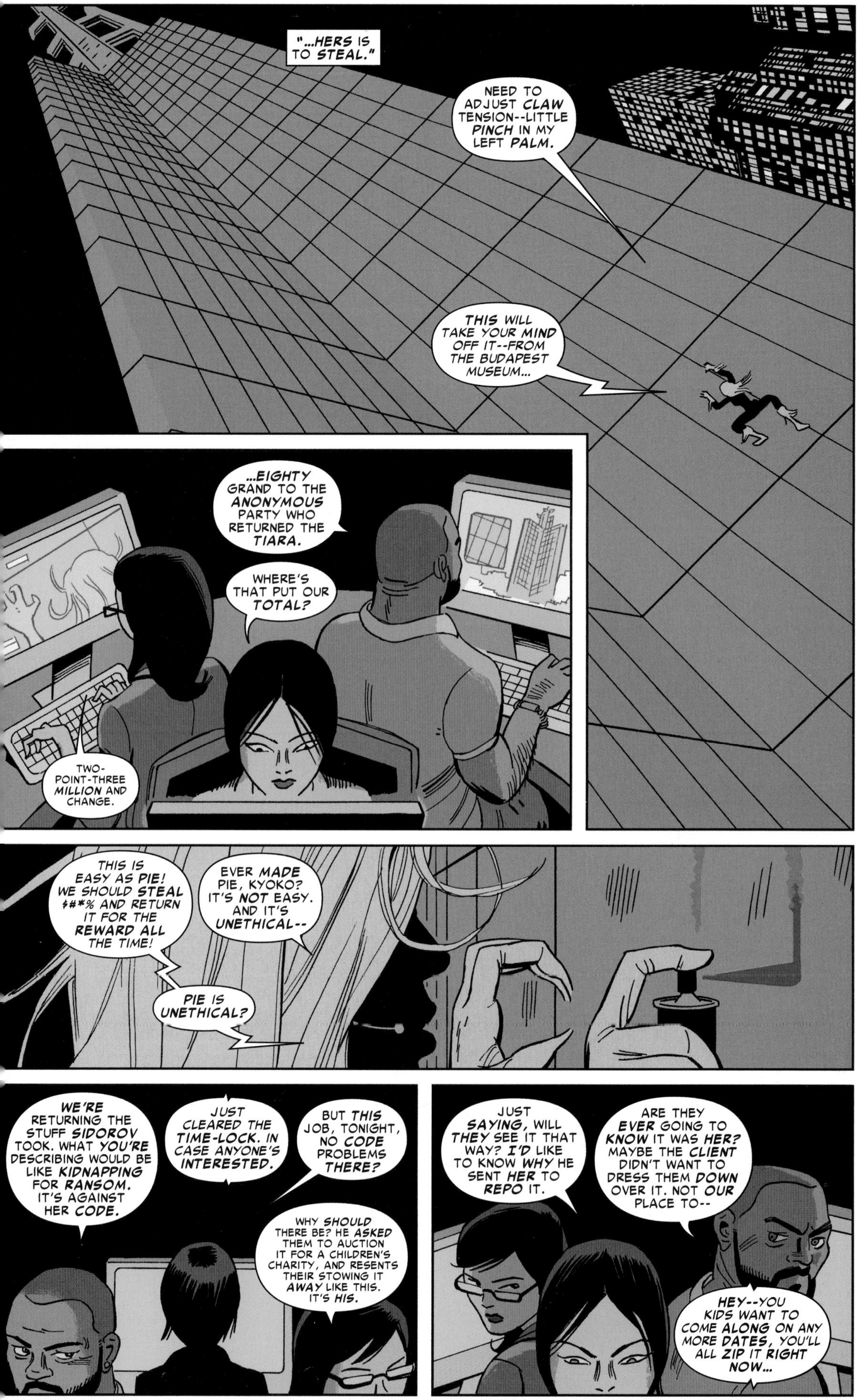
"...HERS IS TO STEAL."
NEED TO ADJUST CLAW TENSION--LITTLE PINCH IN MY LEFT PALM.
THIS WILL TAKE YOUR MIND OFF IT--FROM THE BUDAPEST MUSEUM...
...EIGHTY GRAND TO THE ANONYMOUS PARTY WHO RETURNED THE TIARA.
WHERE'S THAT PUT OUR TOTAL?
TWO-POINT-THREE MILLION AND CHANGE.
THIS IS EASY AS PIE! WE SHOULD STEAL $#*% AND RETURN IT FOR THE REWARD ALL THE TIME!
EVER MADE PIE, KYOKO? IT'S NOT EASY. AND IT'S UNETHICAL--
PIE IS UNETHICAL?
WE'RE RETURNING THE STUFF SIDOROV TOOK. WHAT YOU'RE DESCRIBING WOULD BE LIKE KIDNAPPING FOR RANSOM. IT'S AGAINST HER CODE.
JUST CLEARED THE TIME-LOCK. IN CASE ANYONE'S INTERESTED.
BUT THIS JOB, TONIGHT, NO CODE PROBLEMS THERE?
WHY SHOULD THERE BE? HE ASKED THEM TO AUCTION IT FOR A CHILDREN'S CHARITY, AND RESENTS THEIR STOWING IT AWAY LIKE THIS. IT'S HIS.
JUST SAYING, WILL THEY SEE IT THAT WAY? I'D LIKE TO KNOW WHY HE SENT HER TO REPO IT.
ARE THEY EVER GOING TO KNOW IT WAS HER? MAYBE THE CLIENT DIDN'T WANT TO DRESS THEM DOWN OVER IT. NOT OUR PLACE TO--
HEY--YOU KIDS WANT TO COME ALONG ON ANY MORE DATES, YOU'LL ALL ZIP IT RIGHT NOW...

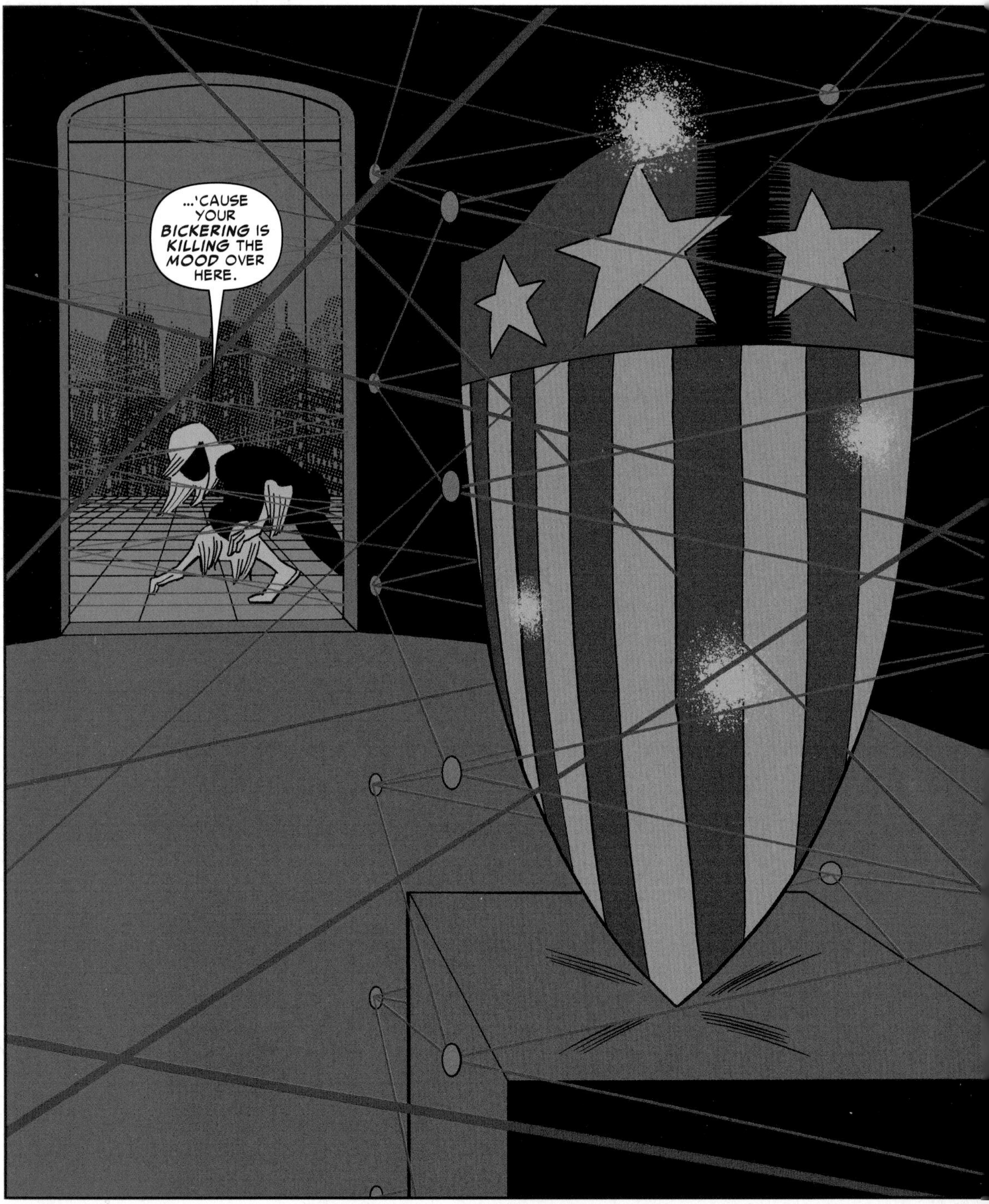
...'CAUSE YOUR BICKERING IS KILLING THE MOOD OVER HERE.

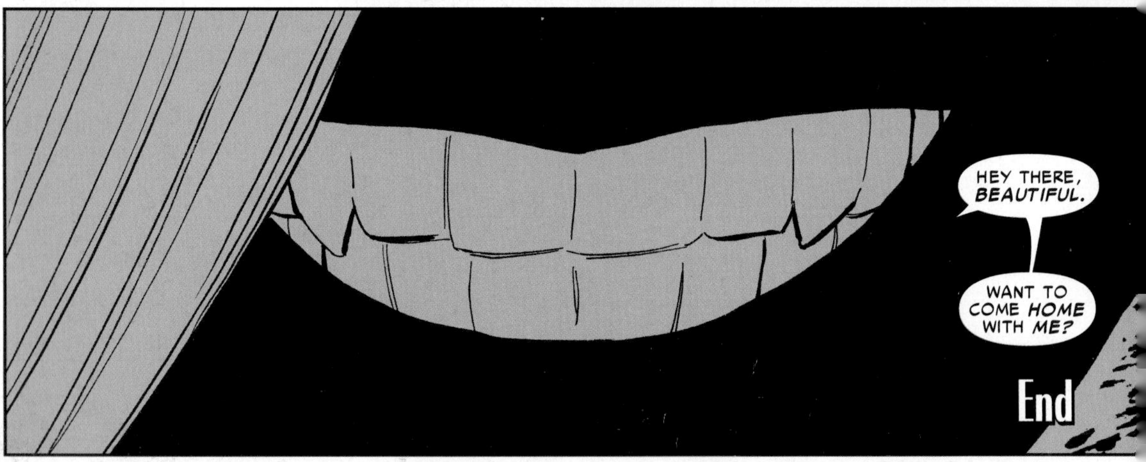
HEY THERE, BEAUTIFUL.
WANT TO COME HOME WITH ME?
End

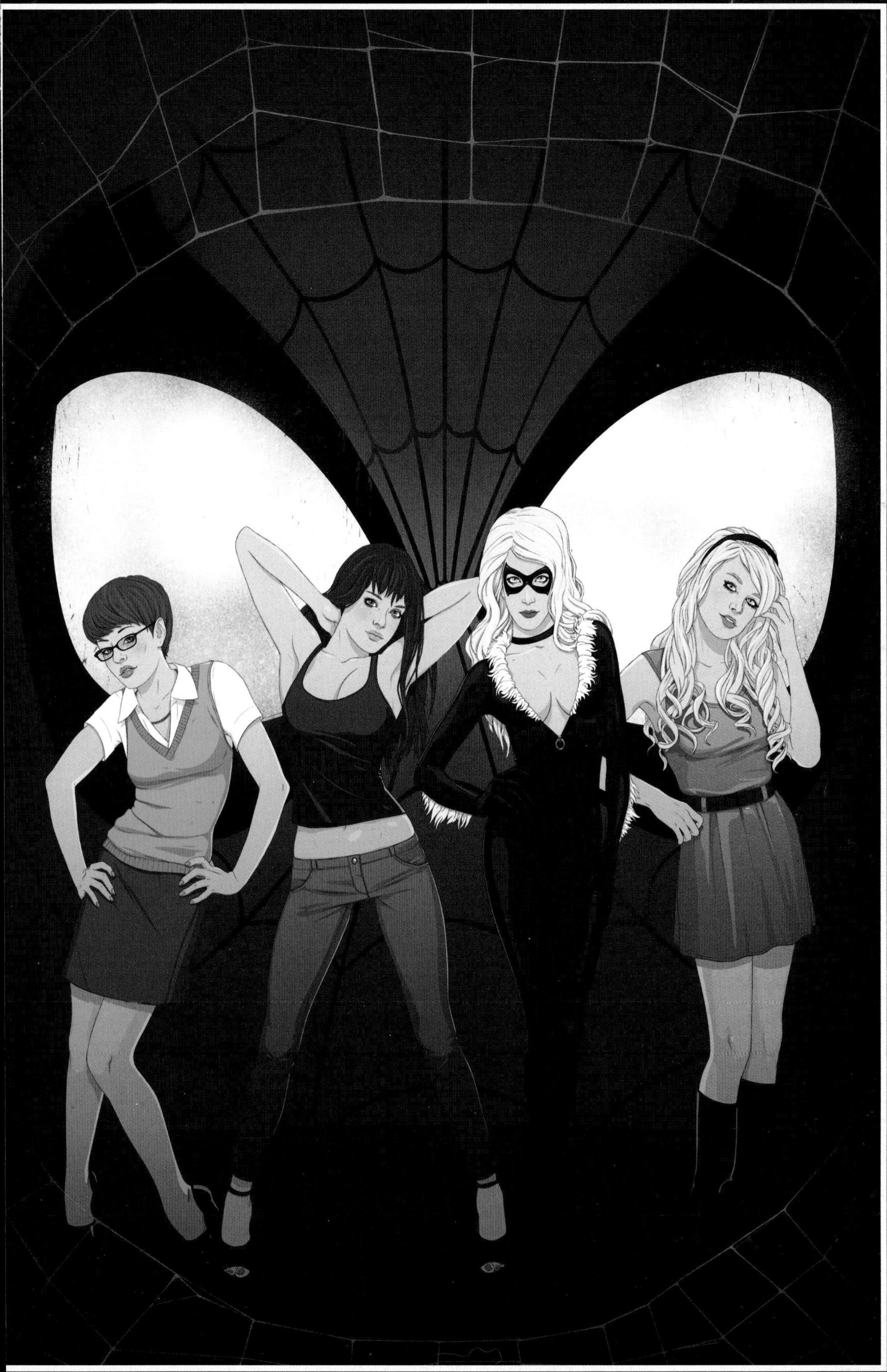

THE MANY LOVES OF THE AMAZING SPIDER-MAN

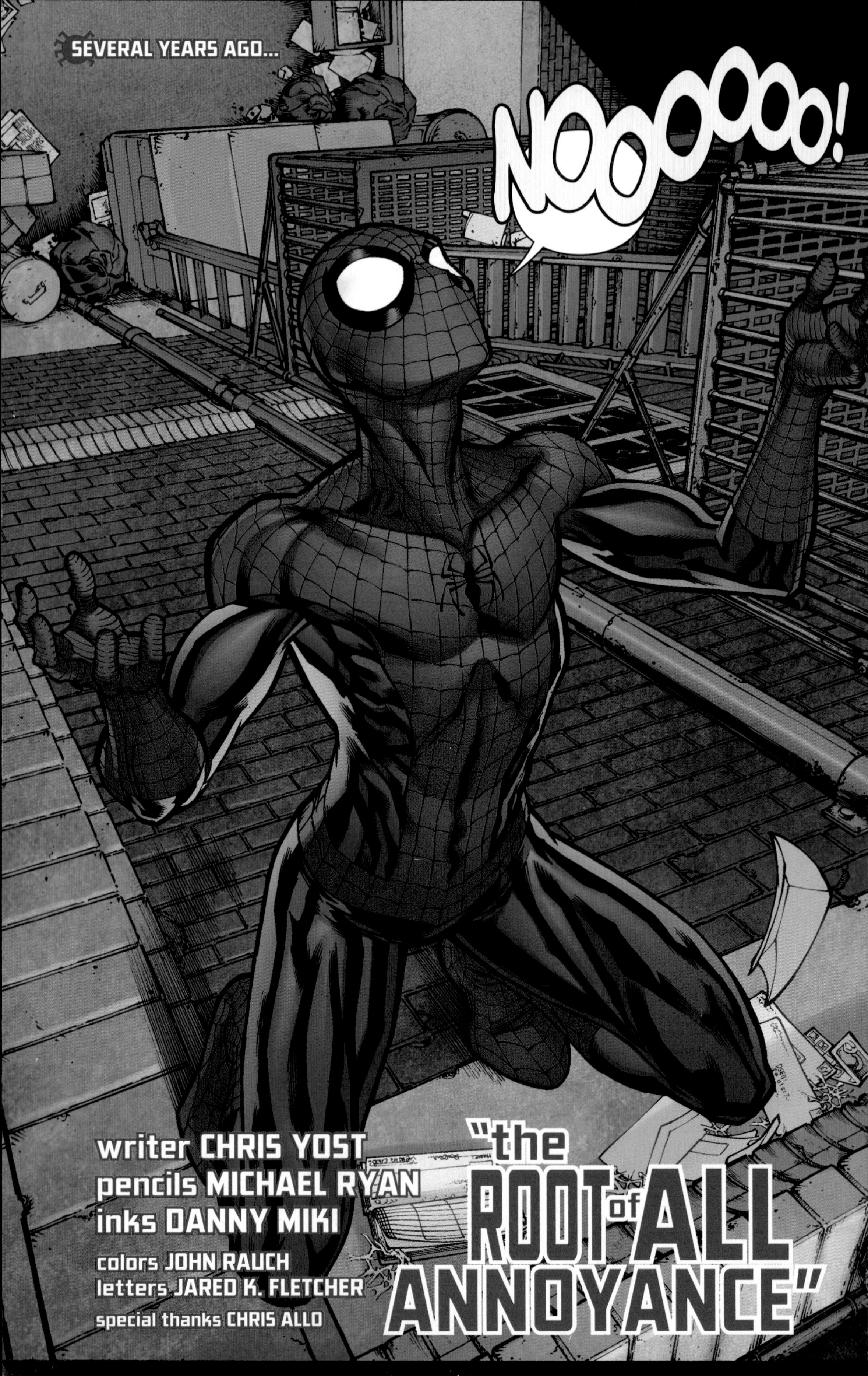
SEVERAL YEARS AGO...
NOOOOOO!
writer CHRIS YOST
pencils MICHAEL RYAN
inks DANNY MIKI
colors JOHN RAUCH
letters JARED K. FLETCHER
special thanks CHRIS ALLO
"the ROOT of ALL ANNOYANCE"

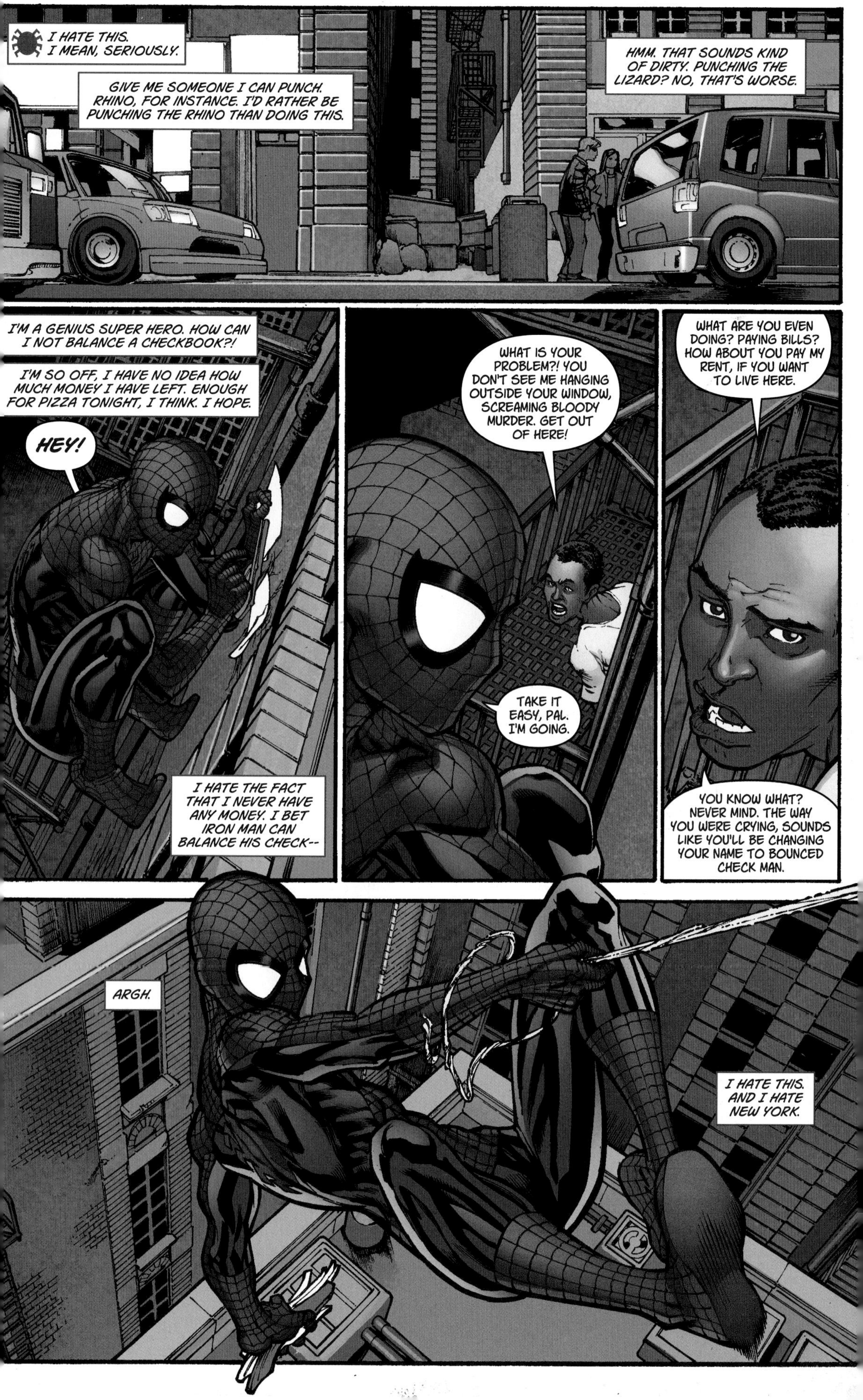
I HATE THIS. I MEAN, SERIOUSLY.
GIVE ME SOMEONE I CAN PUNCH. RHINO, FOR INSTANCE. I'D RATHER BE PUNCHING THE RHINO THAN DOING THIS.
HMM. THAT SOUNDS KIND OF DIRTY. PUNCHING THE LIZARD? NO, THAT'S WORSE.
I'M A GENIUS SUPER HERO. HOW CAN I NOT BALANCE A CHECKBOOK?!
I'M SO OFF, I HAVE NO IDEA HOW MUCH MONEY I HAVE LEFT. ENOUGH FOR PIZZA TONIGHT, I THINK. I HOPE.
HEY!
I HATE THE FACT THAT I NEVER HAVE ANY MONEY. I BET IRON MAN CAN BALANCE HIS CHECK--
WHAT IS YOUR PROBLEM?! YOU DON'T SEE ME HANGING OUTSIDE YOUR WINDOW, SCREAMING BLOODY MURDER. GET OUT OF HERE!
TAKE IT EASY, PAL. I'M GOING.
WHAT ARE YOU EVEN DOING? PAYING BILLS? HOW ABOUT YOU PAY MY RENT, IF YOU WANT TO LIVE HERE.
YOU KNOW WHAT? NEVER MIND. THE WAY YOU WERE CRYING, SOUNDS LIKE YOU'LL BE CHANGING YOUR NAME TO BOUNCED CHECK MAN.
ARGH.
I HATE THIS. AND I HATE NEW YORK.

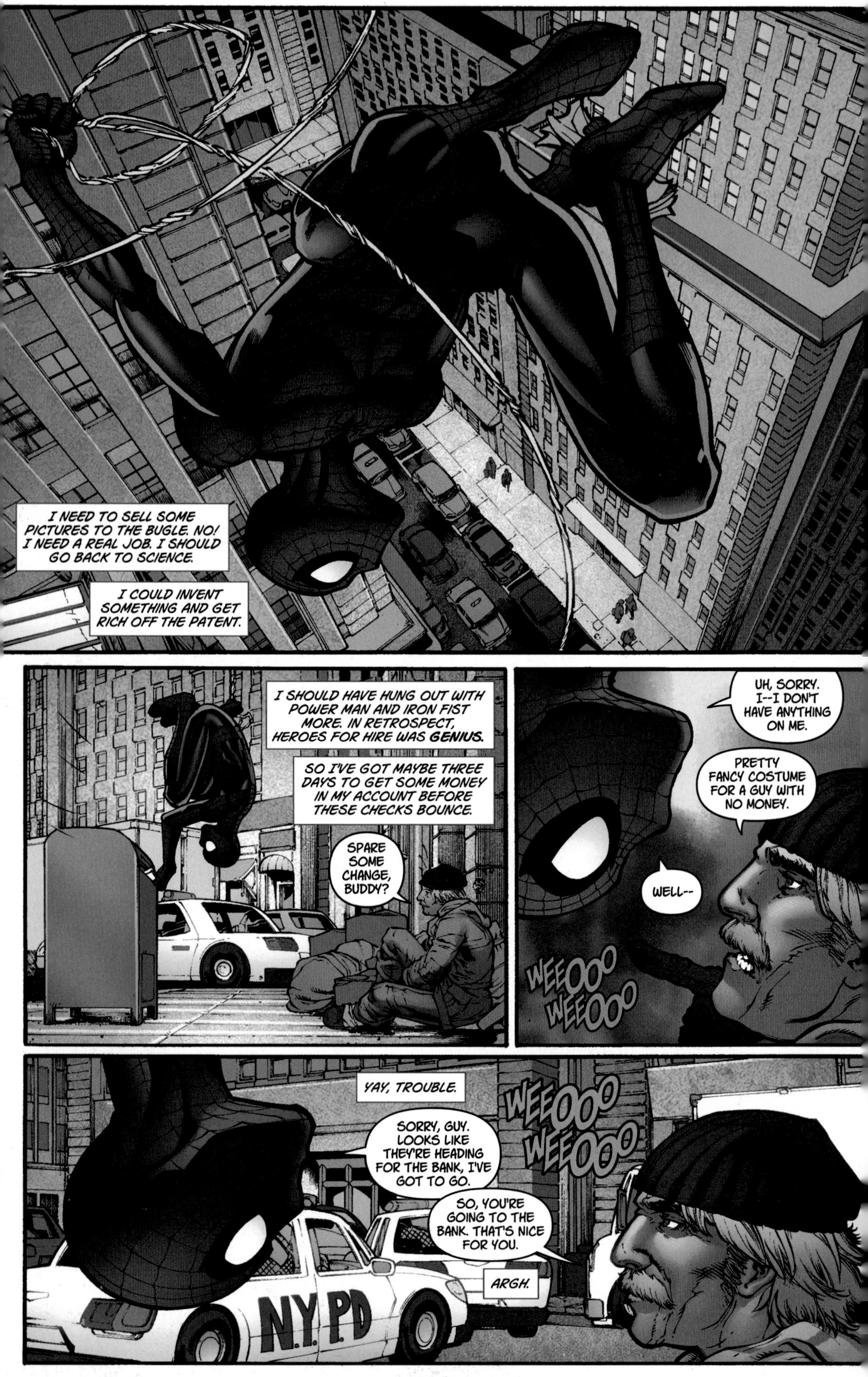
I NEED TO SELL SOME PICTURES TO THE BUGLE. NO! I NEED A REAL JOB. I SHOULD GO BACK TO SCIENCE.
I COULD INVENT SOMETHING AND GET RICH OFF THE PATENT.
I SHOULD HAVE HUNG OUT WITH POWER MAN AND IRON FIST MORE. IN RETROSPECT, HEROES FOR HIRE WAS GENIUS.
SO I'VE GOT MAYBE THREE DAYS TO GET SOME MONEY IN MY ACCOUNT BEFORE THESE CHECKS BOUNCE.
SPARE SOME CHANGE, BUDDY?
UH, SORRY. I--I DON'T HAVE ANYTHING ON ME.
PRETTY FANCY COSTUME FOR A GUY WITH NO MONEY.
WELL--
WEEOOO WEEOOO
YAY, TROUBLE.
WEEOOO WEEOOO
SORRY, GUY. LOOKS LIKE THEY'RE HEADING FOR THE BANK, I'VE GOT TO GO.
SO, YOU'RE GOING TO THE BANK. THAT'S NICE FOR YOU.
ARGH.
N.Y.P.D

ROOOOAAARR!
WHOA! EASY THERE... UH... BANK MONSTER?
LOS ANGELES IS THE BANK ROBBERY CAPITAL OF THE UNITED STATES, THEY SAY.
WELL, NEW YORK IS THE BANK ROBBERY BY CRAZY SUPER POWERED WHACKOS CAPITOL.
HEY! HEY, MAGIC GUY! I'M NOT DONE WITH YOU YET!
IT'S OCCULTIST! THE NAME IS OCCULTIST! NOT MAGIC GUY!
OCCULTIST? IS THAT LIKE AN EYE DOCTOR?
I--NO! SHUT UP AND DIE!
MY GOLEM WILL TAKE CARE OF YOU! NOTHING CAN WITHSTAND MY MAGI--MY OCCULTISM!
...DOOR.

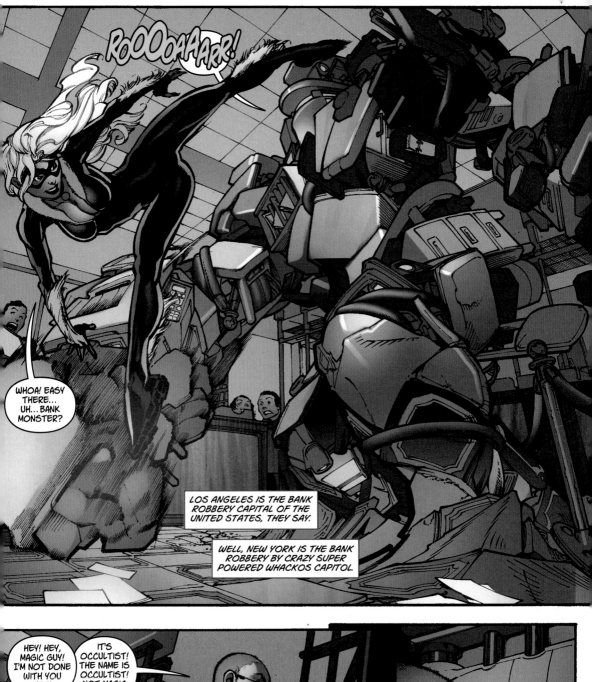

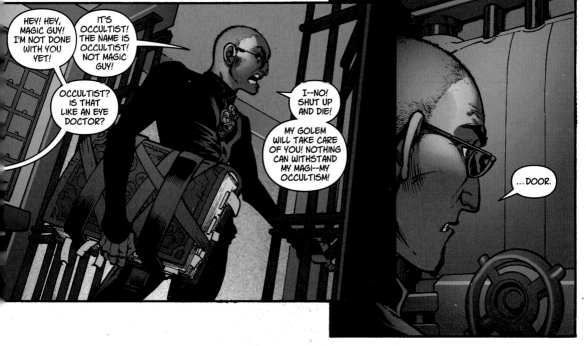

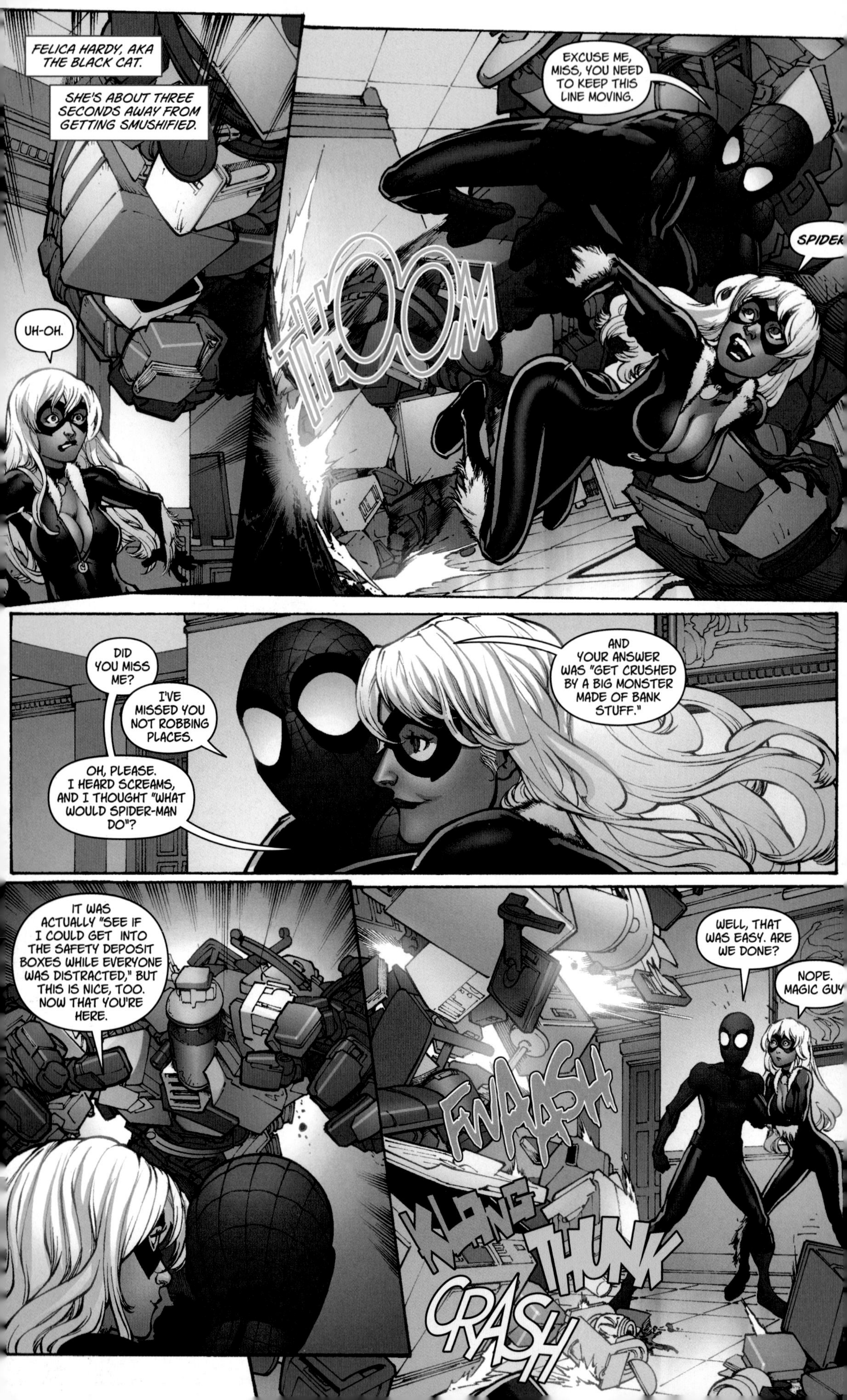
FELICA HARDY, AKA THE BLACK CAT.
SHE'S ABOUT THREE SECONDS AWAY FROM GETTING SMUSHIFIED.
UH-OH.
EXCUSE ME, MISS, YOU NEED TO KEEP THIS LINE MOVING.
THOOM
SPIDER
DID YOU MISS ME?
I'VE MISSED YOU NOT ROBBING PLACES.
OH, PLEASE. I HEARD SCREAMS, AND I THOUGHT "WHAT WOULD SPIDER-MAN DO"?
AND YOUR ANSWER WAS "GET CRUSHED BY A BIG MONSTER MADE OF BANK STUFF."
IT WAS ACTUALLY "SEE IF I COULD GET INTO THE SAFETY DEPOSIT BOXES WHILE EVERYONE WAS DISTRACTED," BUT THIS IS NICE, TOO. NOW THAT YOU'RE HERE.
WELL, THAT WAS EASY. ARE WE DONE?
NOPE. MAGIC GUY
FWASH
KLANG
THUNK
CRASH

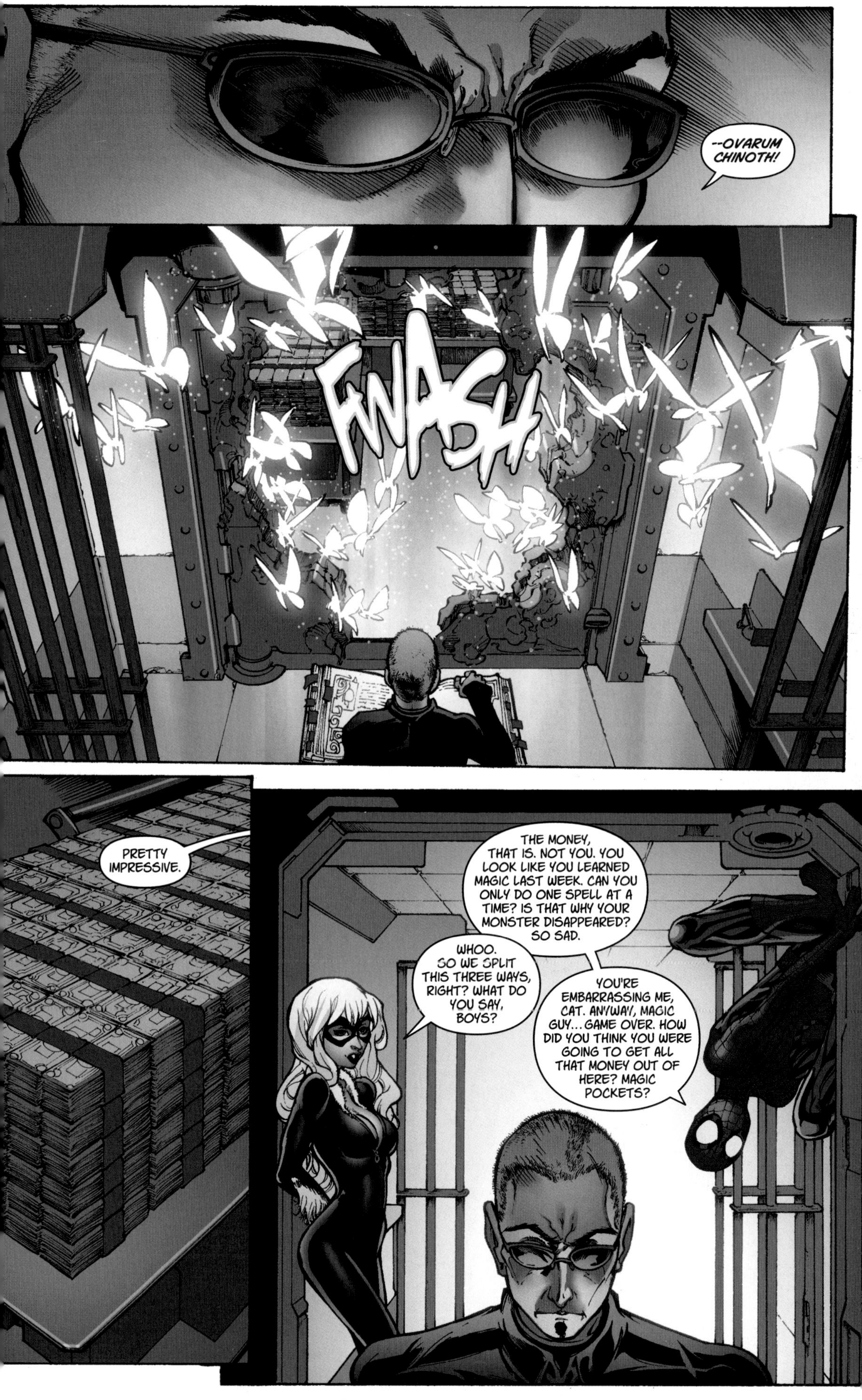
--OVARUM CHINOTH!
FWASH
PRETTY IMPRESSIVE.
THE MONEY, THAT IS. NOT YOU. YOU LOOK LIKE YOU LEARNED MAGIC LAST WEEK. CAN YOU ONLY DO ONE SPELL AT A TIME? IS THAT WHY YOUR MONSTER DISAPPEARED? SO SAD.
WHOO. SO WE SPLIT THIS THREE WAYS, RIGHT? WHAT DO YOU SAY, BOYS?
YOU'RE EMBARRASSING ME, CAT. ANYWAY, MAGIC GUY... GAME OVER. HOW DID YOU THINK YOU WERE GOING TO GET ALL THAT MONEY OUT OF HERE? MAGIC POCKETS?

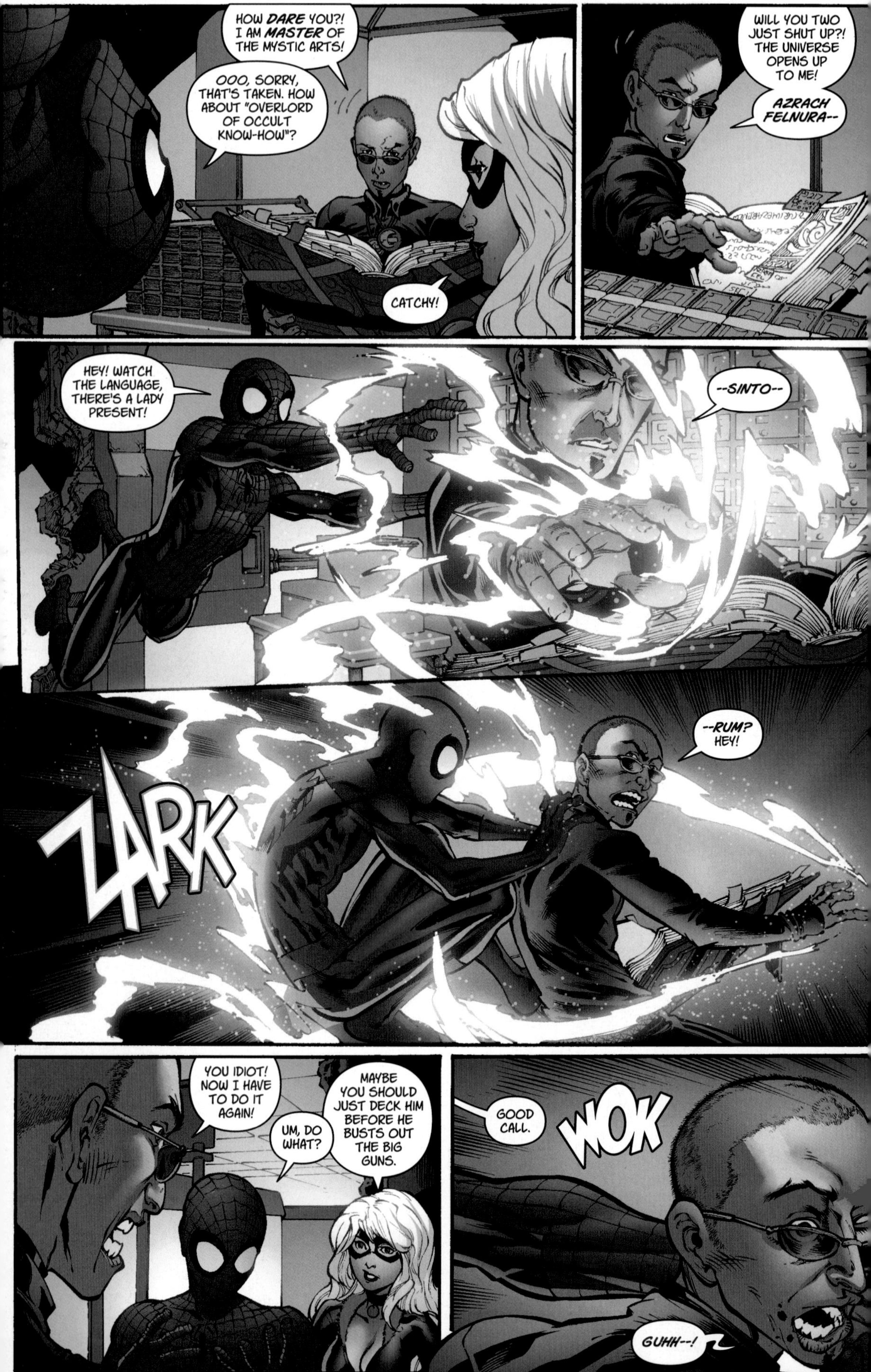
HOW DARE YOU?! I AM MASTER OF THE MYSTIC ARTS!
OOO, SORRY, THAT'S TAKEN. HOW ABOUT "OVERLORD OF OCCULT KNOW-HOW"?
CATCHY!
WILL YOU TWO JUST SHUT UP?! THE UNIVERSE OPENS UP TO ME!
AZRACH FELNURA--
HEY! WATCH THE LANGUAGE, THERE'S A LADY PRESENT!
--SINTO--
ZARK
--RUM? HEY!
YOU IDIOT! NOW I HAVE TO DO IT AGAIN!
UM, DO WHAT?
MAYBE YOU SHOULD JUST DECK HIM BEFORE HE BUSTS OUT THE BIG GUNS.
GOOD CALL.
WOK
GUHH--!

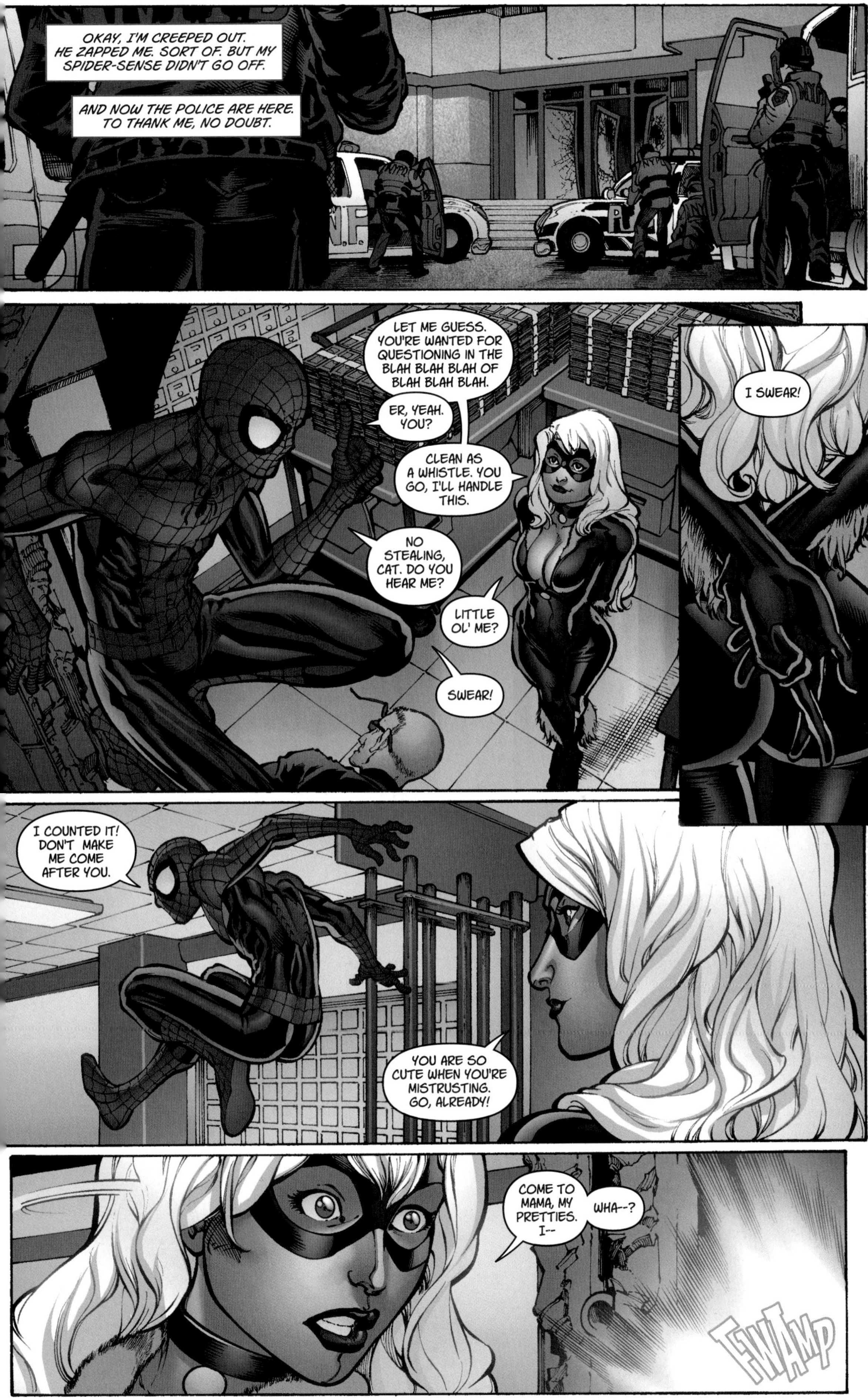
OKAY, I'M CREEPED OUT. HE ZAPPED ME. SORT OF. BUT MY SPIDER-SENSE DIDN'T GO OFF.
AND NOW THE POLICE ARE HERE. TO THANK ME, NO DOUBT.
LET ME GUESS. YOU'RE WANTED FOR QUESTIONING IN THE BLAH BLAH BLAH OF BLAH BLAH BLAH.
ER, YEAH. YOU?
CLEAN AS A WHISTLE. YOU GO, I'LL HANDLE THIS.
NO STEALING, CAT. DO YOU HEAR ME?
LITTLE OL' ME?
SWEAR!
I SWEAR!
I COUNTED IT! DON'T MAKE ME COME AFTER YOU.
YOU ARE SO CUTE WHEN YOU'RE MISTRUSTING. GO, ALREADY!
COME TO MAMA, MY PRETTIES. I--
WHA--?
FWAMP

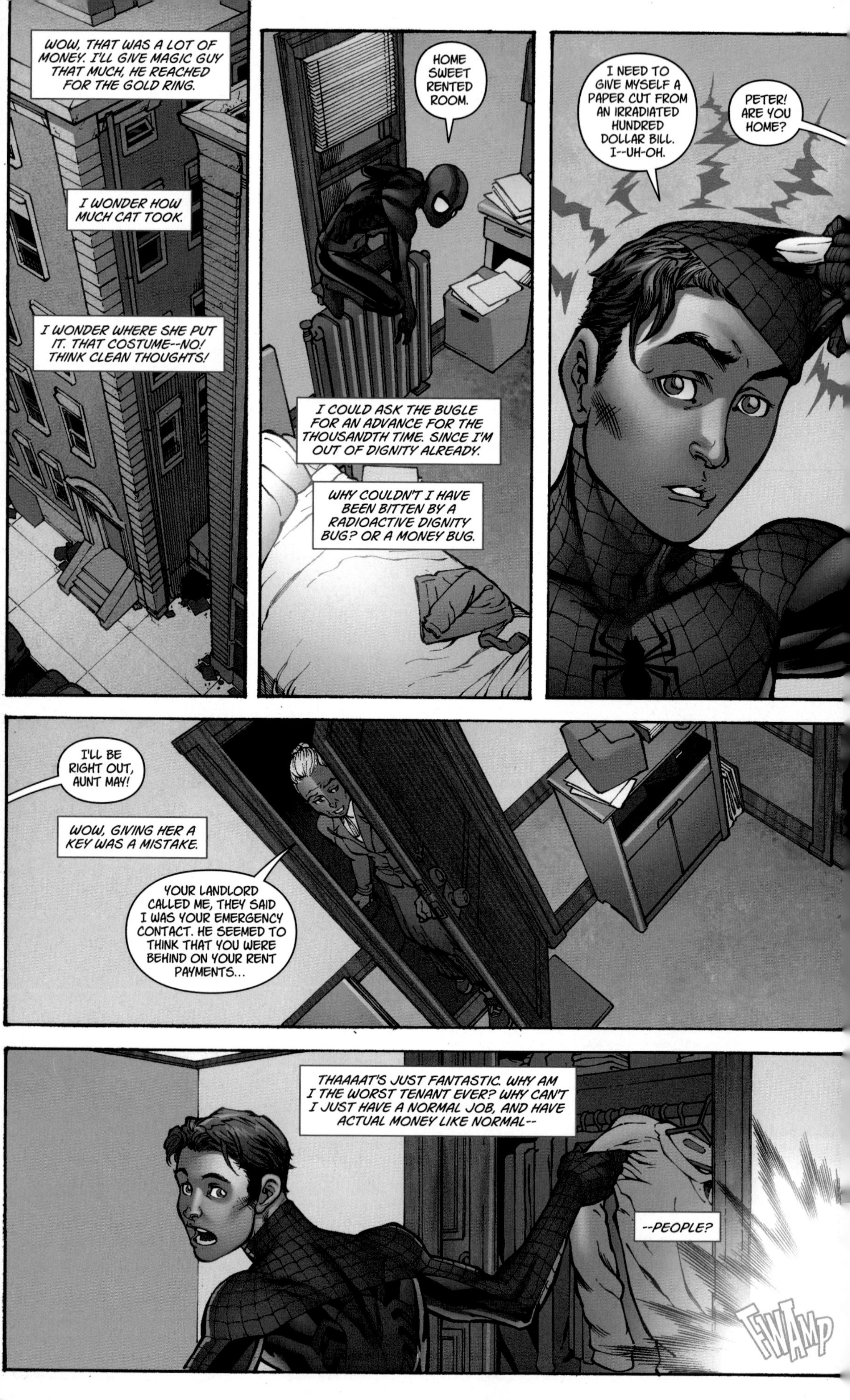
WOW, THAT WAS A LOT OF MONEY. I'LL GIVE MAGIC GUY THAT MUCH, HE REACHED FOR THE GOLD RING.
I WONDER HOW MUCH CAT TOOK.
I WONDER WHERE SHE PUT IT. THAT COSTUME--NO! THINK CLEAN THOUGHTS!
HOME SWEET RENTED ROOM.
I COULD ASK THE BUGLE FOR AN ADVANCE FOR THE THOUSANDTH TIME. SINCE I'M OUT OF DIGNITY ALREADY.
WHY COULDN'T I HAVE BEEN BITTEN BY A RADIOACTIVE DIGNITY BUG? OR A MONEY BUG.
I NEED TO GIVE MYSELF A PAPER CUT FROM AN IRRADIATED HUNDRED DOLLAR BILL. I--UH-OH.
PETER! ARE YOU HOME?
I'LL BE RIGHT OUT, AUNT MAY!
WOW, GIVING HER A KEY WAS A MISTAKE.
YOUR LANDLORD CALLED ME, THEY SAID I WAS YOUR EMERGENCY CONTACT. HE SEEMED TO THINK THAT YOU WERE BEHIND ON YOUR RENT PAYMENTS...
THAAAAT'S JUST FANTASTIC. WHY AM I THE WORST TENANT EVER? WHY CAN'T I JUST HAVE A NORMAL JOB, AND HAVE ACTUAL MONEY LIKE NORMAL--
--PEOPLE?
FWAMP

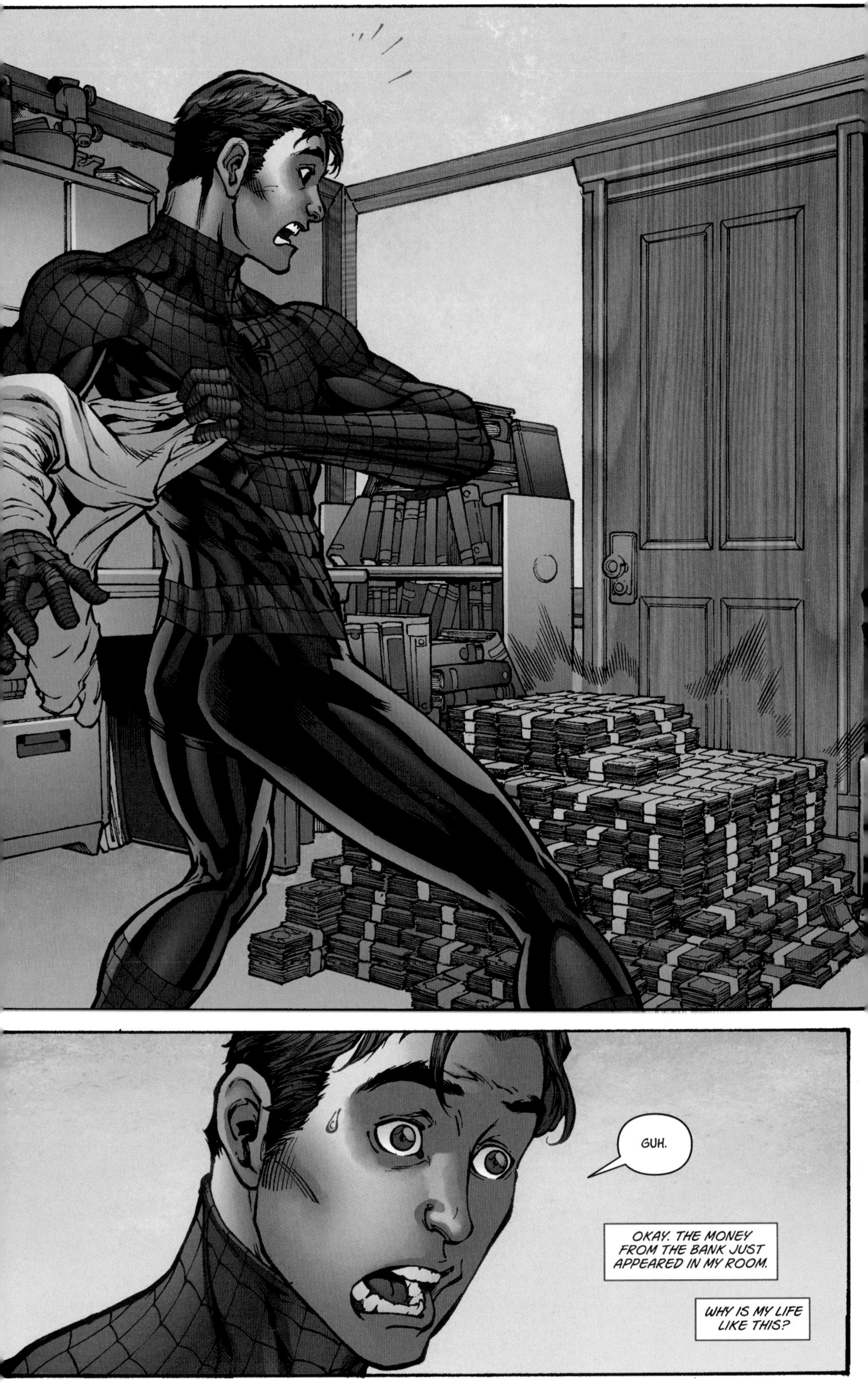
GUH.
OKAY. THE MONEY FROM THE BANK JUST APPEARED IN MY ROOM.
WHY IS MY LIFE LIKE THIS?

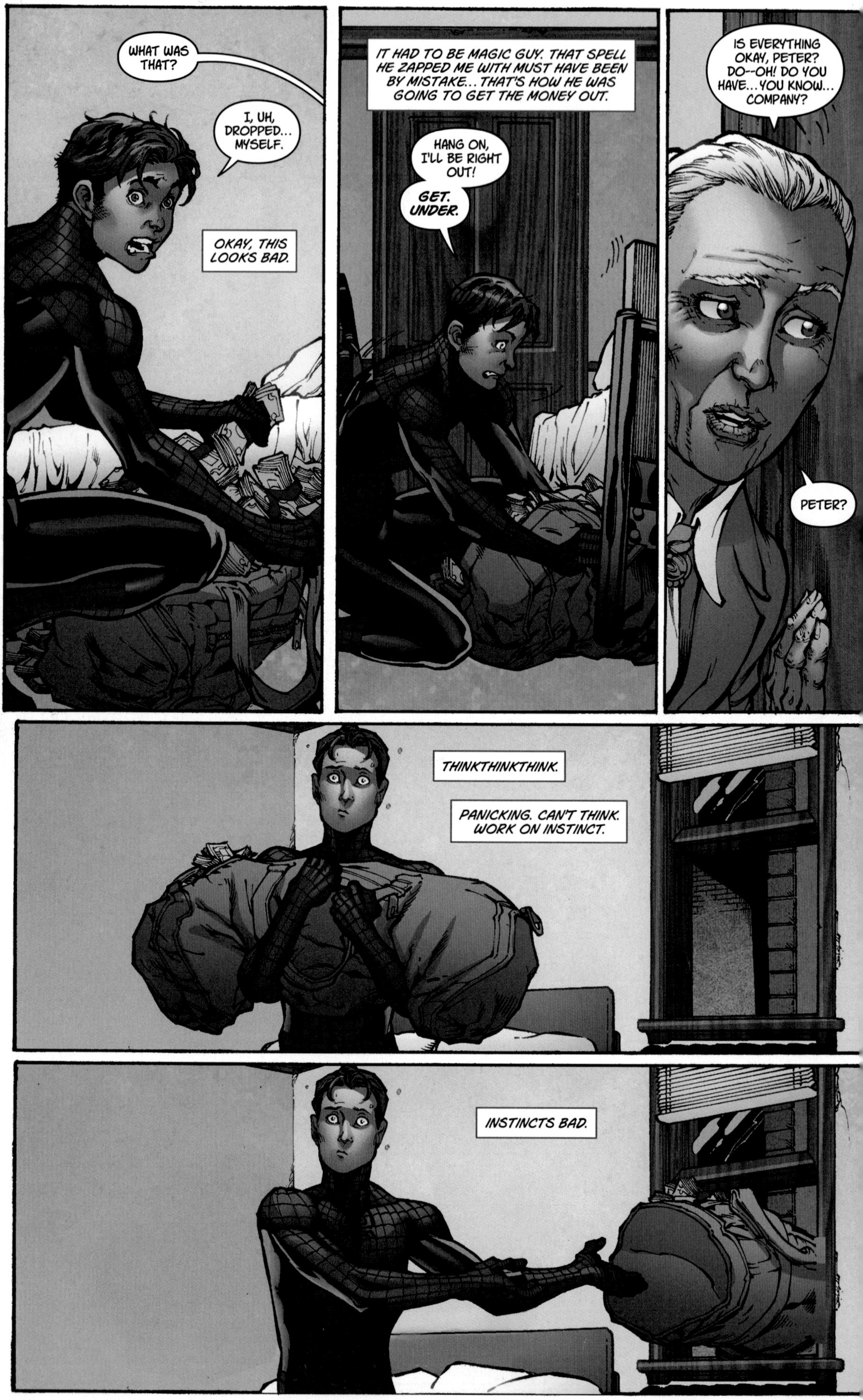
WHAT WAS THAT?
I, UH, DROPPED... MYSELF.
OKAY, THIS LOOKS BAD.
IT HAD TO BE MAGIC GUY. THAT SPELL HE ZAPPED ME WITH MUST HAVE BEEN BY MISTAKE... THAT'S HOW HE WAS GOING TO GET THE MONEY OUT.
HANG ON, I'LL BE RIGHT OUT!
GET. UNDER.
IS EVERYTHING OKAY, PETER? DO--OH! DO YOU HAVE... YOU KNOW... COMPANY?
PETER?
THINKTHINKTHINK.
PANICKING. CAN'T THINK. WORK ON INSTINCT.
INSTINCTS BAD.

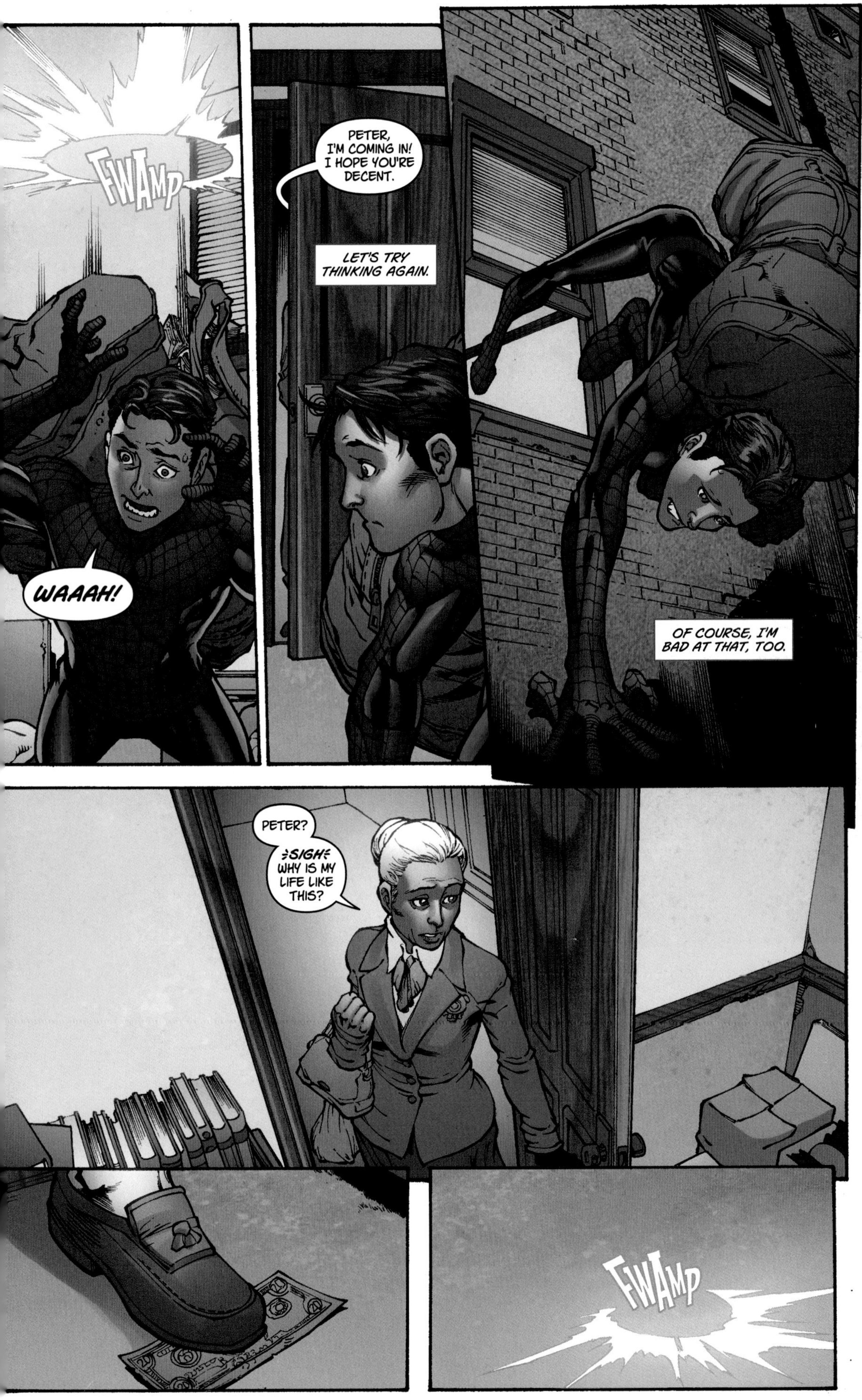
FWAMP
WAAAH!
PETER, I'M COMING IN! I HOPE YOU'RE DECENT.
LET'S TRY THINKING AGAIN.
OF COURSE, I'M BAD AT THAT, TOO.
PETER?
SIGH
WHY IS MY LIFE LIKE THIS?
FWAMP

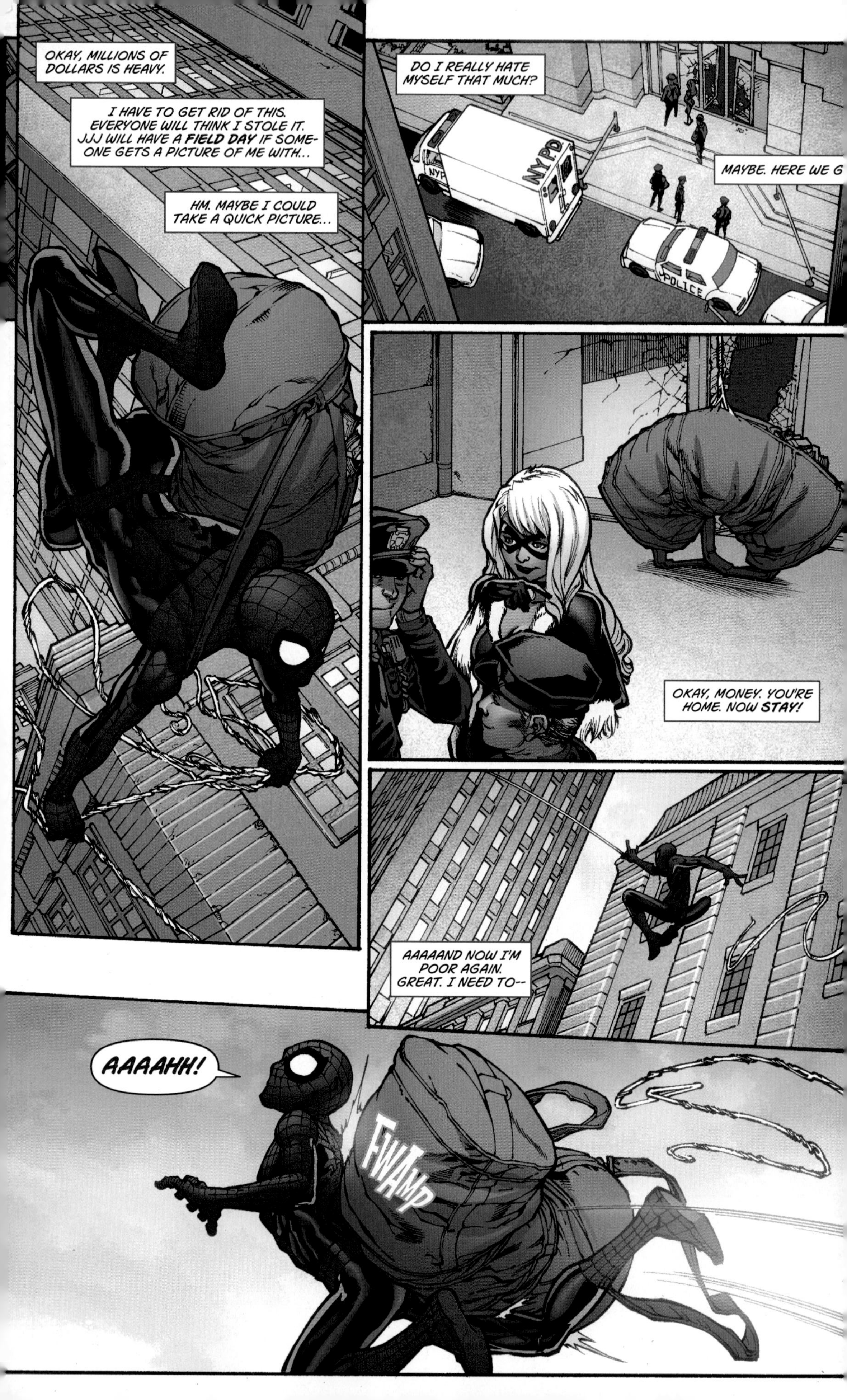

OKAY, MILLIONS OF DOLLARS IS HEAVY.
I HAVE TO GET RID OF THIS. EVERYONE WILL THINK I STOLE IT. JJJ WILL HAVE A **FIELD DAY** IF SOME-ONE GETS A PICTURE OF ME WITH...
HM. MAYBE I COULD TAKE A QUICK PICTURE...
DO I REALLY HATE MYSELF THAT MUCH?
NYPD
POLICE
MAYBE. HERE WE G
OKAY, MONEY. YOU'RE HOME. NOW **STAY!**
AAAAAND NOW I'M POOR AGAIN. GREAT. I NEED TO--
AAAAHH!
FWAMP

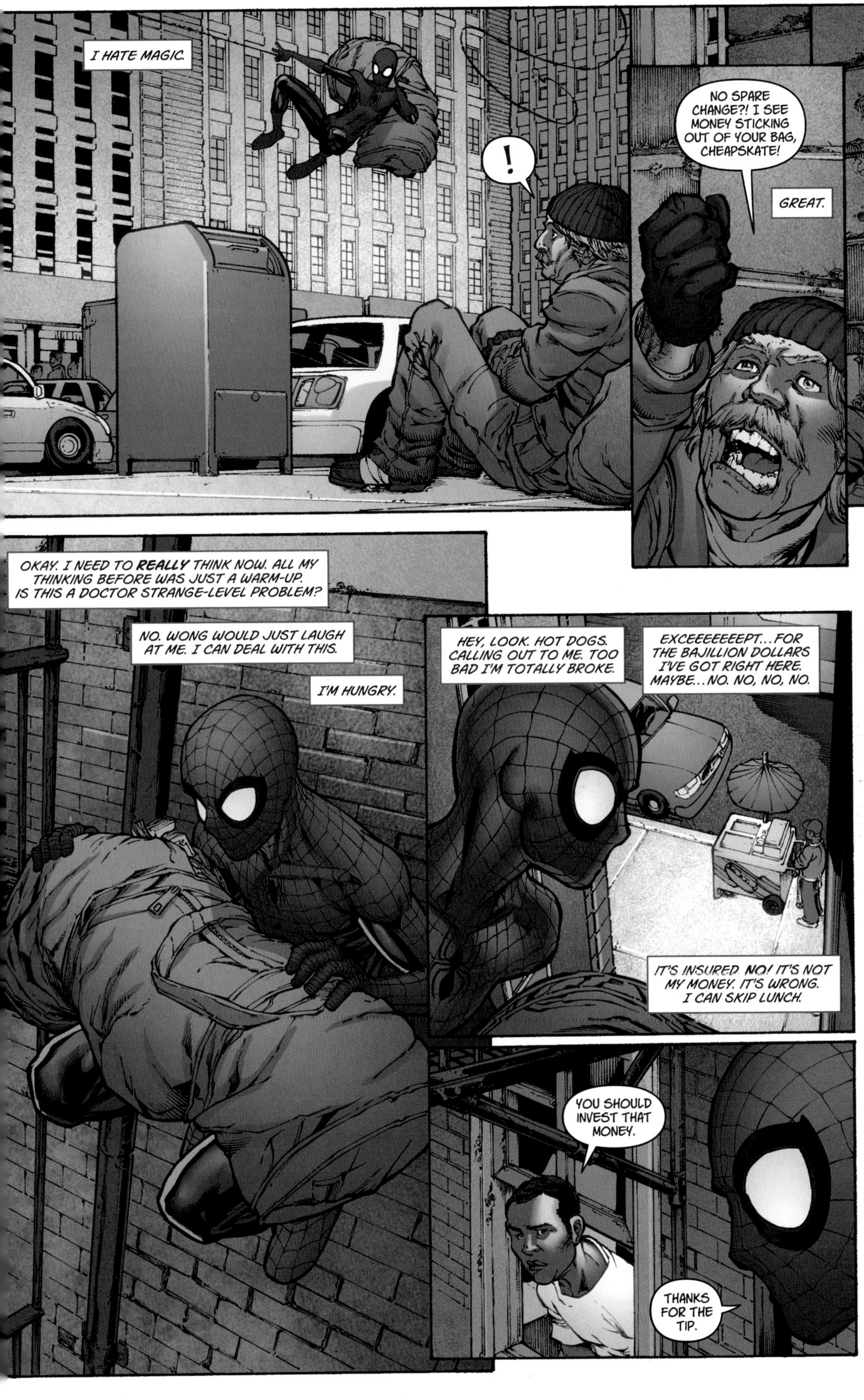
I HATE MAGIC.
!
NO SPARE CHANGE?! I SEE MONEY STICKING OUT OF YOUR BAG, CHEAPSKATE!
GREAT.
OKAY. I NEED TO **REALLY** THINK NOW. ALL MY THINKING BEFORE WAS JUST A WARM-UP. IS THIS A DOCTOR STRANGE-LEVEL PROBLEM?
NO. WONG WOULD JUST LAUGH AT ME. I CAN DEAL WITH THIS.
I'M HUNGRY.
HEY, LOOK. HOT DOGS. CALLING OUT TO ME. TOO BAD I'M TOTALLY BROKE.
EXCEEEEEEEPT...FOR THE BAJILLION DOLLARS I'VE GOT RIGHT HERE. MAYBE...NO. NO, NO, NO.
IT'S INSURED. **NO!** IT'S NOT MY MONEY. IT'S WRONG. I CAN SKIP LUNCH.
YOU SHOULD INVEST THAT MONEY.
THANKS FOR THE TIP.

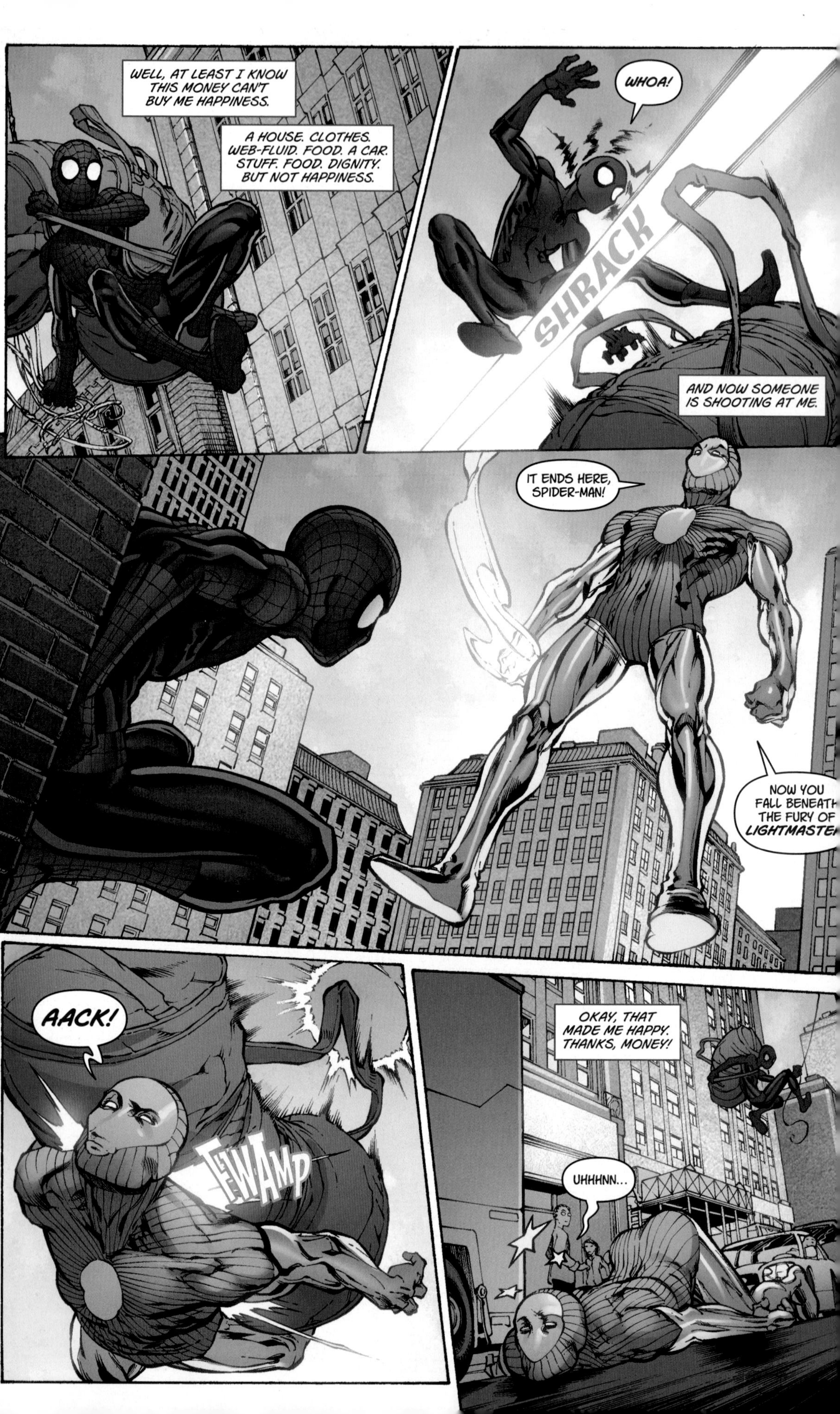

WELL, AT LEAST I KNOW THIS MONEY CAN'T BUY ME HAPPINESS.
A HOUSE. CLOTHES. WEB-FLUID. FOOD. A CAR. STUFF. FOOD. DIGNITY. BUT NOT HAPPINESS.
WHOA!
SHRACK
AND NOW SOMEONE IS SHOOTING AT ME.
IT ENDS HERE, SPIDER-MAN!
NOW YOU FALL BENEATH THE FURY OF LIGHTMASTE
AACK!
TFWAMP
OKAY, THAT MADE ME HAPPY. THANKS, MONEY!
UHHHNN...

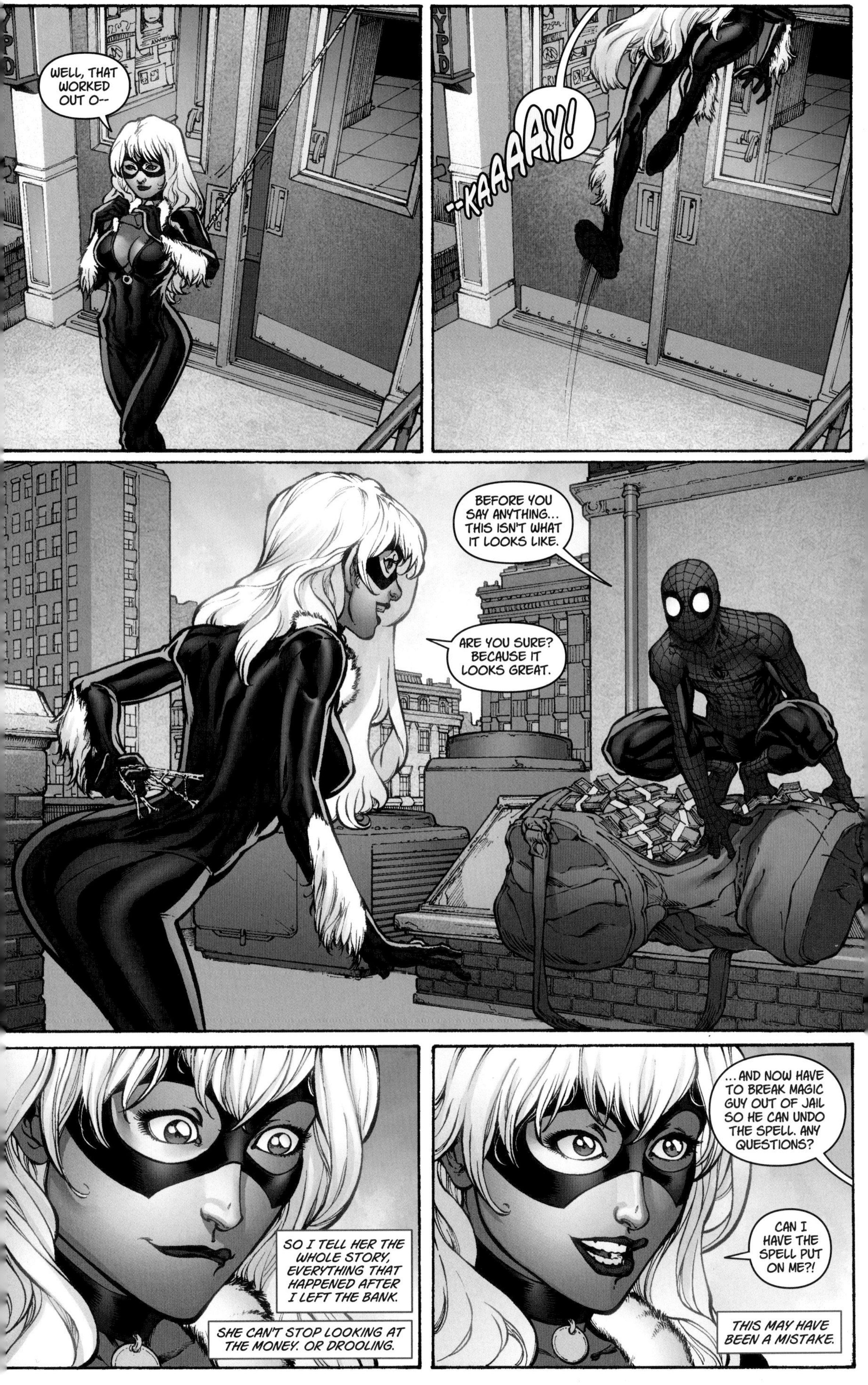
WELL, THAT WORKED OUT O--
--KAAAAAY!
BEFORE YOU SAY ANYTHING... THIS ISN'T WHAT IT LOOKS LIKE.
ARE YOU SURE? BECAUSE IT LOOKS GREAT.
SO I TELL HER THE WHOLE STORY, EVERYTHING THAT HAPPENED AFTER I LEFT THE BANK.
SHE CAN'T STOP LOOKING AT THE MONEY. OR DROOLING.
...AND NOW HAVE TO BREAK MAGIC GUY OUT OF JAIL SO HE CAN UNDO THE SPELL. ANY QUESTIONS?
CAN I HAVE THE SPELL PUT ON ME?!
THIS MAY HAVE BEEN A MISTAKE.

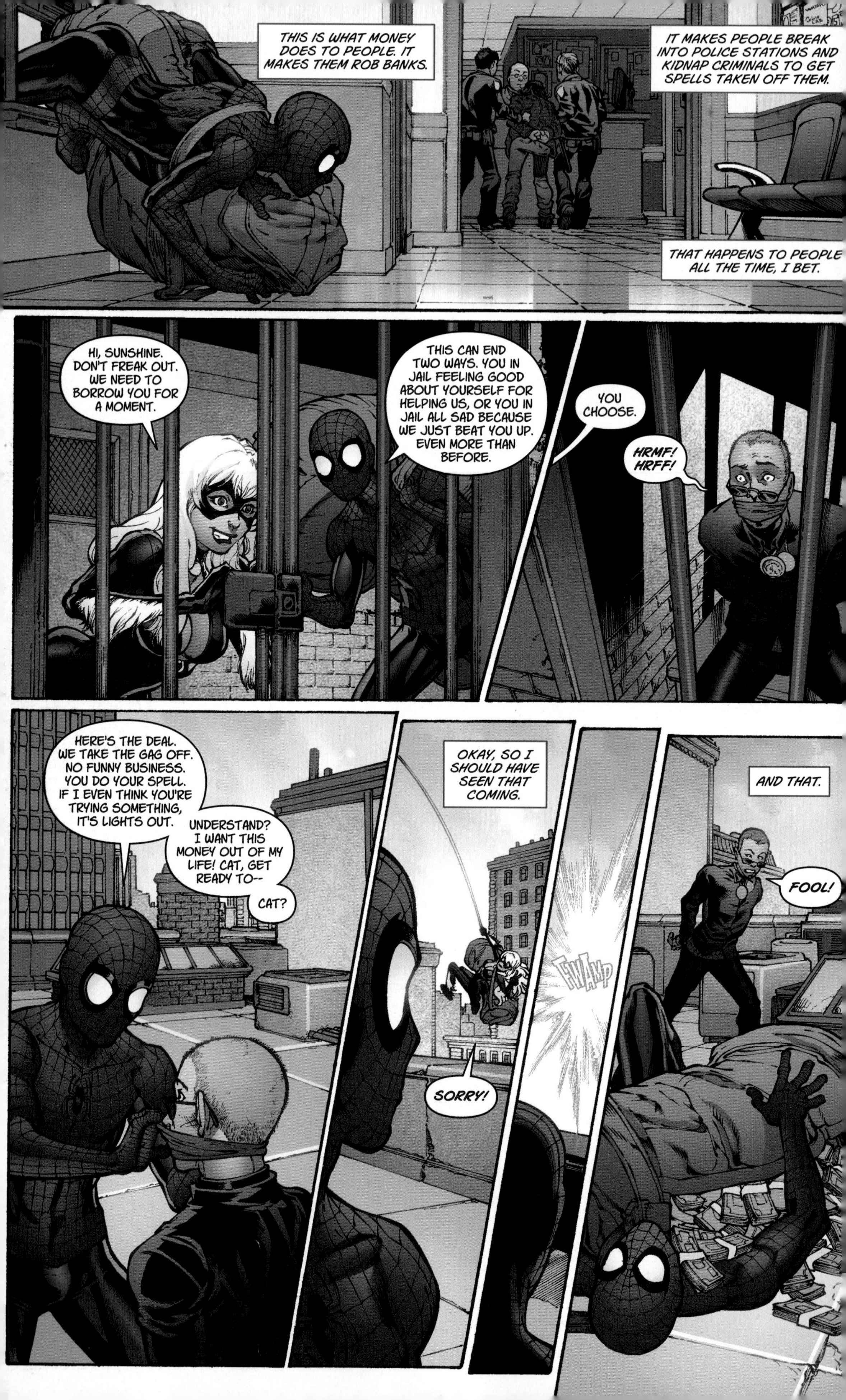
THIS IS WHAT MONEY DOES TO PEOPLE. IT MAKES THEM ROB BANKS.
IT MAKES PEOPLE BREAK INTO POLICE STATIONS AND KIDNAP CRIMINALS TO GET SPELLS TAKEN OFF THEM.
THAT HAPPENS TO PEOPLE ALL THE TIME, I BET.
HI, SUNSHINE. DON'T FREAK OUT. WE NEED TO BORROW YOU FOR A MOMENT.
THIS CAN END TWO WAYS. YOU IN JAIL FEELING GOOD ABOUT YOURSELF FOR HELPING US, OR YOU IN JAIL ALL SAD BECAUSE WE JUST BEAT YOU UP. EVEN MORE THAN BEFORE.
YOU CHOOSE.
HRMF! HRFF!
HERE'S THE DEAL. WE TAKE THE GAG OFF. NO FUNNY BUSINESS. YOU DO YOUR SPELL. IF I EVEN THINK YOU'RE TRYING SOMETHING, IT'S LIGHTS OUT.
UNDERSTAND? I WANT THIS MONEY OUT OF MY LIFE! CAT, GET READY TO--
CAT?
OKAY, SO I SHOULD HAVE SEEN THAT COMING.
SORRY!
FWAMP
AND THAT.
FOOL!

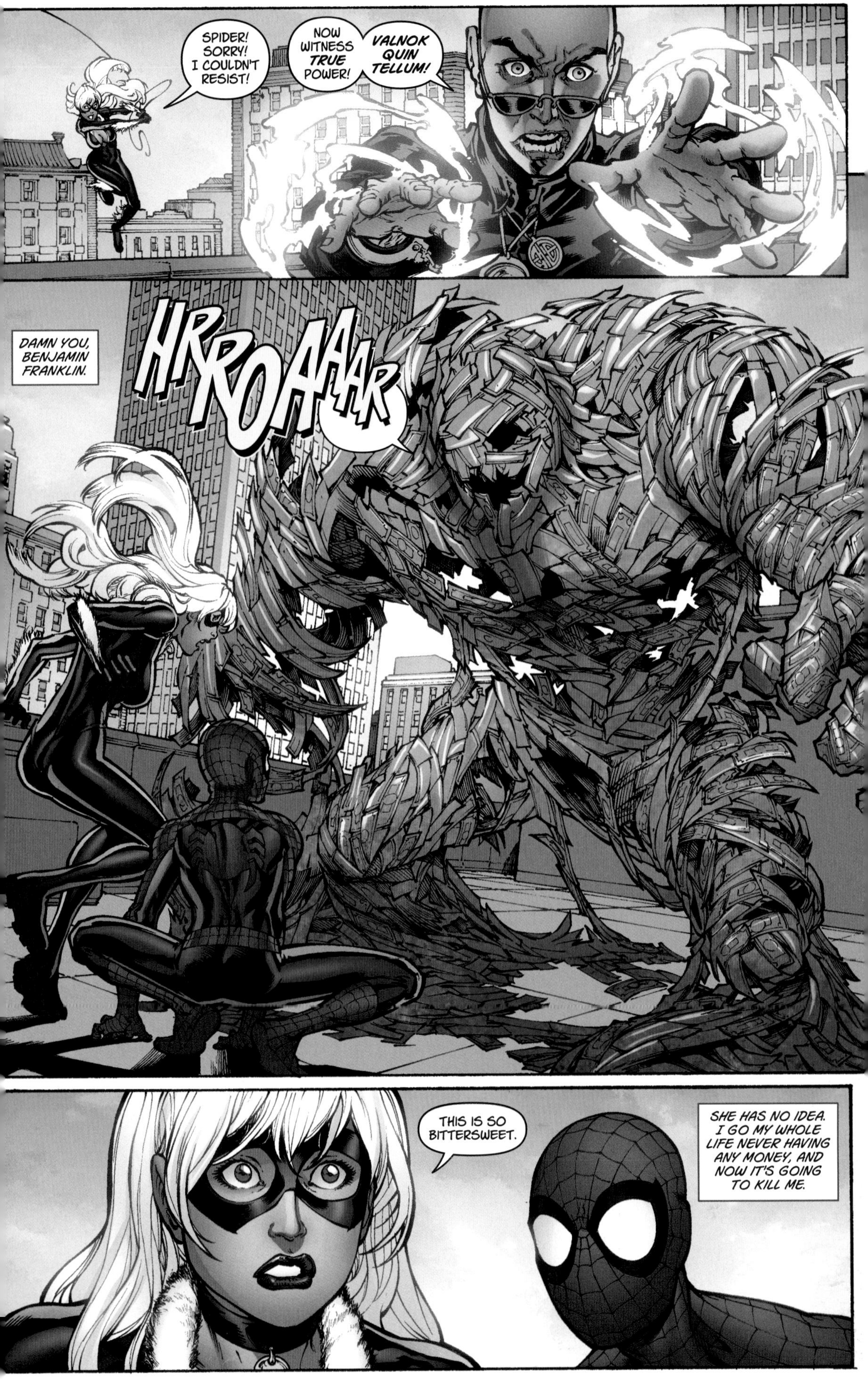
SPIDER! SORRY! I COULDN'T RESIST!
NOW WITNESS TRUE POWER!
VALNOK QUIN TELLUM!
DAMN YOU, BENJAMIN FRANKLIN.
HRROAAAAR
THIS IS SO BITTERSWEET.
SHE HAS NO IDEA. I GO MY WHOLE LIFE NEVER HAVING ANY MONEY, AND NOW IT'S GOING TO KILL ME.

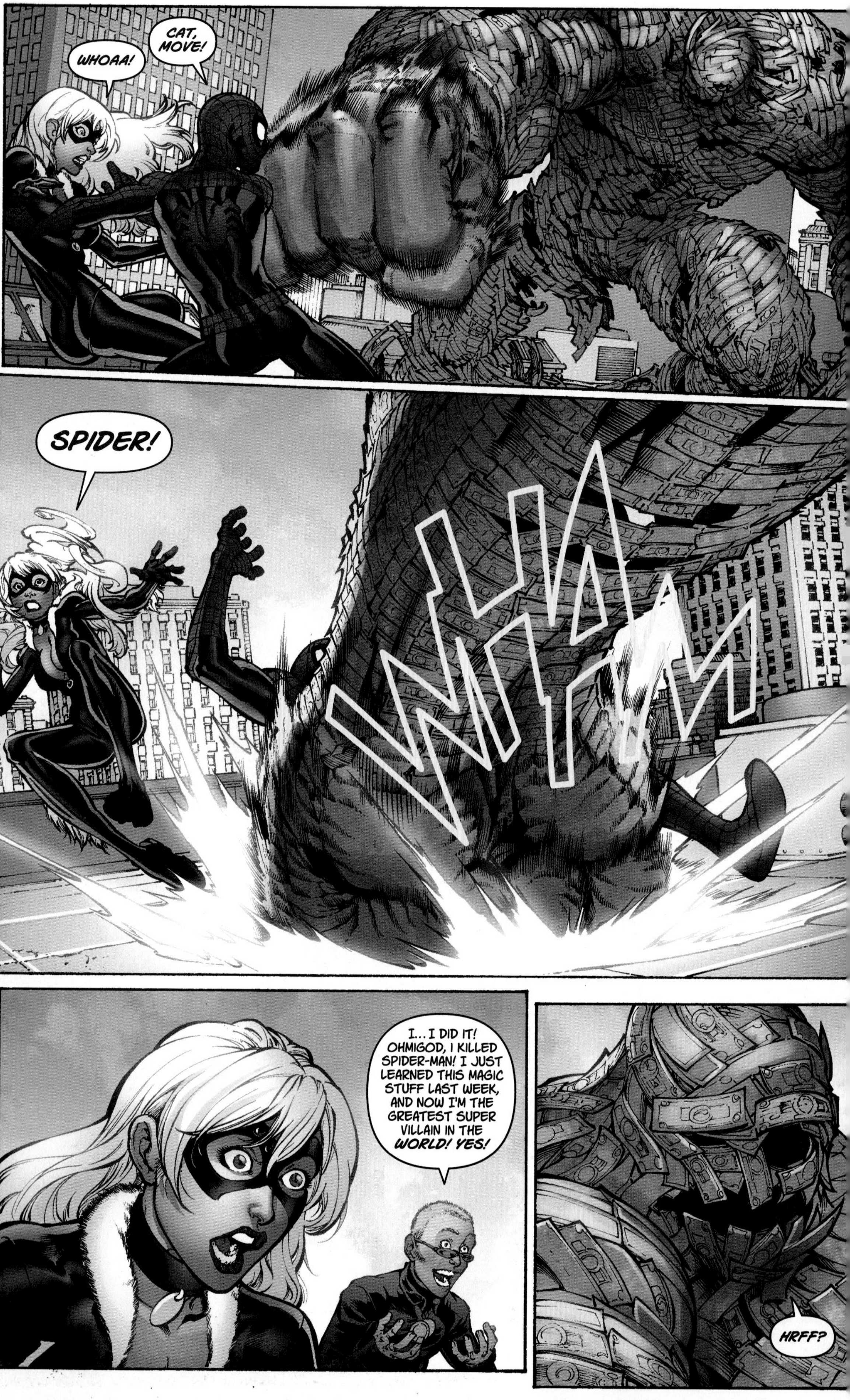
WHOAA!
CAT, MOVE!
SPIDER!
WHAM
I... I DID IT! OHMIGOD, I KILLED SPIDER-MAN! I JUST LEARNED THIS MAGIC STUFF LAST WEEK, AND NOW I'M THE GREATEST SUPER VILLAIN IN THE WORLD! YES!
HRFF?

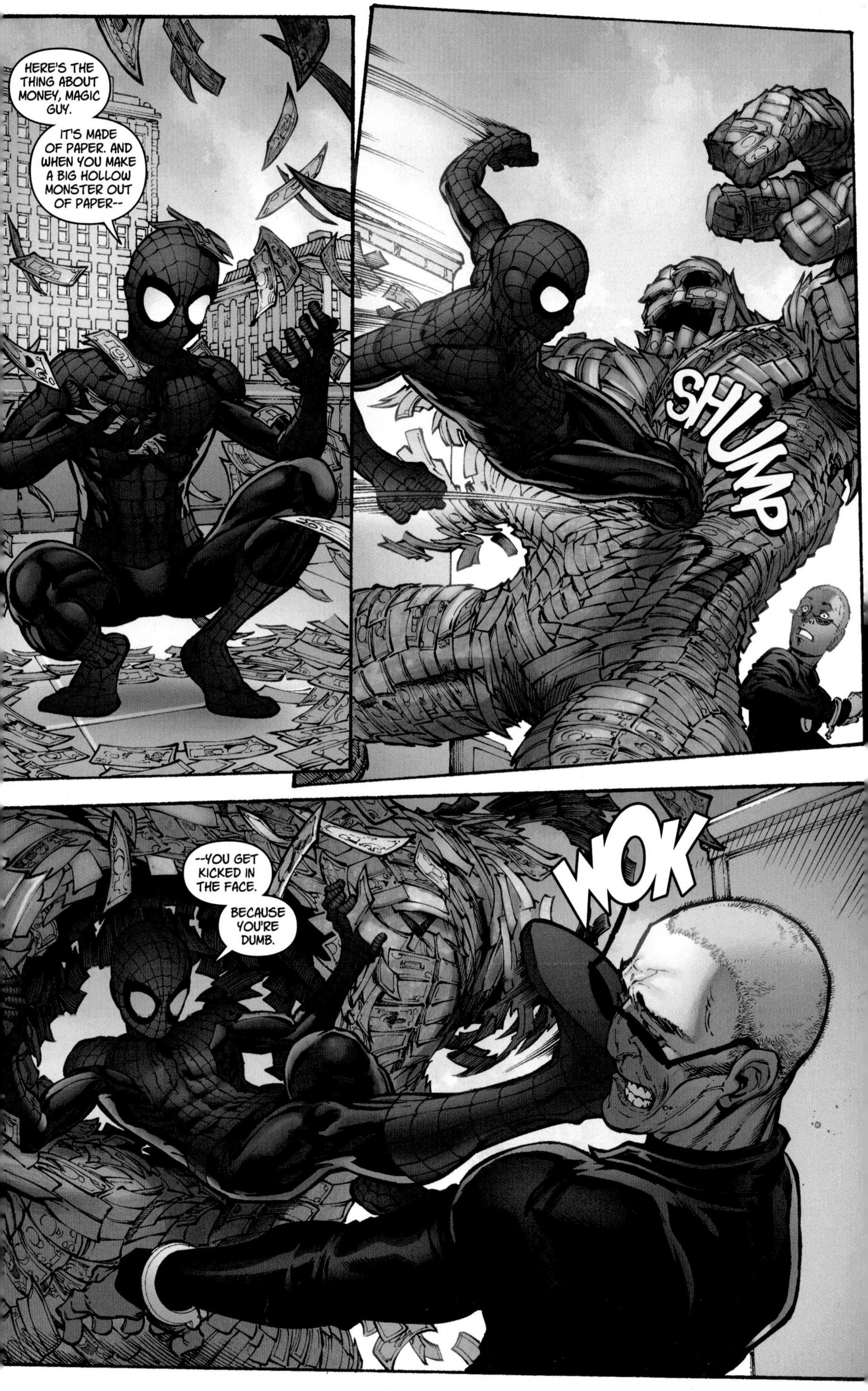
HERE'S THE THING ABOUT MONEY, MAGIC GUY.
IT'S MADE OF PAPER. AND WHEN YOU MAKE A BIG HOLLOW MONSTER OUT OF PAPER--
SHUMP
--YOU GET KICKED IN THE FACE.
BECAUSE YOU'RE DUMB.
WOK

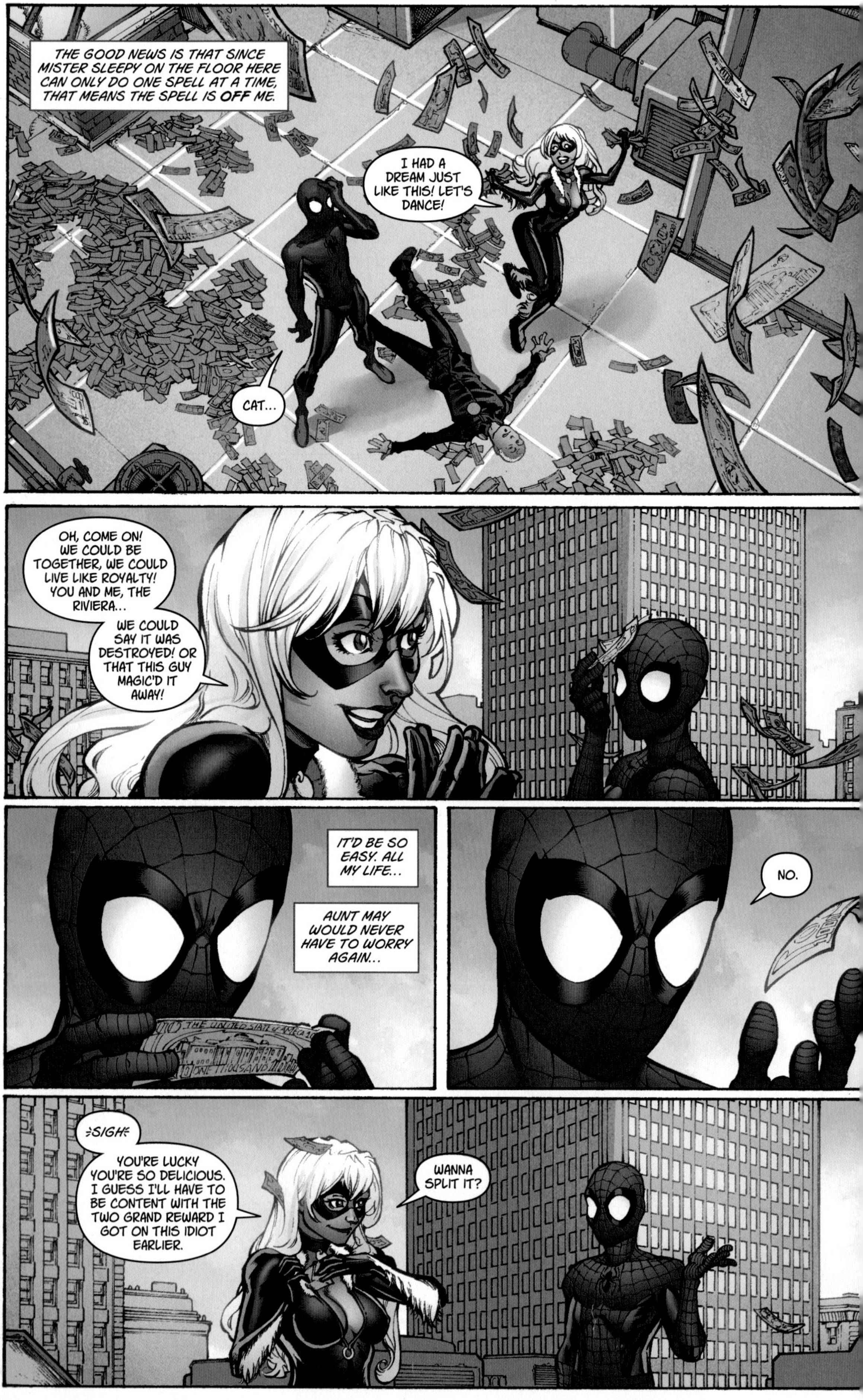
THE GOOD NEWS IS THAT SINCE MISTER SLEEPY ON THE FLOOR HERE CAN ONLY DO ONE SPELL AT A TIME, THAT MEANS THE SPELL IS OFF ME.
I HAD A DREAM JUST LIKE THIS! LET'S DANCE!
CAT...
OH, COME ON! WE COULD BE TOGETHER, WE COULD LIVE LIKE ROYALTY! YOU AND ME, THE RIVIERA...
WE COULD SAY IT WAS DESTROYED! OR THAT THIS GUY MAGIC'D IT AWAY!
IT'D BE SO EASY. ALL MY LIFE...
AUNT MAY WOULD NEVER HAVE TO WORRY AGAIN...
NO.
SIGH
YOU'RE LUCKY YOU'RE SO DELICIOUS. I GUESS I'LL HAVE TO BE CONTENT WITH THE TWO GRAND REWARD I GOT ON THIS IDIOT EARLIER.
WANNA SPLIT IT?

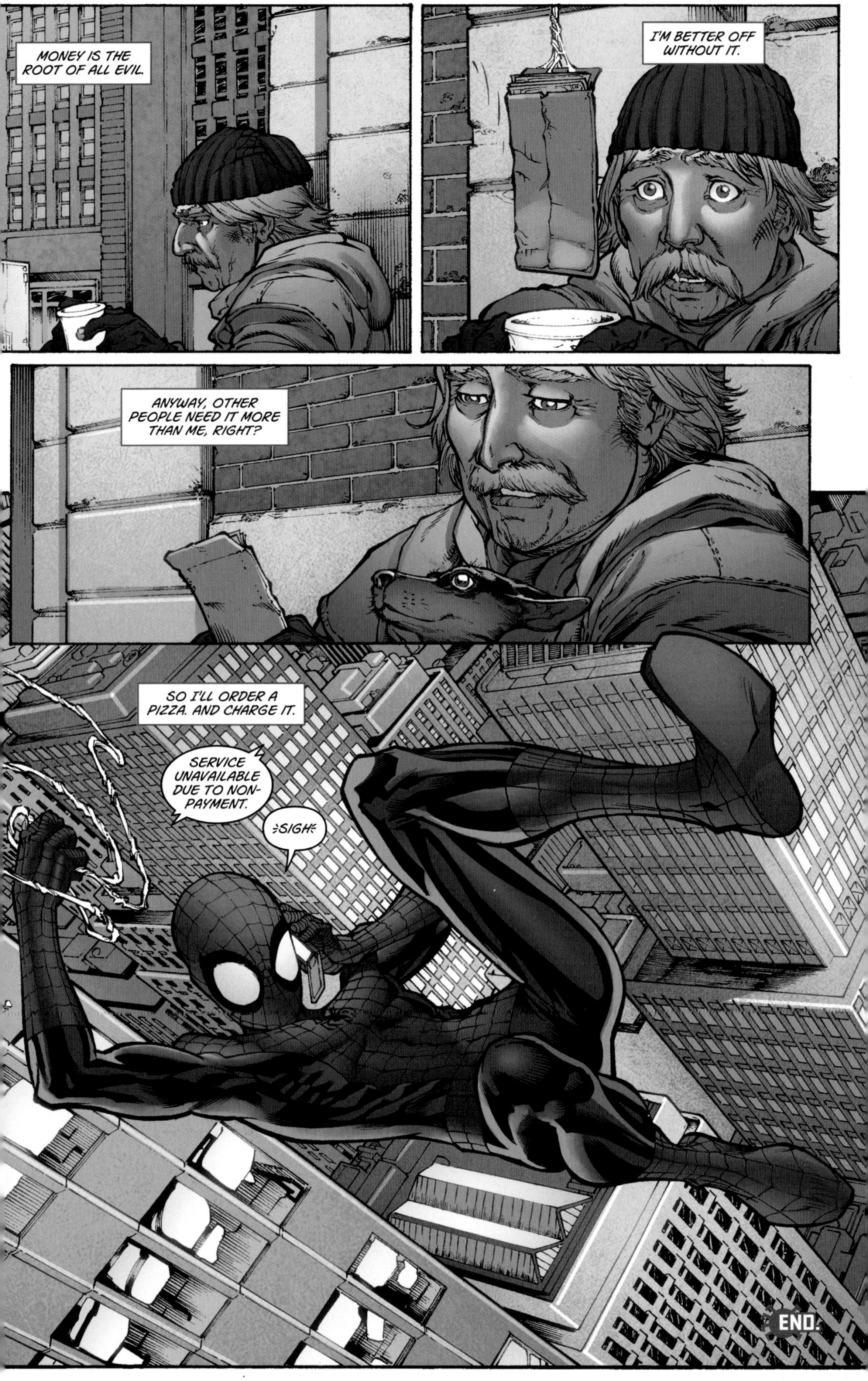
MONEY IS THE ROOT OF ALL EVIL.
I'M BETTER OFF WITHOUT IT.
ANYWAY, OTHER PEOPLE NEED IT MORE THAN ME, RIGHT?
SO I'LL ORDER A PIZZA. AND CHARGE IT.
SERVICE UNAVAILABLE DUE TO NON-PAYMENT.
SIGH
END.

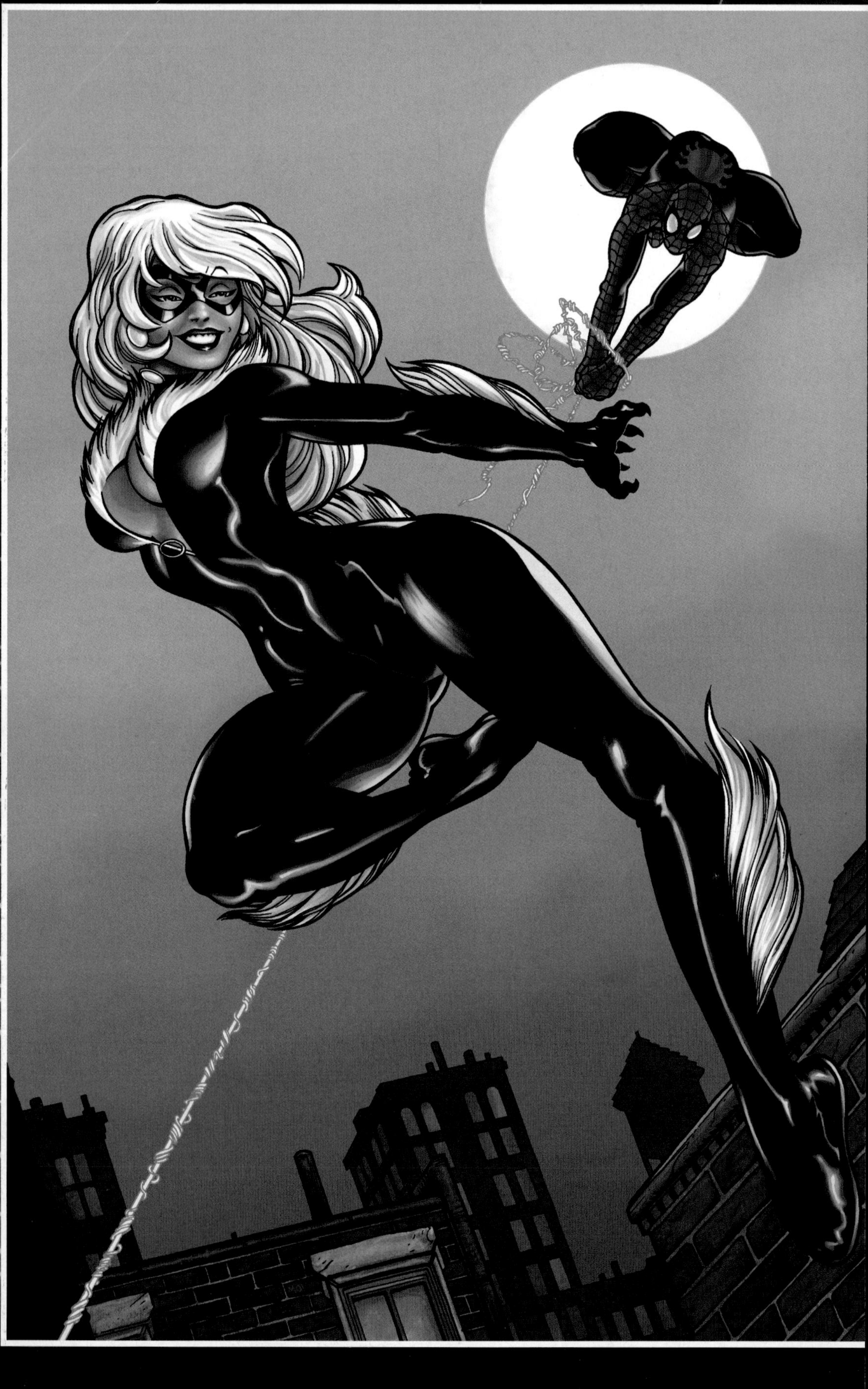

AMAZING SPIDER-MAN #612

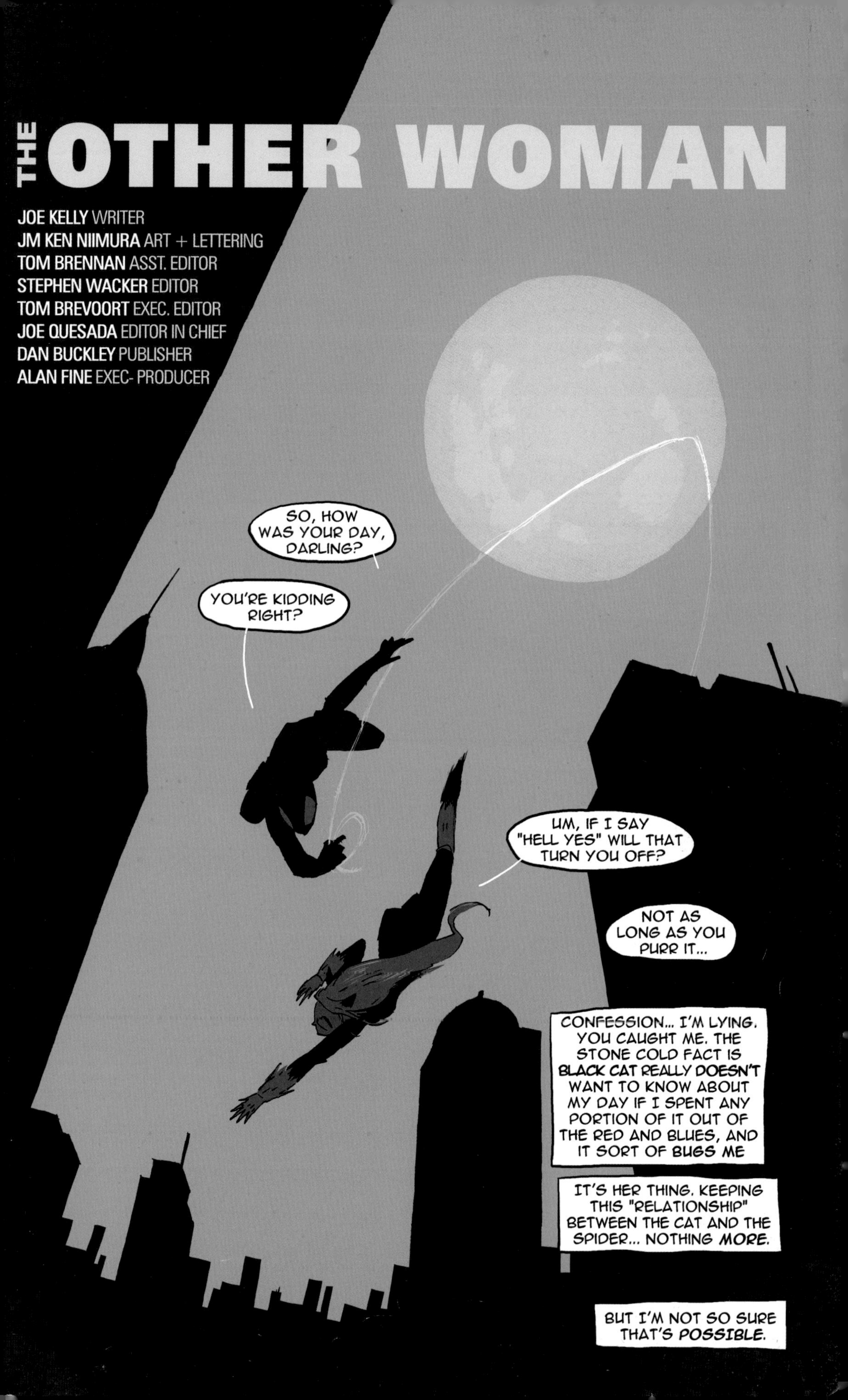
THE OTHER WOMAN
JOE KELLY WRITER
JM KEN NIIMURA ART + LETTERING
TOM BRENNAN ASST. EDITOR
STEPHEN WACKER EDITOR
TOM BREVOORT EXEC. EDITOR
JOE QUESADA EDITOR IN CHIEF
DAN BUCKLEY PUBLISHER
ALAN FINE EXEC- PRODUCER
SO, HOW WAS YOUR DAY, DARLING?
YOU'RE KIDDING RIGHT?
UM, IF I SAY "HELL YES" WILL THAT TURN YOU OFF?
NOT AS LONG AS YOU PURR IT...
CONFESSION... I'M LYING. YOU CAUGHT ME. THE STONE COLD FACT IS BLACK CAT REALLY DOESN'T WANT TO KNOW ABOUT MY DAY IF I SPENT ANY PORTION OF IT OUT OF THE RED AND BLUES, AND IT SORT OF BUGS ME
IT'S HER THING. KEEPING THIS "RELATIONSHIP" BETWEEN THE CAT AND THE SPIDER... NOTHING MORE.
BUT I'M NOT SO SURE THAT'S POSSIBLE.

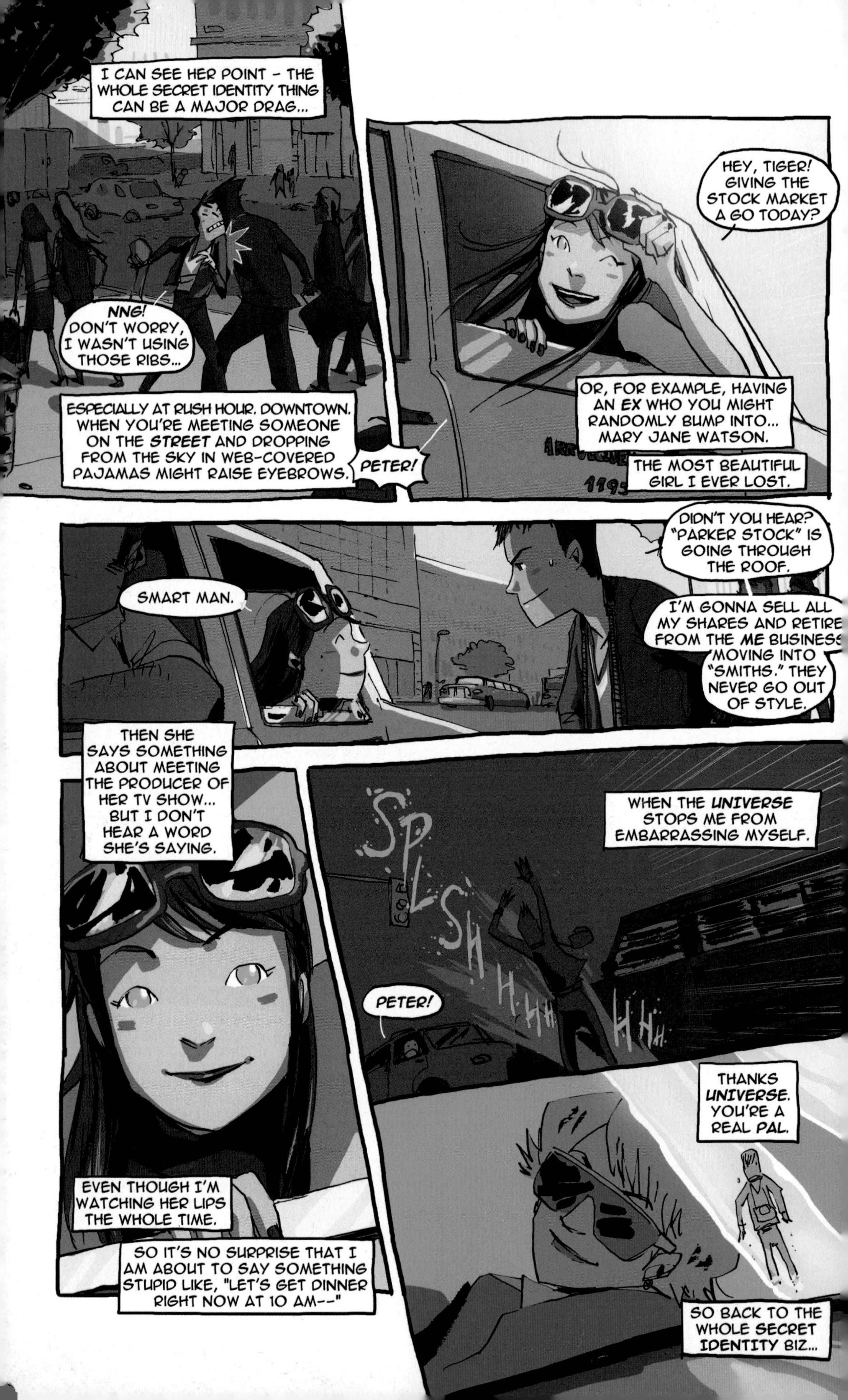

I CAN SEE HER POINT - THE WHOLE SECRET IDENTITY THING CAN BE A MAJOR DRAG...
NNG! DON'T WORRY, I WASN'T USING THOSE RIBS...
ESPECIALLY AT RUSH HOUR. DOWNTOWN. WHEN YOU'RE MEETING SOMEONE ON THE STREET AND DROPPING FROM THE SKY IN WEB-COVERED PAJAMAS MIGHT RAISE EYEBROWS.
PETER!
HEY, TIGER! GIVING THE STOCK MARKET A GO TODAY?
OR, FOR EXAMPLE, HAVING AN EX WHO YOU MIGHT RANDOMLY BUMP INTO... MARY JANE WATSON.
THE MOST BEAUTIFUL GIRL I EVER LOST.
DIDN'T YOU HEAR? "PARKER STOCK" IS GOING THROUGH THE ROOF.
I'M GONNA SELL ALL MY SHARES AND RETIRE FROM THE ME BUSINESS. MOVING INTO "SMITHS." THEY NEVER GO OUT OF STYLE.
SMART MAN.
THEN SHE SAYS SOMETHING ABOUT MEETING THE PRODUCER OF HER TV SHOW... BUT I DON'T HEAR A WORD SHE'S SAYING.
EVEN THOUGH I'M WATCHING HER LIPS THE WHOLE TIME.
SO IT'S NO SURPRISE THAT I AM ABOUT TO SAY SOMETHING STUPID LIKE, "LET'S GET DINNER RIGHT NOW AT 10 AM--"
WHEN THE UNIVERSE STOPS ME FROM EMBARRASSING MYSELF.
SPLSHHHHHHHH
PETER!
THANKS UNIVERSE. YOU'RE A REAL PAL.
SO BACK TO THE WHOLE SECRET IDENTITY BIZ...

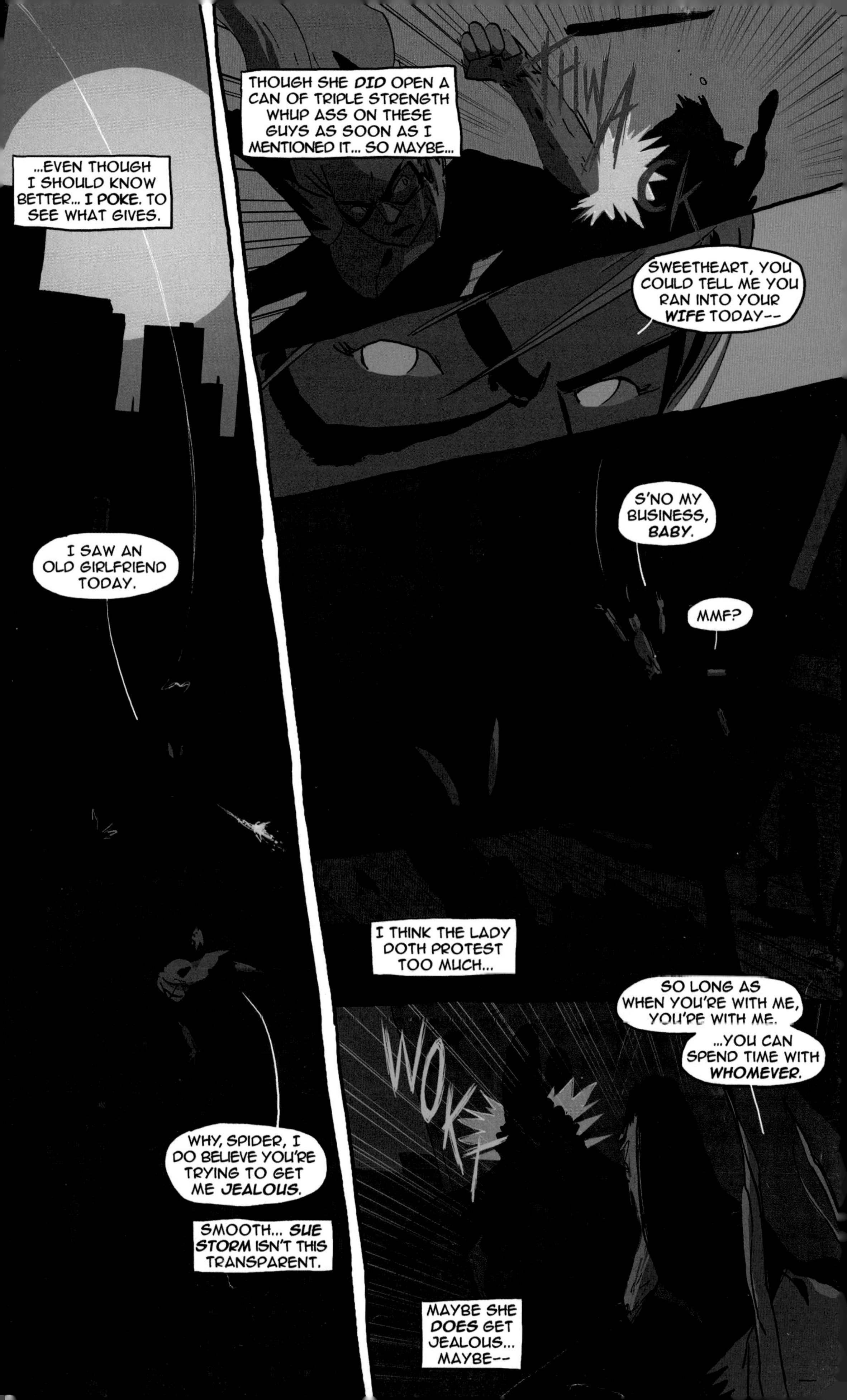

...EVEN THOUGH I SHOULD KNOW BETTER... I POKE. TO SEE WHAT GIVES.
I SAW AN OLD GIRLFRIEND TODAY.
WHY, SPIDER, I DO BELIEVE YOU'RE TRYING TO GET ME JEALOUS.
SMOOTH... SUE STORM ISN'T THIS TRANSPARENT.
THOUGH SHE DID OPEN A CAN OF TRIPLE STRENGTH WHUP ASS ON THESE GUYS AS SOON AS I MENTIONED IT... SO MAYBE...
THWACK
SWEETHEART, YOU COULD TELL ME YOU RAN INTO YOUR WIFE TODAY--
S'NO MY BUSINESS, BABY.
MMF?
I THINK THE LADY DOTH PROTEST TOO MUCH...
SO LONG AS WHEN YOU'RE WITH ME, YOU'RE WITH ME.
...YOU CAN SPEND TIME WITH WHOMEVER.
MAYBE SHE DOES GET JEALOUS... MAYBE--

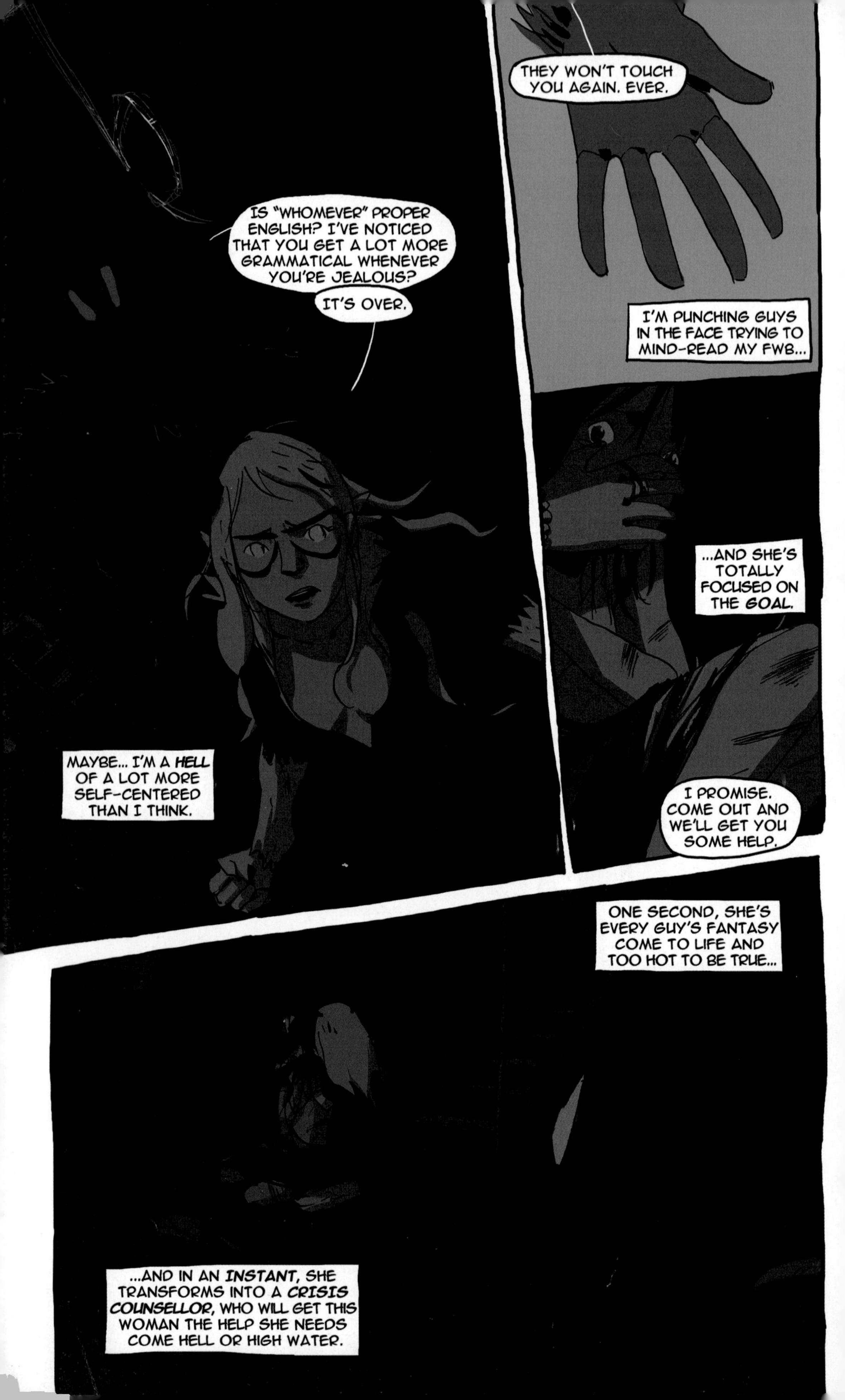

IS "WHOMEVER" PROPER ENGLISH? I'VE NOTICED THAT YOU GET A LOT MORE GRAMMATICAL WHENEVER YOU'RE JEALOUS?
IT'S OVER.
MAYBE... I'M A HELL OF A LOT MORE SELF-CENTERED THAN I THINK.
THEY WON'T TOUCH YOU AGAIN. EVER.
I'M PUNCHING GUYS IN THE FACE TRYING TO MIND-READ MY FWB...
...AND SHE'S TOTALLY FOCUSED ON THE GOAL.
I PROMISE. COME OUT AND WE'LL GET YOU SOME HELP.
ONE SECOND, SHE'S EVERY GUY'S FANTASY COME TO LIFE AND TOO HOT TO BE TRUE...
...AND IN AN INSTANT, SHE TRANSFORMS INTO A CRISIS COUNSELLOR, WHO WILL GET THIS WOMAN THE HELP SHE NEEDS COME HELL OR HIGH WATER.

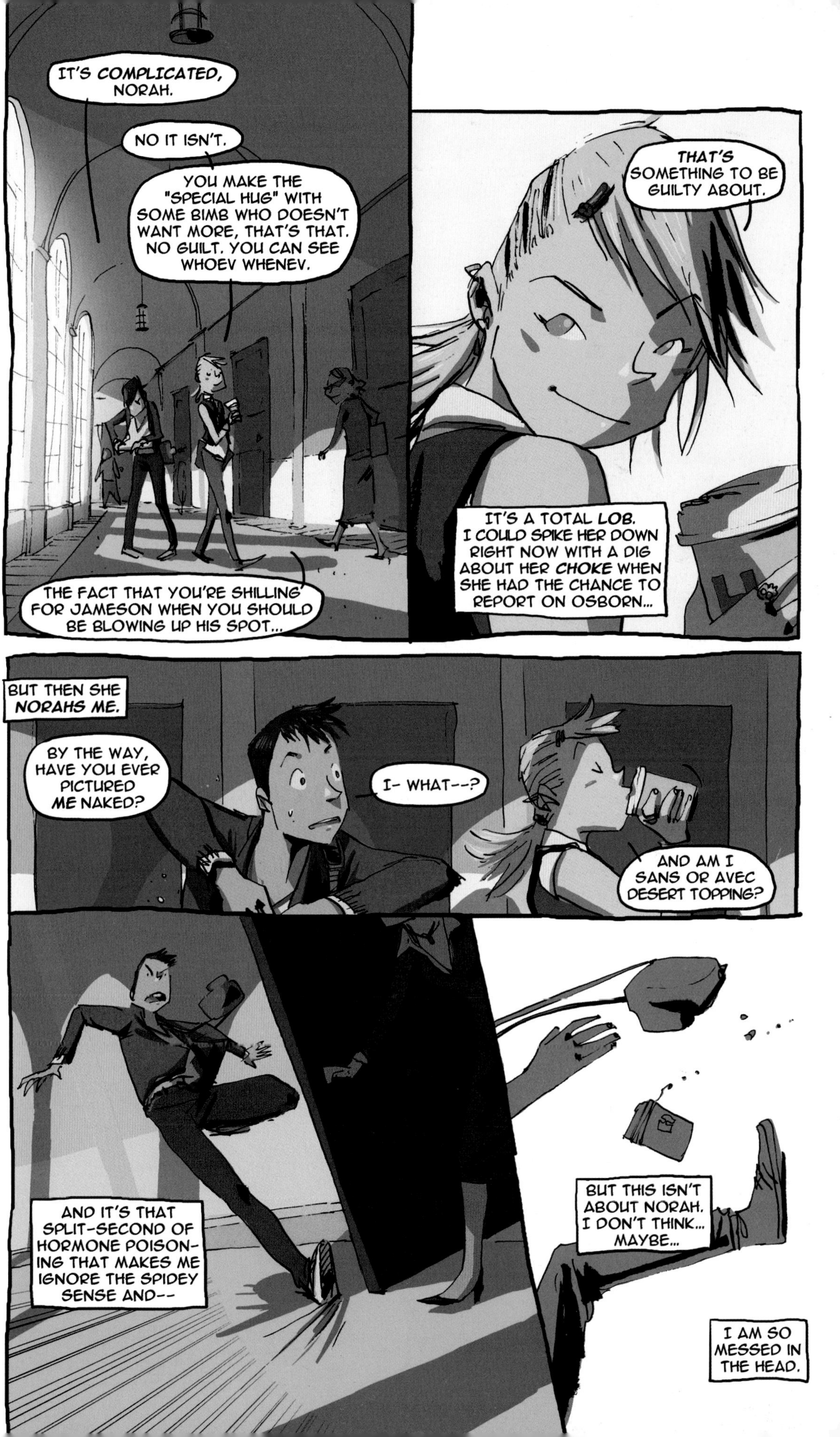
IT'S COMPLICATED, NORAH.
NO IT ISN'T.
YOU MAKE THE "SPECIAL HUG" WITH SOME BIMB WHO DOESN'T WANT MORE, THAT'S THAT. NO GUILT. YOU CAN SEE WHOEV WHENEV.
THE FACT THAT YOU'RE SHILLING FOR JAMESON WHEN YOU SHOULD BE BLOWING UP HIS SPOT...
THAT'S SOMETHING TO BE GUILTY ABOUT.
IT'S A TOTAL LOB. I COULD SPIKE HER DOWN RIGHT NOW WITH A DIG ABOUT HER CHOKE WHEN SHE HAD THE CHANCE TO REPORT ON OSBORN...
BUT THEN SHE NORAHS ME.
BY THE WAY, HAVE YOU EVER PICTURED ME NAKED?
I- WHAT--?
AND AM I SANS OR AVEC DESERT TOPPING?
AND IT'S THAT SPLIT-SECOND OF HORMONE POISONING THAT MAKES ME IGNORE THE SPIDEY SENSE AND--
BUT THIS ISN'T ABOUT NORAH. I DON'T THINK... MAYBE...
I AM SO MESSED IN THE HEAD.

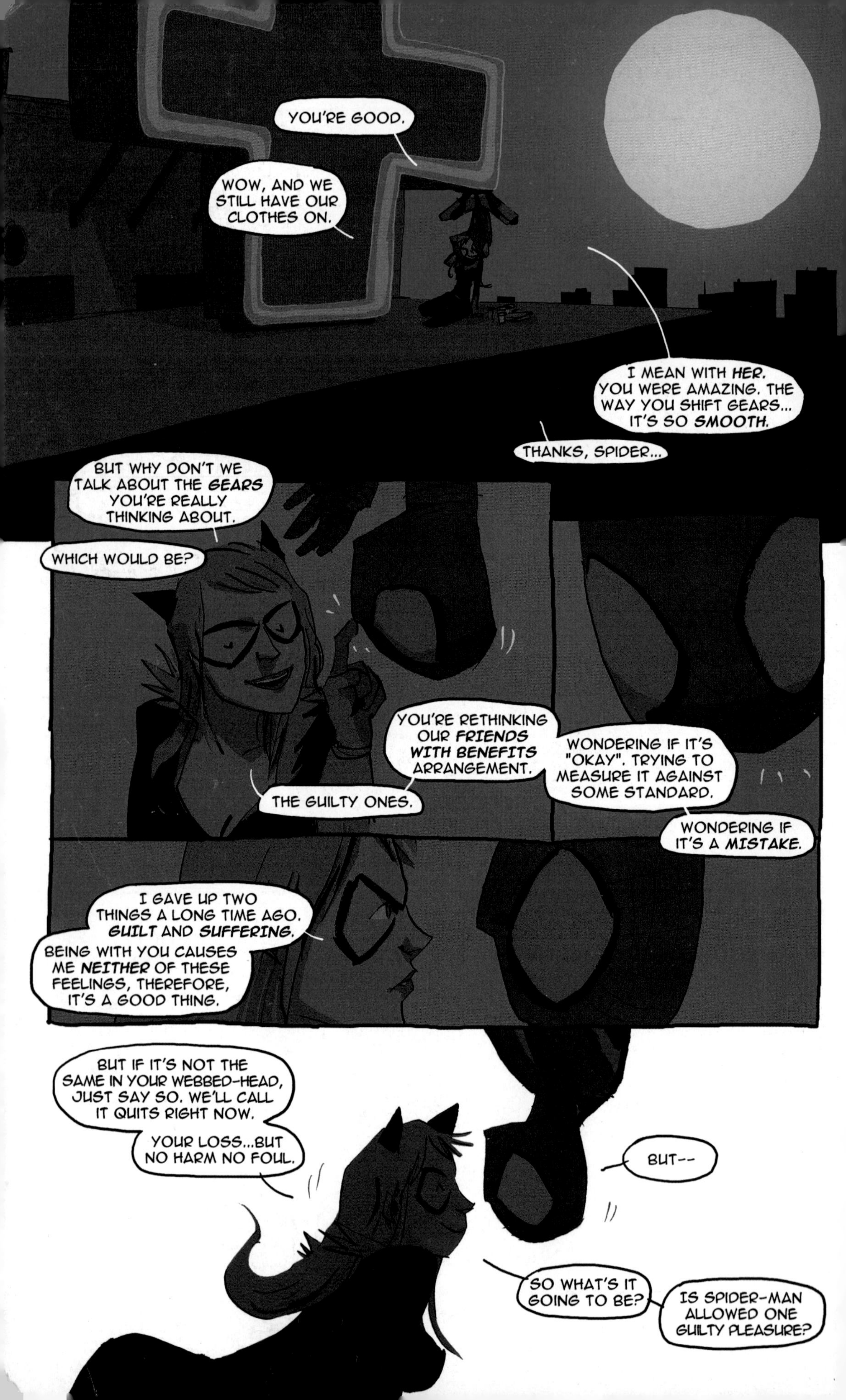
YOU'RE GOOD.
WOW, AND WE STILL HAVE OUR CLOTHES ON.
I MEAN WITH HER. YOU WERE AMAZING. THE WAY YOU SHIFT GEARS... IT'S SO SMOOTH.
THANKS, SPIDER...
BUT WHY DON'T WE TALK ABOUT THE GEARS YOU'RE REALLY THINKING ABOUT.
WHICH WOULD BE?
THE GUILTY ONES.
YOU'RE RETHINKING OUR FRIENDS WITH BENEFITS ARRANGEMENT.
WONDERING IF IT'S "OKAY". TRYING TO MEASURE IT AGAINST SOME STANDARD.
WONDERING IF IT'S A MISTAKE.
I GAVE UP TWO THINGS A LONG TIME AGO. GUILT AND SUFFERING.
BEING WITH YOU CAUSES ME NEITHER OF THESE FEELINGS, THEREFORE, IT'S A GOOD THING.
BUT IF IT'S NOT THE SAME IN YOUR WEBBED-HEAD, JUST SAY SO. WE'LL CALL IT QUITS RIGHT NOW.
YOUR LOSS...BUT NO HARM NO FOUL.
BUT--
SO WHAT'S IT GOING TO BE?
IS SPIDER-MAN ALLOWED ONE GUILTY PLEASURE?

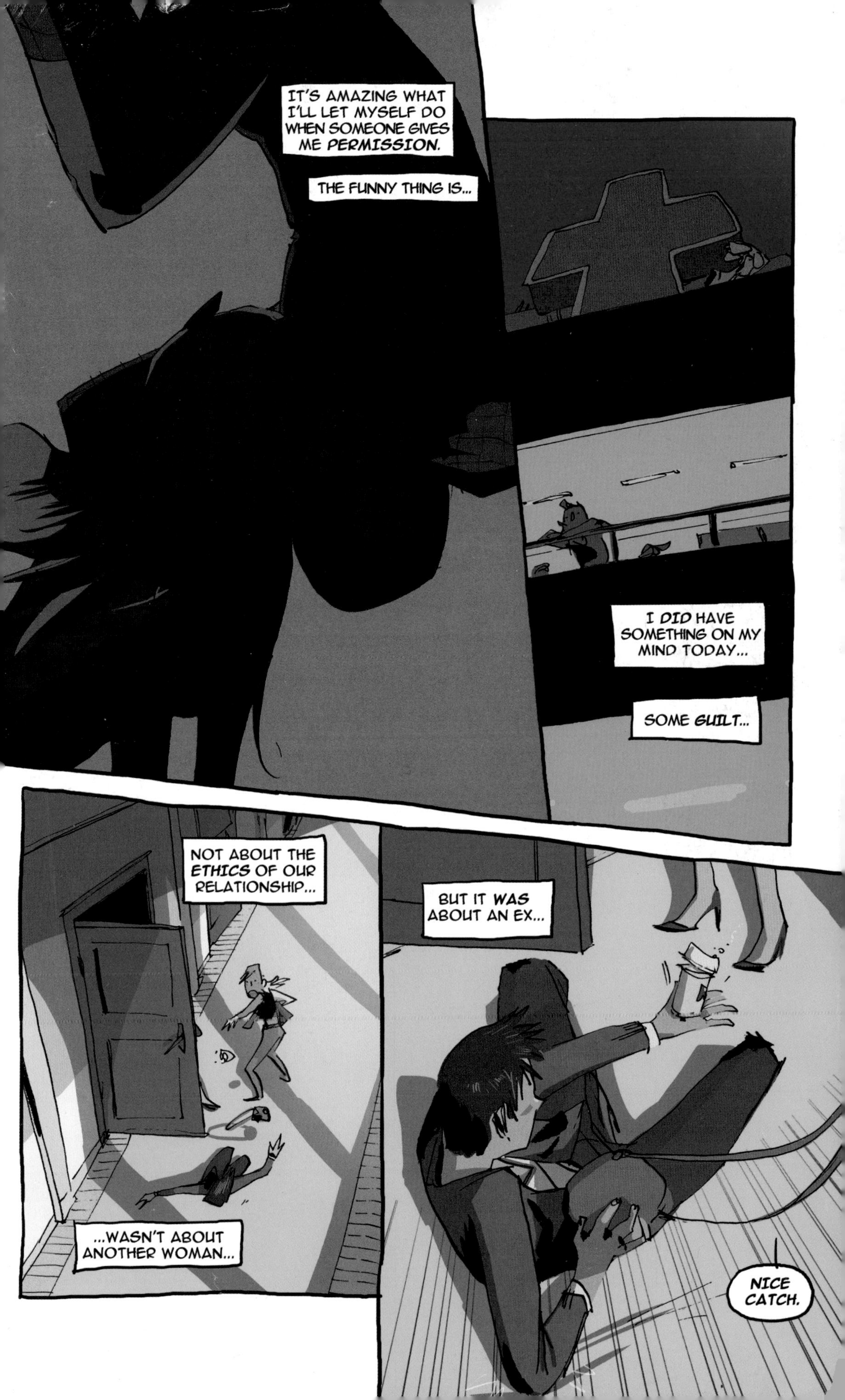
IT'S AMAZING WHAT I'LL LET MYSELF DO WHEN SOMEONE GIVES ME PERMISSION.
THE FUNNY THING IS...
I DID HAVE SOMETHING ON MY MIND TODAY...
SOME GUILT...
NOT ABOUT THE ETHICS OF OUR RELATIONSHIP...
...WASN'T ABOUT ANOTHER WOMAN...
BUT IT WAS ABOUT AN EX...
NICE CATCH.

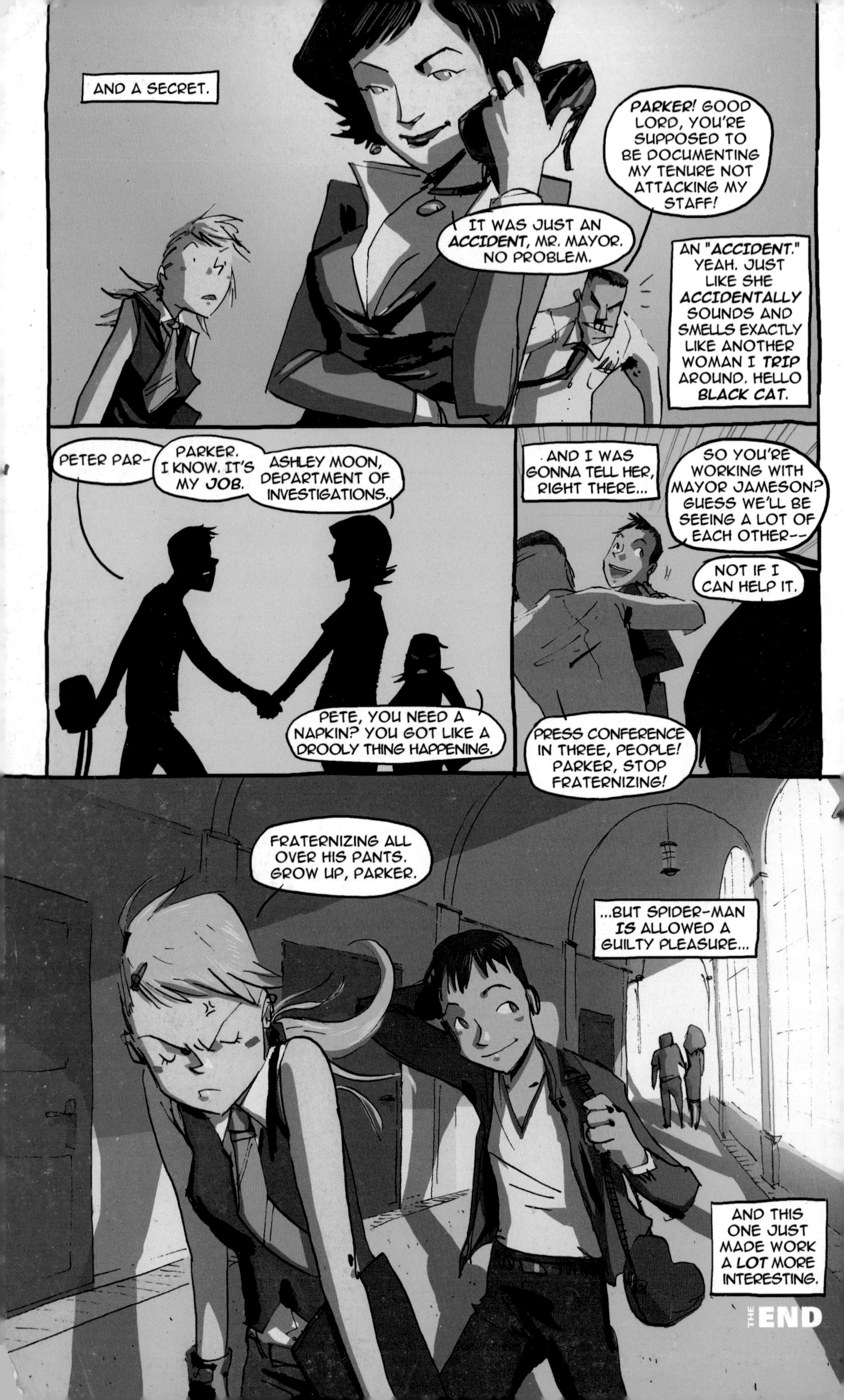
AND A SECRET.
PARKER! GOOD LORD, YOU'RE SUPPOSED TO BE DOCUMENTING MY TENURE NOT ATTACKING MY STAFF!
IT WAS JUST AN ACCIDENT, MR. MAYOR. NO PROBLEM.
AN "ACCIDENT." YEAH. JUST LIKE SHE ACCIDENTALLY SOUNDS AND SMELLS EXACTLY LIKE ANOTHER WOMAN I TRIP AROUND. HELLO BLACK CAT.
PETER PAR–
PARKER. I KNOW. IT'S MY JOB.
ASHLEY MOON, DEPARTMENT OF INVESTIGATIONS.
PETE, YOU NEED A NAPKIN? YOU GOT LIKE A DROOLY THING HAPPENING.
AND I WAS GONNA TELL HER, RIGHT THERE...
SO YOU'RE WORKING WITH MAYOR JAMESON? GUESS WE'LL BE SEEING A LOT OF EACH OTHER--
NOT IF I CAN HELP IT.
PRESS CONFERENCE IN THREE, PEOPLE! PARKER, STOP FRATERNIZING!
FRATERNIZING ALL OVER HIS PANTS. GROW UP, PARKER.
...BUT SPIDER-MAN IS ALLOWED A GUILTY PLEASURE...
AND THIS ONE JUST MADE WORK A LOT MORE INTERESTING.
THE END